African American theatre had a dual origin – first came the indigenous theatre consisting of folk tales and songs, as well as music, dance, and mimicry that African Americans performed in cabins, at camp meetings, and in open parks. These forms of expression were African in spirit that were transformed by the American environment. Then in 1821 Mr. William Henry Brown established the African Grove Theatre. Though Brown began with Shakespeare, he also staged a sketch on slavery and his own play, *The Drama of King Shotaway*. Other African American companies emerged after the American Civil War. African Americans first appeared on Broadway in dramatic roles in *Three Plays for a Negro Theatre* in 1917. The thirties witnessed an upsurge of socially relevant plays, and the short-lived Federal Theatre Project sponsored black playwrights and productions. After the Second World War, the civil rights movement gained momentum and fostered what eventually became African American theatre of today.

Professor Hay charts the history of African American theatre and examines such fundamental questions as its origins, its impact, its short life span, and its salvation. This book not only adds insights to the general literature in the area, but also provides a useful overview that is not currently available.

D0217404

African American Theatre

CAMBRIDGE STUDIES IN AMERICAN THEATRE AND DRAMA

Series Editor

Don Wilmeth, *Brown University*

Advisory Board

C. W. E. Bigsby, *University of East Anglia*
Errol Hill, *Dartmouth College*
C. Lee Jenner, independent critic and dramaturge
Bruce A. McConachie, *College of William and Mary*
Brenda Murphy, *University of Connecticut*
Laurence Senelick, *Tufts University*

BOOKS IN THE SERIES:

Samuel Hay, *African American Theatre*
Amy Green, *American Directors Re-Invent the Classics*

African American Theatre
A Historical and Critical Analysis

SAMUEL A. HAY

CAMBRIDGE
UNIVERSITY PRESS

PUBLISHED BY THE PRESS SYNDICATE OF THE UNIVERSITY OF CAMBRIDGE
The Pitt Building, Trumpington Street, Cambridge, United Kingdom

CAMBRIDGE UNIVERSITY PRESS
The Edinburgh Building, Cambridge CB2 2RU, UK   http://www.cup.cam.ac.uk
40 West 20th Street, New York, NY 10011-4211, USA   http://www.cup.org
10 Stamford Road, Oakleigh, Melbourne 3166, Australia
Ruiz de Alarcón 13, 28014 Madrid, Spain

First published 1994
Reprinted 1994, 1996, 1999

Typeset in Ehrhardt

Library of Congress Cataloging-in-Publication Data is available.

British Library Cataloging in Publication applied for.

ISBN 0 521 46585 0 paperback

Transferred to digital printing 2003

To the memory of my mother,
Mrs. Maebell Glover Hay

Contents

Contents

Acknowledgments

I wish to thank the following people for criticizing draft manu-
scripts: playwright Ed Bullins, Professor Marvin Carlson of the
Graduate Center at the City University of New York, Professor
Harry Elam of Stanford University, Professor Errol Hill of
Dartmouth College, Professor Thomas Pawley of Lincoln Univer-
sity in Missouri, and Professor Arnold Rampersad of Princeton
University. Professor Don Wilmeth and the Advisory Board.

Garry Gray at the Library of Congress helped considerably by
locating documents. The other libraries that provided valuable research assistance included the Moorland-Spingarn Research Center at Howard University, the Horace Howard Furness Memorial
Library at the University of Pennsylvania, the National Archives,
the Schomburg Center for Research in Black Culture in New York,
and the Hatch-Billops Collection in New York.

ix

Among the hundreds of people to be thanked for their assistance and encouragement are Professor Addell Austin Anderson of Wayne State University, Professor William Branch of Cornell University, Professor Winona Fletcher of Indiana University, Professor James V. Hatch of the City University of New York, Bertrum Bernard Hay of Riviera Beach, Florida, Professor Floyd W. Hayes III of Purdue University, Professor Herb West of Columbia, Maryland, Professor Margaret Wilkerson of the University of California, Berkeley, artistic director Samuel Wilson, Jr., of the Baltimore Arena Players, and director Antonio Zamora of the Purdue University Black Cultural Center. I am greatly indebted to former associate editor Julie Greenblatt, assistant editor T. Susan Chang, and production editor Camilla Palmer of Cambridge University Press. I owe a special debt to copyeditor Susan Greenberg. I assume full responsibility for any shortcomings of this book.

African American Drama and Theatre: Outline of Schools, Periods, Classes, Subclasses, and Types

I. The Black Experience School of Drama
   A. Early Musicals Period of Art-Theatre (1898–1923)
   B. Early Serious Drama Period of Art-Theatre (1923–38)
   C. Experimentation and Diversification Period of Art-Theatre (1938–68)
      1. Inner Life versus Outer Life Class
         a. Expressionism Subclass
         b. Protest Realism Subclass
         c. Satire/Farce Subclass
      2. Binding Relationships Class
      3. Flow Class
      4. Inner Life versus Inner Life Class
   D. Black Experience Theatre Period (1968–75)
      1. New Inner Life versus Outer Life Class
      2. New Binding Relationships Class
      3. New Flow Class
      4. New Inner Life versus Inner Life Class

Introduction

I F it were simply a question of the survival of African American theatre, there would be no need for yet another historical and critical analysis of African American plays, theatre people, and theatrical organizations. Up to today, this theatre has wheezed through more than one hundred seventy years, thanks to generous patching and propping. Given the circumstances, such a long existence is no small achievement. This prompts the question, What can be done to improve prospects for the further long-term health of this repository of African American life and history? To find answers requires a thorough examination of African American drama and theatre. Getting a fix on the plays demands, for example, a complete understanding of the general principles governing the works' methods, aims, functions, and characteristics.[1] In this checkup, therefore, the first two chapters separate into schools, periods, and classes most of the plays written by African Americans between 1898 and 1992. The criteria are based on theories espoused by the philosopher Alain Locke (1886–1954) and the sociologist William E. B. DuBois (1868–1963) during the 1920s and the 1930s. The purpose of classification is to set terms and impose limits. Chapter 3 studies African American theatre people. Their condition today looks better than it actually is – thanks to the well-known few actors trained in community theatres during the thirties and the forties. These theatres now are on their deathbeds, however, because there are too few young people willing to brave the uncertainty of the theatre profession and the racial prejudice in the preparation. The third chapter, then, is a pep talk to the young and the tired. They must be made aware that historically the major contributions to African American theatre have come from people whose backs have been spiked to the wall. Their stories might be just the medicine needed to improve even the management of theatre organizations. This is the purpose of the fourth chapter, which analyzes historical examples of management schemes, pointing out their advantages and disadvantages. The benefits of these strategies are reviewed in Chapter 5, which rummages through history to find abundant and fresh remedies.

Getting this health examination under way requires looking at the tenets of developments in, and nineteenth-century sources for DuBois's and Locke's respective schools of theatre. DuBois wandered into the theatrical arena in 1911 in order to teach "the colored people" the meanings of their history and of their rich emotional life. Most importantly, he wanted to use theatre to reveal the Negro to the white world as "a human, feeling thing."[2] These were also the objectives of his *Suppression of the African Slave Trade* (1896) and precedent-setting *Philadelphia Negro* (1899). He realized, however, that to change the race situation in the United States required capturing the mass imagination. Theatre was the most accessible medium for this purpose. DuBois tried his hand at writing, submitting to the American Pageant Association in 1911 his stiff *The Star of Ethiopia*. The association ignored him, although not totally for racial reasons. DuBois was happy to appear before a special committee of the U.S. Senate on February 2, 1912. The committee was holding hearings on a planned exposition to celebrate the fiftieth anniversary of the Emancipation Proclamation. DuBois proposed a permanent – and "distinctly educational" – exhibit, whose "main scheme should try to show the condition of the colored people throughout the United States."[3] He said, for obvious reasons, that a historical pageant might be just what was needed. By 1913 DuBois was staging his *Star of Ethiopia* in New York; it opened in Washington in 1915, in Philadelphia in 1916, and in Los Angeles in 1924. During these same years, DuBois, an almost tireless man, organized three Pan-African congresses (1919, 1921, and 1923), founded and edited four national periodicals, and developed two theatre companies – all to give first-class citizenship to African peoples. The DuBois school of theatre, therefore, was strictly political. DuBois attacked the popular Broadway musical comedies of the time, calling them "decadent" stories about "clowning people." His "new theatre" consisted of characters and situations that depicted the struggle of African Americans against racism, which he called "Outer Life." This struggle, DuBois believed, required that the drama show people not only as they actually were but also as they wished to be.

Locke found DuBois's school of Protest theatre indigestible, particularly his going on at length about African Americans who were "ignoring or discrediting their cultural contributions and spiritual resources."[4] The most interesting thing about Locke's complaint was that he did not go public with it for twelve years. Instead, he tried to change the DuBois school from within, to shift it from protest to art-theatre. He began soon after DuBois performed his *Star of Ethiopia* in Washington. Locke was not among the many who believed that the pageant was the best thing since cornbread, fatback, and millet syrup. Locke wanted believable characters and situations that sprang from the real life of the people, from what DuBois called "Inner Life." Instead of loudly publicizing his feelings, Locke quietly pushed dramatists away from protest writing. Nevertheless, the DuBois school flourished until, in 1922, Locke published his "Steps Toward the Negro Theatre" – in DuBois's own *Crisis* magazine no less. Locke obliquely criticized DuBois for not recognizing that "sowing the future" of African American cultural arts depended on

distinguishing between the movement toward race drama and the quite distinguishable movement toward the Negro Theatre. In the idea of its sponsors, the latter includes the former, but goes further and means more; it contemplates an endowed artistic center where all phases vital to the art of the theatre are cultivated and taught.[5]

Warming to the task, Locke unloaded a double-barrel with his "Enter the New Negro" and "Youth Speaks" in the March 1, 1925, issue of *The Survey:* "The Sociologist, the Philanthropist, and The Race-leader" must understand that the "New Negro" was not "swathed in their formulae." This younger generation, which was "younger" not because of its age, but because of its new aesthetic and philosophy of life, did not see itself through the distorted perspective of a social problem. These young had shed the old chrysalis of the Negro problem and had been spiritually emancipated. Locke recommended that artists lay aside the status of beneficiary and ward, that they become collaborators and participants in American civilization, and that they tap the gifts of the folk-temperament – its humor, sentiment, imagination, and tropic nonchalance.[6]

In October 1926, eleven months after the publication of Locke's *The New Negro* (1925), the manifesto of the Art-Theatre School, DuBois answered Locke in "Criteria of Negro Art." He said in this treatise of the Protest School that by agreeing to focus on Inner Life themes and people, Locke's New Negro artists were being hoodwinked into stopping agitation on the African American question. These young artists, who were but "accidents of education and opportunity," had to search first for Truth and Beauty. If that search caused the artists' work to be labeled propaganda, people should dismiss the charge:

All Art is propaganda and ever must be, despite the wailing of the purists. I stand in utter shamelessness and say that whatever art I have for writing has been used always for propaganda for gaining the right of black folk to love and enjoy. I do not care a damn for any art that is not used for propaganda. But I do care when propaganda is confined to one side while the other is stripped and silent.[7]

Locke shot back that Truth and Beauty in art demanded a balanced, interesting, and detached depiction of things as they were. Instead of DuBois's plots, which "revealed" African Americans, Locke demanded plots that were full of these people's "lusty" lives, myths, legends, and histories. Locke wanted characters who were off the streets, who came out of joints and dives – people who, while "cuttin the fool," expressed honest and personal emotions, irrespective of politics. DuBois wished for characters who came from the same mold as model human beings and historical figures, characters who pined because of frustrated hope. Locke directed his themes almost exclusively toward African Americans. Without sentimentalizing issues, he sometimes indicted whites. DuBois's themes pricked the consciences of white people. The language in Locke's Art-Theatre was that of ordinary folk – dressed up with poetry, music, and dance. DuBois spoke up for "literate and thought-provoking" language. Despite their differences, the tenets of the two schools still inform African American drama. Within the particular contexts of their origins and development, neither school appears more obviously right or wrong, modern or outdated, than the other.

Although Locke and DuBois drew up the ground plans for modern African American drama, their schools really originated with the African Company productions of Shakespeare's *Richard III* in 1821 and William Brown's *The Drama of King Shotaway* in 1823.[8] The stories about the productions of Mr. Brown and his African Grove Theatre of New York City are well-known. Few know, however, about the productions' political and economic contexts, which lend significance not only to the stories but also to the modern schools. Brown, a retired seaman of means (he had served as a chief steward), built his successful theatre organization in three phases. During its initial stage, 1816 to 1821, he molded such Inner Life "exhibitions" as singing, dancing, and reciting into shows designed solely for audience escapism. The acts presented by Brown were the fountainhead of Locke's Art-Theatre (later, the Black Experience School). The birthplace of Brown's theatre was the backyard of his Thomas Street home in Greenwich Village. The 1816 birth year, significantly, coincided with the transformation of ten thousand free Africans in New York City into a political force. These Africans, voting overwhelmingly with the Federalist party, often swung close elections: In 1813, for example, three hundred Africans decided the city's Assembly elections in favor of the Federalists, changing the political character of the state.[9] Africans had no African-based entertainment, however, until Brown opened his rough-hewn tea garden. The Africans flooded Brown's Sunday-afternoon affairs, so much so that within five years the police had forced Brown to move. In 1821 he built the African Grove Tea-Garden at 56 Mercer Street, an elaborate place with little boxes, each seating four, as well as space for the garden band. There was even a second-story apartment.

For the August 1, 1821, opening, Brown invited not only his own considerable following but also the press. One person to accept the invitation was Mordecai Manuel Noah (1785–1851), the sheriff of New York City. Noah was also a judge, consul, politician, playwright, and critic, and the editor of the powerful *National Advocate* newspaper. When he invited Noah, Brown probably did not know that he was a proslavery official in the city's Tammany Hall political organization. In fact, at the 1821 New York State constitutional convention Noah was responsible for whipping up support to change considerably the qualifications an African American had to meet in order to vote (a freed African man was eligible to vote, as was a white man, if he paid taxes, or owned a freehold valued at twenty pounds, or rented a tenement for at least forty shillings).[10] Noah's reasons for seeking to raise the qualifications were as much political and economic as they were racial. His Tammany Hall

Democrats, many of whom were mechanics, believed that universal suffrage drew African Americans to New York, where, as they "changed butler's coat for cap and jeans, or salver for a saw," they took good-paying jobs away from whites.[11] The political ramifications of this increased African American vote were the loss of Assembly seats and political appointments by the Democrats. Tammany Hall nearly panicked, therefore, when it realized that the tide at the 1821 convention was running in favor of maintaining the less-stringent voting requirements. As the September 19 first vote approached, Noah desperately needed ammunition with which to stop approval.

The invitation to the opening of the tea garden was just what Noah needed. As soon as Mr. Brown read Noah's article on the opening in the August 3 *Advocate*, Brown knew his enterprise was in trouble. Instead of a review, Noah wrote a political notice that also questioned African American intelligence: "People of colour generally are very imitative, quick in their conceptions and rapid in execution; but it is in the lighter pursuits requiring no intensity of thought or depth of reflection. It may be questioned whether they could succeed in the abstruse sciences."[12] This was also the theme of the Democrats at the convention as was keynoted by a Mr. Ross: "[African Americans] are a peculiar people, incapable, in my judgment, of exercising that privilege [of voting] with any sort of discretion, prudence, or independence."[13] Noah's article personalized this theme: He made fun of African Americans, describing the men's "shining faces, protuberant eyes, and widening mouths."[14] He debased the women, paraphrasing Shakespeare ("Black beauties 'making night hideous' "). He reported overhearing a conversation that he used to prove that Brown's friends could do nothing but "ape their Federalist masters and mistresses in every thing." Here again Noah echoed Ross's opening address: "A petition in behalf of Negro votes now on your table, in all probability, had been instigated by gentlemen of a different colour who expect to control their votes." Noah ended his notice on the opening of the tea garden with fodder for the conventioneers: "They fear no

Missouri plot, care for no political rights; they are happy in being permitted to dress fashionable, walk the streets, visit the African Grove, and talk scandal."

The fallout from Noah's article, which led to the second phase, 1821 to 1822, of Brown's theatre organization, initially created a financial bonanza for Brown. So many people – including whites – crowded into the tea garden that the neighbors allegedly complained to the police. In response, Sheriff Noah closed the establishment, which left Brown with a useless piece of property. Brown, however, seized upon a notion that came to him when he saw, in the *Advocate,* that the Park, the city's leading theatre, which was being rebuilt, had booked the English actor Junius Brutus Booth (1796–1852) to star in *Richard III* for its October 21, 1821, reopening. Sheriff Noah's order had forbade the reopening of the tea garden; the order had said nothing about a theatre. Thus Brown staged his own version of *Richard III* in his upstairs apartment, which was now the African Grove Theatre. Noah attended the opening on September 20, the day after proslavery Democrats at the convention had lost on the voting question by sixty-three to fifty-nine. Infuriated by the loss, Noah avenged it with a scurrilous review of *Richard III.* He hoped this tactic would win him the five votes he needed to reverse the decision on the second reading. Noah stated in the review that African Americans, whom he called "imitative inmates of the kitchen and pantries," were already too assertive because of "the great charter that declares 'all men are equal.' "[5] Noah did not let up: Before and after the convention, he published only five articles about African Americans – all were negative. During the convention, however, he published ten articles detailing crimes committed by African Americans, in addition to three reviews of the African Company. He even attached the following editorial to Brown's announcement of an opera that opened on September 24:

The following is a copy of a printed play bill of gentlemen of *colour.* They now assemble in groups; and since they have crept in favour in the convention, they are determined to have balls and quadrille parties, establish a forum, solicit a seat in the assembly, or in the common council, which, if refused, let them look to the elections. They can outvote the whites, as they say.[16]

Noah had every reason to feel desperate: The debate in the convention still favored giving all men the right to vote – thanks to the expert leadership of Peter A. Jay, whose father, Governor John Jay, had founded in 1785 the Society for Promoting the Manumission of Slaves. In the meantime, all of Noah's publicity about the African Grove Theatre drew people to it – especially white people, who, according to the actor Ira Aldridge, came to ridicule but stayed to admire. These crowds meant lower ticket sales at the Park Theatre. This, too, very much concerned Noah, whose friend, Stephen Price (1783–1840), owned the Park. In fact, Price and his assistant manager, Edmund Shaw Simpson (1784–1848), produced Noah's plays:

I became in a manner domiciliated in the greenroom. My friends, Price and Simpson, who had always been exceedingly kind and liberal, allowed me to stray about the premises like one of the family, and always anxious for their success, I ventured upon another attempt for a holyday occasion, and produced *Marion, or the Hero of Lake George*. It was played on the 25th of November – Evacuation day, and I bustled about among my military friends, to raise a party in support of a military play, and what with generals, staff-officers, rank and file, the Park theatre was so crammed that not a word of the play was heard, which was a very fortunate affair for the author. The managers presented me with a pair of handsome silver pitchers, which I still retain as a memento to their good will and friendly consideration.[17]

Significantly, this close friendship motivated Noah, as sheriff, to close the African Grove Theatre. The reason-of-record was that the theatre caused riots. But according to Aldridge, the disturbances were sparked by Price:

Price, a manager of some repute, became actually *jealous* of the success of the "real Ethiopian," and emissaries were employed to put them down. They [the African Company] attracted considerable notice; and people who went to ridicule remained to admire, albeit there must have been ample scope for the suggestion of the ridiculous. Riots ensued, and destruction fell upon the little theatre.[18]

The real reason Price wanted the African Grove closed was that Brown was hurting the Park Theatre financially.[19] The political reason for closing the African Grove was that it made good copy for poisoning conventioneers' minds against African Americans. Noah even turned into a political act Brown's practice of seating troublesome whites behind a partition – done in a desperate effort to stop his theatre from being closed.[20]

Following the closing, Brown developed the first guerilla theatre: Throughout 1822 he moved his actors to different rented spaces, including a hotel next door to the Park Theatre. Noah pursued, closing performance after performance, making some arrests right off the stage. The arrests became so commonplace that the actors continued performing, even in the jail cells. These arrests – duly reported by Noah in the *Advocate* as well as by the other dailies – also had the effect of isolating Mr. Brown from the city's African American preachers and other community leaders. The tragedy was that these leaders had worked tirelessly to retain the liberal voting criteria, and Brown was undermining their efforts. In the end, the constitutional convention limited voting to those men who "shall have been in New York for three years, and for one year next preceding any election, shall be seized and possessed of a freehold estate of the value of two hundred fifty dollars over and above all debts."[21] African American leaders probably felt little sympathy for Brown, either for his having been harassed in 1822 or for his decision to retaliate in 1823 and begin his organization's final developmental phase. It was during this stage that Brown used theatre, as DuBois would later advocate it be used, to protest racism. Brown even defied Noah's ban: Not only did Brown return to the closed African Grove Theatre, but he also widely advertised his return on playbills, as well as with lanterns out front. Furthermore, he changed his offerings from the Inner Life entertainment plays of the earlier phases to Outer Life protest plays. He first added abolitionist scenes to his version of Pierce Egan's melo-drama, *Tom and Jerry* (1821), which opened at the African Grove on June 7, 1823. Then, on June 20, 1823, Brown opened his own play, *The Drama of King Shotaway*, the first African American play known to have been written strictly for political purposes. Although it is not extant, the play, according to a bill, dramatized the events of the 1795 Garifuna Insurrection against the British on the island of Saint Vincent.[22] Following the opening of *King Shotaway*, however, Brown disappears from history.[23]

The Brown story raises important questions: Who were these people who started and attended this first theatre? How did Man-uel Noah so easily manipulate them? What lessons can be learned? Brown and his audience were middle-income property owners who, according to one contemporary, Dr. James McCune Smith, held "respectable and responsible positions."[24] The stewards trav-eled widely. They had style, exquisite taste, and "stately courtesy," gained in part from serving and entertaining on the high seas such people as the Vanderbilts.[25] Straightforward and competitive, the Brown fraternity of stewards often vied to see who could best en-tertain them and their wives. It was probably this one-upmanship that compelled Chief Steward Brown, on his retirement, to found a theatre. In order to leave no doubt among his brother stewards that he was still the Chief, he added "exhibitions" to his backyard teas. According to Dr. Smith, these backyard teas overflowed with "brandy and gin-toddies, wine-negus, porter and strong ale" – no wonder Noah reported that men in the audiences had shiny faces and bug eyes. Clearly, these middle-income African Americans founded their theatre so that they could have a good time. Noah could exploit this group with ease because they probably tended to be apolitical and irreligious: These particular African Americans likely did not care whether or not they could vote. The truth was that even under the more conservative voting restrictions, Brown and his class still qualified. They did not need all of the forums, where preachers were hustling the poor by connecting voting to economic conditions. These audiences had no political, economic, or religious reason to attend church. The poor, on the other hand, had good reason to stay away from the Brown people, who cared little about how the church regarded them. Their self-absorption and isolation, however, set Brown's people up to be manipulated.

Mr. Brown, especially, was made to realize the error of his ways. Stephen Price taught him that theatre was not play, but a cutthroat business. This was a hard lesson for Brown, who had won his early matches with Price so easily. Brown simply had opened his own versions of Price's advertised plays one month before Price, thereby securing the African American market as well as pulling in Price's white audience, which "slummed" at the African Grove, looking for exotica. Price, who was losing his audience not only to Brown but also to the new James West Circus, which targeted the thrill-seeking mechanics and industrial workers, was finally able to stop the decline in his business. First, he literally stole the West Circus. He told West that the Park Theatre planned to build an amphitheater on Broadway similar to Astley's in London. Fearing that he could not compete with such a large enterprise, West sold out to Price, including all of his leases, buildings, engagements, horses, and materials. Price even got West to agree not to establish another circus in the United States.[26] Once West was out of the way, Price probably turned the Brown problem over to his friendly sheriff. Brown now himself needed powerful friends. Had he cultivated the goodwill of such individuals as Bishop James Varick of the Mother Zion AME Church and Father Peter Williams of the Episcopal church, Brown would have had access to Peter Jay, who would have welcomed the opportunity to undo Noah's dirt dealing in the city. Then Brown, whose overhead was considerably lower, could have given Price a run for his shillings. But because Brown had no such support, he had to resort to guerilla theatre. It must have been quite exciting to witness Noah's deputies arresting Brown's actors, who continued to recite their lines. Brown must have gotten immense satisfaction from passing out playbills to patrons about to enter the Park and literally pull those people from the Park's doors. Yet this was a poor substitute for what the playwright Richard Wesley called the "painstaking and self-deflating political analysis of the situation." Brown released his anger at Price by writing a revolutionary play about a foreign rebellion. In doing so, Brown was propagating revolution without first clearly analyzing how truly desperate and defensive he himself was. A disturbing question arises, Where were all of Brown's good-timing, style-setting friends? Not one answered his call to arms: There are no news accounts of protests, demonstrations, or uprisings in support of Brown. Friends did not even write open letters. The significance of this was that if Brown had not ignored low-income people during his good days, then they, unlike the good-timers, would not have deserted him.

From the Brown saga one can understand why DuBois feared that African Americans who portrayed "decadent" stories about "clowning" people simply were arming their "traditional enemies." Although Brown could not have known it at the time, the death knell of his theatre was tolling along with the sounds of the thousands of coins that he was collecting because of Noah's negative publicity. Noah's financial shot in the arm, in other words, proved to be poison not only for Brown but also for generations of African Americans. Noah originated negative African American stereotypes in drama by lifting out of their context Brown's depictions of what Locke would later call "lusty" lives. Noah's slanders not only ruined Brown's thriving business but also infected the American body politic. From Noah's pen came the overdressed "Black beauties" and the head-scratching, happy, Federalist apes – the imitative kitchen inmates with oily faces, surprised eyes, and triple lips. The English actor Charles Mathews first brought Noah's words to the stage in 1824, making Noah – not Thomas D. Rice – the father of Negro minstrelsy. Noah's images played the boards for more than a century. Tragically, African Americans themselves picked up and projected these images for the next seventy-five years, including them even in the early musical comedies that made up the first period of Locke's Art-Theatre. It was with Noah, then, that DuBois battled to recast the African American as a human being worthy of full citizenship. It was against both Noah and DuBois, however, that Locke struggled to develop his Art-Theatre.

I

~~~~~~~~~~~~~~

The Black Experience School of Drama

By the earnest solicitation of some in whose judgment I have the greatest confidence, I now present [my play] in a printed form to the public. As I never aspired to be a dramatist, I ask no favor for it, and have little or no solicitude for its fate. If it is not readable, no word of mine can make it so; if it is, to ask favor for it would be needless.

William Wells Brown

THE goal of philosopher Alain Locke's active interest in African American theatre was conversion of a smattering of protest race plays and an overabundance of musical comedies into endowed theatre-training centers. He knew that he would have to overcome objections from the William E. B. DuBois Protest theatre, which would be quite difficult. Locke underestimated, however, how attached the spectators themselves had become to Manuel Noah's "nigra" images. People loved the revues and things of the Early Musicals Period of Art-Theatre (1898–1923), the first of five stages in the development of the Black Experience School. The quintessential question concerning this period is Why did Locke – and even DuBois – have such a difficult time persuading African Americans to repudiate the clown images in the musicals? One answer might be that Locke overlooked how thoroughly Noah had studied African American life in

15

order to originate, develop, and popularize the original Negro stage types. Close readings of Noah's reviews of the African Grove Tea-Garden and the African Grove Theatre show that Noah extracted the images he parodied from carefully selected aspects of *real* African American life. Although colored by his political agenda, his descriptions were an accurate record of what he saw and heard. Noah's reports on appearance and dress, for example, match what we know of African Americans' popular dress during the early nineteenth century:

The gentleman, with his wool nicely combed, and his face shining through a coat of sweet oil, borrowed from the castors; cravat tight to suffocation; . . . blue coat, fashionably cut; red ribbon and a bunch of pinchback seals; wide pantaloons; shining boots, gloves, and a tippy rattan. The lady, with her pink kid slippers; her fine Leghorn, cambric dress with open work; corsets well-fitted; reticule, hanging on her arm.[1]

Even his accounts of the misbehavior of these stylishly dressed people (throwing crackers on the stage and cracking jokes with the actors) were protocol for nineteenth-century theatre audiences.[2]

The conversations Noah allegedly overheard possibly were true: African Americans, after a drink or twenty, probably did put on a few airs, split a couple of dozen verbs, and smack their ample lips. Noah's work at rendering these images shows up in a comparison of his first and second efforts at writing African American speech. His August 3 commentary on the opening of Brown's tea garden has African American women speaking almost standard English: "Can't say I like it [music] much. I once could play Paddy Cary on the Piano; our young ladies learnt me."[3] Noah pokes fun at the men's speech, however, which he uses to hammer home his political message: "Harry, who did you vote for at de election? De fedrillists to be sure; I never wotes for de mob. Our gentlemen brought home tickets, and after dinner, ve all vent and woted."[4] What is funniest about this speech is that Noah has made his African Americans sound German. By the time he writes his September 21 review of James Hewlett in *Richard III*, Noah has almost captured nigraese:

The courting scene was inimitably fine, particularly when Richard confesses his passion.

"Ah take de pity in dy eye
And see um here. *Kneels.*
Ann. Woud dey were brass candlesticks
To strike de dead."[5]

The change – in only seven weeks – lends credibility to critic Noah's account of how Hewlett actually performed the role of Richard III:

The tent scene was the *chef d'ouevre:* the darkness of the night, the black face of the king, the flourish of drums and clarionetts, the start from the dream, the "Gib me noder horse," and finally, the agony of the appalled Richard, the rolling eye, white gnashing teeth, clenched fists, and phrenzied looks, were all that the author could have wished.[6]

Hewlett had studied the English actor Edmund Kean (1787/ 90–1833), and he adopted Kean's romantic acting style (rolling eyes, gnashing teeth, clenched fists, and frenzied looks). Noah's review showed that Hewlett was simply Kean with a colored face, which Noah later blackened. What evolved into minstrelsy, then, was effective not only because Noah based the speech and the character in reality but also because he was able to market his creation so well. In 1824 Noah solicited the help of the actor Edwin Forrest (1806–72). Forrest was the first and the best white actor to represent the African American on the stage. Between 1819 and 1824 Forrest studied African Americans in the Midwest, and he was able to perfect his representation of the "Southern plantation negro peculiarities of dress, gait, accent, and manners."[7] Forrest not only played the Negro Ruban in a sketch by Sol Smith, but Forrest played the role with a real African American washerwoman portraying his wife.[8] The significance of Noah's and Forrest's mixtures of reality and make-believe was that in each case the latter quality reinforced the former. By later marrying the make-believe representation to elements of African American popular culture, Noah made it all but impossible for Locke to eradicate what had emerged as well-honed stereotypes. The use of popular figures, tunes, and activities in minstrelsy and early musical comedies caused spectators to approve overwhelmingly of these kinds of entertainment. Such pieces as Bob Cole's *A Trip to Coontown* (1898), at the beginning of the Early Musicals Period, or *Shuffle Along* (1921), *Liza* (1922), and *Runnin' Wild* (1924), which came near the end, – whether or not Locke thought them "tawdry trappings" – tapped into African and early African American cultural retentions.[9] The musicals recalled the shouts and songs from the Congo Place in New Orleans; the Pinkster dances from New York; and the jubilees from Philadelphia. It was not surprising, therefore, that the people boogied in the music halls for almost two hundred fifty continuous years (1700–1950). The musicals made it possible for thousands of self-taught African American theatre professionals, such as the actor Tom Fletcher (1872–1954), to support and educate their families. In their turn, ordinary people made cultural heroes out of actors like Sam Lucas (1848–1916), a fifth-grade-educated barber and the dean of African American performers. Neither the actors nor the audiences took umbrage at the stereotypes. Fletcher even expressed the hope that the clowning would help to "break down the ill feeling that existed toward the colored people."[10] Actors and spectators alike understood that minstrel and musical-comedy characters were but collections of the same peculiarities that often provoked laughter in real life. This was why, as the critic Sterling Brown observed, the people would start laughing literally as soon as they paid for their ticket.[11] They wanted – and would have – escapism, notwithstanding DuBois's complaint that their "loud ejaculations and guffaws of laughter broke out in the wrong places."[12] It was DuBois's problem that he was "bewildered" by their "shouts of merriment" as Othello strangled Desdemona.[13]

Locke soon accepted the immortality of the musicals and their stereotypes. He asked himself how best to utilize them. DuBois too had posed this question. DuBois had asked Bob Cole in 1909 to write Protest musicals.[14] Such musicals would have turned Noah in on himself. There were, however, dramaturgical safeguards against this use of negatives to create positives: DuBois wanted themes to be clarified; musical theatre simplified issues. DuBois loved making people ponder the significance of an action or a belief. Musicals delighted and entertained without making people think.[15] Cole declined DuBois's request, possibly because he understood the difficulties in changing totally the formula common to minstrelsy, vaudeville, and musical comedy. Not even Edwin Forrest could breach the convention. Forrest did not come right out and say that African Americans were "inherently incompetent people who had the same opportunities as everyone else, but who could do nothing with them," he merely implied it with his widened eyes, gaping lips, ill-fitting clothes, "nigger" dialects, and contorted movements.[16] Even African American minstrels and vaudevillians obeyed the rules of simplification and implication. In his famous "Grand Central Station" sketch, Bert Williams, for example, could only imply that African Americans were not stupid: Bert, a husky redcap, carries the bags of a British tourist. Their quite hazardous trip to the upper level of the train station is through temporary passages, exposed girders, and unfinished iron work. Bert ties a rope to the neat little British tourist, and he encircles his own waist with the other end. They proceed cautiously. The little tourist, not paying attention, chatters away about things that bore Bert. The tourist falls. Bert hauls him up. The tourist gives a nickel to Bert, who scornfully mutters to himself. The tourist falls again. Bert, still grumbling, unties his end of the rope. He even throws the suitcase after the tourist.[17]

Although DuBois would undoubtedly have laughed at this sketch, he also would have wanted speeches about the importance of Bert's act. Such speeches, DuBois believed, struck a balance between the spectacle of African American life and the potential for changing that life. Even if the speeches were to become songs, musicals required still other fundamental changes to suit DuBois's need. Themes – flashed like fire-engine lights – should appear early and often. In Cole's *Trip to Coontown*, for example, Willie

Wayside would have to have saved the gullible old Silas Green much earlier from the con artist Jim Flimflammer's scheme to bilk Green out of his pension of five thousand dollars.[18] Cole would then have had the problem of finding a new body for the musical, beyond the singing, dancing, and clowning. In addition to inventing another happy ending, Cole would have to have written entertaining DuBoisian sermonettes, a contradiction in terms. Had he agreed to DuBois's request, Cole would have had to disregard as well the people's tastes and expectations, which dictated the DuBois-hated imbalance between music and serious theme. The asymmetry must be present – even if, as in the case of Cole's *The Red Moon* (1909), the subject is serious. DuBois did not understand that the convention would continue to shape musical comedies, even such a later one as Flournoy E. Miller, Aubrey Lyles, Noble Sissle, and Eubie Blake's *Shuffle Along* (1921), which appeared almost twenty-five years after *Coontown*. Only at the end of *Shuffle Along* does the community expel the two crooked Reconstruction Era–type political candidates who steal from their jointly-owned grocery store to finance their opposing mayoral campaigns. The tomfoolery overshadows the election of a reform candidate and makes quite forgettable the theme of "crime does not pay." Because most dramatists adhered strictly to the imbalances, most early musicals were objects of disgust for such erudite African Americans as Locke and DuBois. The significance of the theme-simplification rule was that it actually fostered the creation of stereotypes. Only by changing the very form of the musical could DuBois hope to use the stereotypes to better ends – for improving racial pride and self-esteem. Locke deemphasized the necessity of such a change in 1924. The German director Max Reinhardt (1873–1943) persuaded Locke that musical comedies were "American treasures":

It is intriguing, very intriguing, these musical comedies of yours that I have seen. But, remember, not as achievements, not as things in themselves artistic, but in their possibilities, their tremendous artistic possibilities. They are most modern, most American, most expressionistic.

They are highly original in spite of obvious triteness, and artistic in spite of superficial crudeness. To me they reveal new possibilities of technique in drama, and if I should ever try to do anything American, I should build it on these things.[19]

Instead of continuing to rail against the musicals, Locke now saw them as "new possibilities" to help African American theatre "develop its own idiom, to pour itself into new molds, . . . to grow in its own soil, cultivate its own intrinsic elements, and cease being a rootless derivative."[20] Locke even referred to the early musicals as the taproot of his Art-Theatre. By 1936 he had anointed Bob Cole as the "guiding genius" of the musicals.[21] Granted, Locke's turn-about might have been so he could claim for his own in his continuing debates with DuBois the person James Weldon Johnson had already acclaimed the most talented and versatile African American ever connected with the stage.[22] What was most important, however, was that Locke had finally accepted the early musicals – stereotypes and all – as the foundation of his Art-Theatre.

Disgusted with the early musicals, Locke turned to works by Willis Richardson (1889–1977) and S. Randolph Edmonds (1900–83) as models for his Art-Theatre. Richardson and Edmonds, typical playwrights of Locke's second period, the Early Serious Drama Period of Art-Theatre (1923–38), disproved – for Locke – DuBois's Outer Life theory: In their plays, believable plots came *solely* from depictions of African Americans either in confrontation with whites about racism or as they "[put] the best face forward" for whites.[23] The depiction of *real* African American plots, characters, and themes, which Locke called "Inner Life," was necessary – irrespective of white misinterpretations. Locke held that from such representations African Americans developed "a positive self-respect and self-reliance."[24] Inner Life portrayals, furthermore, repudiated social dependence and healed "hypersensitiveness."[25] The importance of this Inner Life versus Outer Life debate was that it decided the extent to which theatre would be a cultural tool for gaining political and economic rights. DuBois feared that were Locke to win, young dramatists would abandon writing about political issues for degenerate plots about buffoons.[26] Locke, on the other hand, was tired of plots and characters who were but crude embodiments of political themes. Politics, Locke believed, freeze-dried drama. Richardson and Edmonds promised an easing of both men's anxieties, first by balancing Inner Life and Outer Life episodes in their plots. Edmonds's *The Bad Man* (1934) typified such a balance. The beginning and middle episodes feature a wicked sawmill-camp roughneck, Thea Dugger, bullying his co-workers, as well as aiming his eyes and his loins at one fellow's sister. These Inner Life actions are, however, but antecedents to the touching final episode: Thea sacrifices his life to save his buddies from a white lynch mob, which intends to avenge a white man's death. In this plot the scale of the "Inner" and "Outer" episodes is large and symmetrical enough to prevent "our traditional enemies," as DuBois put it, from seizing the play "for the purposes of the ancient and hateful propaganda."[27]

This same mixing of the immoral and the honorable could appear in the development either of a single character or of a cast. In Richardson's *The Idle Head* (1929), George Broadus, for example, is both the no-account, trouble-loving type disliked by DuBois and the heroic figure that bored Locke. Richardson's and Edmonds's socially deviant characters do undergo well-motivated changes for the better toward the ends of their plays, however, thereby ameliorating the objectionable behavior. Not only does Broadus pawn an expensive pin to pay his mother's church dues, but, in Richardson's *The Chip Woman's Fortune* (1923), the character Jim gives to a poor family the money that his mother had saved for his release from the penitentiary.[28] This fusing of Outer Life and Inner Life traits in a single character pointed out the definitive differences between characterizations in the Art-Theatre and the Protest schools: Whereas the characters in the DuBois Protest theatre were what poet and critic Sterling Brown called "plaster saints," the major characters in Art-Theatre were well-developed characters who were only themselves.[29] If the dramatists chose not to develop Inner Life and Outer Life traits in a single character, they sought to balance the traits within the cast. In Richardson's *House of Sham*

(1929), for example, real-estate dealer John Cooper steals, and does "everything else crooked," in order to give his family "fine clothes, new cars, parties, trips to Europe, and everything to try to imitate millionaires."[30] When found out, Cooper does not repent – his spirit breaks only because of the discovery. Richardson, however, makes Mrs. Cooper and her daughter Enid more virtuous than Vertu. These balanced treatments were in all of Richardson's and Edmonds's plays dealing with such themes as racism, manhood, bravery, urban family strife, unemployment, unrequited love, and intraracial exploitation. This pleased both Locke and DuBois, who nevertheless feuded about how these themes were developed. DuBois demanded a didactic treatment of the Outer Life, white-oppression theme, which would appear in plays in voluminous set speeches. Locke, on the other hand, wanted writers to avoid these long, flowery, and carefully composed monologues in expressing "the heart of the play."[31] Most Inner Life authors followed Locke's advice. Like Frank Wilson in *Sugar Cane* (1926) and John Matheus in *'Cruter* (1929), Richardson seldom indulged himself with set speeches, even when the theme invited them, as in his *Compromise* (1925). In this play the son of a white neighbor rapes and impregnates Annie, the daughter of an African American widow. Richardson provides background for the widow's troubles with this neighbor by having him "accidently" kill her older son, which precipitates her husband's suicide-by-drinking. Having set up this volatile situation, Richardson has the younger son, Alec, avenge the rape, but only to the extent of breaking the white boy's arm and leaving the South. Although DuBois encouraged such plays as *Compromise,* he thought the many monologues that Angelina Grimke wrote for *Rachel* (1916) succeeded better in pricking white consciences and inciting African American emotions. Because by the end of Art-Theatre's second period, in 1938, most dramatists had adopted DuBoisian plots, themes, and characters, Locke's Art-Theatre School was principally defined by what it was not.

Definition came to the school during the Experimentation and Diversification Period of Art-Theatre, 1938 to 1968. Locke's theories about the natures of Beauty and Truth birthed four classes of plays. The Inner Life versus Outer Life class trumpeted Locke's tenet that protest could occur without being moralistic and sickeningly sentimental:

Not all the new art is in the field of pure art values. There is poetry of sturdy social protest, and fiction of calm, dispassionate social analysis. But reason and realism have cured us of sentimentality: instead of the wail and appeal, there is challenge and indictment. Satire is just beneath the surface of our latest prose, and tonic irony has come into our poetic wells. These are good medicines for the common mind, for us they are necessary antidotes against social poison. And so the social promise of our recent art is as great as the artistic. It has brought with it, first of all that wholesome, welcome virtue of finding beauty in one self. . . . Gradually, too, under some spiritualizing reaction, the brands and wounds of social persecution are becoming the proud stigmata of spiritual immunity and moral victory. It is no longer true that the Negro mind is too engulfed in its own social dilemmas for control of the necessary perspective of art, or too depressed to attain the full horizons of self and social criticism.[32]

So many young writers tried to mix protest and self-beauty that the Inner Life versus Outer Life class broke into three subclasses: Expressionism, Protest Realism, and Satire/Farce. The start of this third period was marked by the hit *Don't You Want to Be Free?* (1938), by Langston Hughes (1902–67), which not only introduced expressionism to African American theatre but also smudged the line of demarcation between Art-Theatre and Protest theatre.[33] Hughes used untried Inner Life and Outer Life elements to satisfy Locke's and DuBois's opposing objectives. Hughes chose as his Outer Life component the plot outline from DuBois's pageant, *The Star of Ethiopia* (1913). That plot traced the history of African Americans from West Africa to the Americas. Hughes's Outer Life plot fulfilled DuBois's goal of having theatre show life as it could be: African Americans and whites joining hands to struggle for equal opportunities. With his Inner Life ingredients (drums, Negro spirituals, the blues, traditional songs, and dance, along with Hughes's own poems), Hughes voiced his deep feelings about the battle against racial discrimination. Hughes, therefore, proved correct Locke's theory that drama could offer "challenge and indictment." In addition, Hughes added Locke's prerequisite satire and tonic irony "just beneath the surface." The significance of this Locke-and DuBois-inspired Hughes concoction, which obeyed no rule of dramatic structure, was that the play eradicated the technical differences between the two schools. Whereas Richardson and Edmonds invested elements of both schools into their plot and character development, Hughes combined all the structural and theoretical constituents. His characters, for example, were more than just the mixtures of good and evil traits found in the characters and casts of Richardson and Edmonds or in the characters in Theodore Browne's *Natural Man* (1941) and J. Augustus Smith and Peter Morell's *Turpentine* (1936). A Hughes character was both Locke's "real person" and DuBois's "idealized type." For example, Hughes made the characters A Young Man and Overseer engaging individuals *and* allegorical representations. A Young Man thus was both the bright and caring narrator as well as the pitiful enslaved people. He guided the audience through the thickets of the Hughes-DuBois theme that African Americans and poor whites had to "unite" because they were "in the same boat."

To make his unprecedented point, Hughes needed a scenography different from the then-typical two-dimensional backdrops and three-dimensional box sets. He borrowed again, this time from the Soviet directors Vsevelod Meyerhold (1874–1943) and Nikolai Okhlopov (1900–66). They had invited the visiting Hughes to sit in on their rehearsals in 1937, which gave him the opportunity to study their new arena staging.[34] Hughes's use of arena staging in his own Suitcase Theatre in Harlem (1938–9) was one of the first such stagings in the United States. Hughes's expressionistic staging and drama narrowed the differences between Locke and DuBois. It was almost tragic, therefore, that the influential Federal Theatre Project (FTP) (1935–9) re-ignited the dissension. The FTP was uninterested in such expressionistic – but unproduced – plays of the period as Marita Bonner's *Purple Flower* (1928) and

Abram Hill and Frank Silvera's *Liberty Deferred* (1936). FTP officials believed that the late thirties was not the time for depictions
of race issues. The FTP did not have to worry about producing
Hughes because he had decided quite early to have nothing to do
with this Workers Progress Administration program. The New
York Unit's "in-fighting and inner intrigue" were simply too much
for him.[35] Hughes might have felt differently about getting involved had the actress Rose McClendon, whom he respected, accepted FTP director Hallie Flanagan's invitation to direct the
Negro Unit.[36] Because the FTP refused to address the race issue
substantively, Art-Theatre dramatists tackled the task through the
second (Protest Realism) and the third (Satire/Farce) subclasses of
Inner Life versus Outer Life plays.

By developing the hybrid Protest Realism, the Locke school really trespassed on the turf of the DuBois people. The Locke dramatists postponed the inevitable battle with adherents of the
DuBois school by making their plots and characters different.
Locke's followers wrote plots with clearly distinguished beginnings, middles, and ends and created major characters who were
fully developed. Most Locke dramatists of the period shied away
from the difficult job of addressing political issues through forms
that favored colorful characters. The actor Alice Childress, however, welcomed the change. She was "sick and tired" in 1950 of
white people who grinned at her when they were in the audience
but, in the larger society, denied her opportunities to display the
full range of her considerable acting talent. She continually complained to her co-actors about having to portray suffering Mamas,
Mammies, Madames, and Mulattoes. When she was challenged by
one friend to do something about it, Childress wrote *Florence*
(1950) – overnight.[37] This play, which typified the Protest Realism
subclass, radically altered the African American "Mama" stereotype. Although this Mama appears "Mama-ly," she confronts a
northern white liberal woman, Mrs. Carter, over racism. Childress
makes Mama a typically devoted mother, having her wait in a
southern train depot to bring home from New York her starving-

actress daughter Florence. Childress further embellishes appearances by introducing the prototypical white liberal, a helping-hand northerner who "eats with Negroes." Having complied with the formula for her beginning, Childress now "messes" with it: Mrs. Carter's help to Florence is to offer the girl maid work. Instead of having Mama "praise the Lord" for Mrs. Carter's offer, Childress has her raise hell: Mama grabs Helping-hand's wrist, almost pulling it out of its socket. When told that she is hurting the woman, Mama becomes sarcastic: "I mustn't hurt you, must I?" Then she sends Florence some "keep-on-trying" money. Childress cut Mama from the same cloth as William Wells Brown's Cato in *Escape; or, A Leap for Freedom* (1858). The difference between the two characters is that Mama never masks her feelings. Her *appearance*, which comes out of Noah's negative stereotype, misleads the audience. One significant aspect of this play is that in it Childress proves that the Mama character does not have to be a stereotype. More importantly, Childress flashes an early warning to African Americans to stop mistaking *signs* for *symbols:* "Eating together" was for Mama, at midcentury, as well as it was for other African Americans, a one-to-one representation (i.e., a symbol) of equality. The Bible and the southern oligarchy made it so by respectively commanding and outlawing that the races break bread together. To Mrs. Carter, however, "eating together" simply drew attention to a situation (i.e., it was a sign). The sign often deceived, as indicated by Mrs. Carter's equating sharing a table with sisterhood. Childress's theme – which was far ahead of its 1950 appearance – was that the movement during the forties and fifties for public accommodations was too myopic. Money was the real source of the struggle, Childress said. This theme drew Childress's Protest Realism subclass, like Hughes's Expressionism, quite close to DuBois's objectives, if not to his dramatic methods.

The Satire/Farce subclass was even further away from DuBois's views on Protest theatre. DuBois had *said*, in a tribute to Bert Williams, that those deserving the "highest praise" for helping "most" in the struggle for race equality were the ones who "made the world laugh": "For this is not mere laughing: It is the smile that hovers above blood and tragedy; the light of happiness that hides breaking hearts and bitter souls. This is the top of bravery; the finest thing in service."[38] DuBois believed, however, that this laughter should come "in the calm afterday of thought and struggle to racial peace."[39] The DuBois people frowned, therefore, at such non-"afterday" plays as Ossie Davis's *Purlie Victorious* (1961) and Douglas Turner Ward's *Day of Absence* and *Happy Ending* (1965). Plays that asked their audiences to laugh at evil conditions violated DuBois's central notion that drama must portray people being frustrated by obstacles. The Locke school, of course, rejoiced at Davis's and Ward's respective farce and satire about people who defeated racial segregation – even at times when too few people did. The Locke people cared less about DuBois's fear that African Americans were still reeling from the effects of having been painted in the minstrels as jesters and clowns.[40] The Locke theatre admired Ossie Davis's nerve in having the Reverend Purlie, in *Purlie Victorious*, mastermind the takeover of Big Bethel from the white master, Cap'n Cotchipee. The DuBois people worried about Davis's further alienating southern whites and upsetting middle-income African Americans. The latter had already insisted, as Sterling Brown pointed out, that they would have nothing to do with such "down home" folks as Reverend Purlie.[41] Also, Ward should have known better than to have African Americans "carryin' on in public" in *Day of Absence* and *Happy Ending*. The DuBois people believed that "The Race" was not far enough away from Noah's negative stereotypes to be making fun of these types. Nevertheless, Davis's and Ward's gambles paid off. African Americans made anthems of these plays because they were what the author and critic Jessie Fauset called "our emotional salvation."[42] Locke's followers completely dismissed the DuBois claims both that the characters in farces and satires reinforced white people's beliefs and that African Americans were only "lay figures whose business it was to be funny and sometimes pathetic."[43] This

Satire/Farce subclass concluded the Inner Life versus Outer Life class, therefore, by calling for renewed attention to Locke–DuBois theoretical disputes.

The Binding Relationships class of drama illustrated Locke's belief that social pressure welded together the African American community. This class even further widened the gap between the two schools because, except to motivate actions, it rarely addressed any race relations (or, Outer Life) issues. Instead, the class invoked the Locke concept that societal forces inextricably bound African Americans:

All classes of a people under social pressure are permeated with a common experience; they are emotionally welded as others cannot be. With them, even ordinary living was epic depth and lyric intensity, and this, their material handicap, is their spiritual advantage. So, in a day when art has run to classes, cliques and coteries, and life lacks more and more a vital common background, the Negro artist, out of the depths of his group and personal experience, has to his hand almost the conditions of a classical art.[44]

Transposed into plays, Locke's notion became the class that showed African peoples to be so linked by blood, law, or friendship that they simply could not walk away from their relationships, regardless of how unpleasant or destructive they might be. Locke's explanation of the bond clarified and unioned life sources as African American "classical art." Constrained by the definitive rule always to write from one's own experience, dramatists could not continue to comply with DuBois's wish that they create characters only of the message-making type. The writers had no choice, Locke implied, but to put on the stage every character in the community, from historical figures to street freaks. Locke said as well that authors should not make characters into race models or types, but should allow them to be themselves. DuBois was correct, however, when he reasoned that audiences – and "our traditional enemies" – would not distinguish between classic-art representa-

tions and caricatural stereotypes. Within these contexts, the nature
of the Binding Relationships play solidified during this third
period. Dramatists explored family tensions. Dramatic conflict
arose when the family's code of expectations was broken by one
or more of its "contrary" members, precipitating a showdown.
Lena, for example, has to batter heads when Walter Lee, in
Lorraine Hansberry's classic, *A Raisin in the Sun* (1959), does not
live up to the family's hopes. The tension between Walter and
Mama, according to the critic Margaret B. Wilkerson, was important because it drove the plot and revealed the human contradictions and complexities of African Americans.[45] Spectators found
"the truth and sense of their condition in this tension," which
made this class of drama so popular; the family dilemmas were as
recognizable as they were varied.[46] The tensions sprang up between mothers and daughters (Sophia vs. Esther in Errol John's
Moon on a Rainbow Shawl [1962]), grandmothers and couples
(Grandmother vs. Lem and May Scott in Louis Peterson's *Take a
Giant Step* [1953]), and husbands and wives (Sister Margaret vs.
Luke in James Baldwin's *The Amen Corner* [1965]). These Binding
Relationships plays differed from the English domestic tragedies
and melodramas of the seventeenth and eighteenth centuries in
that the African American families were nuclear, extended, and assembled. The family could include, for example, not only close
friends, such as Aunt Nancy, the chip woman in Richardson's *The
Chip Woman's Fortune,* but also clusters of people such as the sawmill workers in Edmonds's *The Bad Man* and the turpentine workers in Smith and Morell's *Turpentine.* During this third period,
because audiences identified so closely with such characters and
conflicts, these plays became the all-time most popular class of
African American drama.[47]

Partly responsible for this upsurge in interest in Binding Relationships plays were the college professors who preferred these
plays over Dubois's Protest plays. According to Professor A. Clifton Lamb, college administrators did not allow much protest or
other theatre, except for an occasional commencement Shakes-

peare production.[48] The professors in the early programs at schools in the Intercollegiate Theatre Association (ITA) did not contest such prohibitions because they did not want to risk their shaky places on the faculty.[49] Theatre programs were only a probationary part of these college curricula. Their introduction resulted from Locke's intense and successful lobbying in 1921 of the Howard University administration. The theatre educators decided, therefore, to write their own, "safe," plays. These American versions of the sixteenth-century English University Wits produced a highly respected body of Binding Relationships plays that conformed to what Wilkerson has called the Euro-American literary tradition.[50] The plays and collegiate theatre programs multiplied under the leadership of Randolph Edmonds, founder of the ITA in 1930 and the National Association of Dramatic and Speech Arts (NADSA) in 1936.[51] Programs dating from the mid-thirties could be found at Florida Agricultural and Mechanical University in Tallahassee, where Edmonds then taught, and at Howard University, where Anne Cooke Reid, James W. Butcher, and Owen Dodson at various times assisted the founding director, Montgomery Gregory. By the fifties programs existed in colleges as far north as Morgan State University in Baltimore, headed there by A. Clifton Lamb and Waters E. Turpin; as far west as Lincoln University in Jefferson City, Missouri, directed by Thomas D. Pawley; and as far south as Bethune-Cookman College in Daytona Beach, Florida, led by Thurman W. Stanback. Among the representative works by these educators were Pawley's *Judgment Day* (1938), Edmonds's *Gangsters over Harlem* (1942), Stanback's *The Delicate Thread* (1957), Dodson's *The Christmas Miracle* (1955), and Lamb's *Roughshod up the Mountain* (1956). The widespread acceptance of such plays in both college and community theatres solidified the differences between the DuBois and the Locke theatres. The professors totally ignored DuBois's principles.

Flow class plays, which displayed Locke's view that drama must be vibrant, disregarded DuBois even more than did Binding Relationships plays. These plays conformed to Locke's belief that drama, ignoring politics, had to be a "delightfully rich transfusion of essential folk-arts"[52]:

The newer motive . . . in being racial is to be so purely for the sake of art. Nowhere is this more apparent, or more justified, than in the increasing tendency to evolve from the racial substance something technically distinctive, something that as an idiom of style may become a contribution to the general resources of art. In flavor of language, flow of phrase, accent of rhythm in prose, verse and music, color and tone of imagery, idiom and timbre of emotion and symbolism, it is the ambition and promise of Negro artists to make a distinctive contribution.[53]

The DuBois Protest theatre considered Locke's call for "young Negro writers [to] dig deep into the racy peasant undersoil of the race life" flawed in that it thwarted all meaningful protest.[54] Indeed, analysis of the plot synopses of the more than seven hundred musical comedies produced between Cole's *Coontown* in 1898 and Hughes's *Simply Heavenly* in 1957 shows almost no evidence of social consciousness. Although the musicals felt somewhat "duty bound to carry messages in defense of their race," as Sterling Brown put it, they did so at the expense of making the half-hearted defense look like "an incongruous addition to their [song-and-dance] glorification of the Negro girl."[55] Added to this criticism was the fact that the Flow class included gospel musicals and comedies, as well as folk opera and poetic drama, none of which appealed to the DuBois people. As the Flow class plays gained in popularity, adherents of the DuBois theatre felt obliged to take action. They believed that the mid-forties was not the time to parade on the stage again Noah's spooks from the Early Musicals Period. A long-delayed battle erupted between the DuBois and Locke schools. During the low point of their relationship, in 1924, DuBois and Locke had laid the groundwork for the 1946 warfare. Locke repeatedly backhanded DuBois because, quite frankly, Locke believed that DuBois was smothering theatre. DuBois, too, could have done without Locke: DuBois made it quite clear that, although he thought "Locke was by long odds the best trained man among the younger American Negroes," he also was "a bit leery about Locke."[56] DuBois's feelings probably stemmed from Locke's having requested, accepted, then refused to publish DuBois's important essay "The Negro and Social Reconstruction," which argues that the African American has never been considered an integral part of the nation, either in industry, politics, or civil rights. The suspicion was that Locke thought DuBois's "views were too radical, too challenging, and too unusual."[57] Locke topped this off by being openly rude to DuBois.[58] Locke belittled DuBois in *The New Negro:* Although honoring DuBois by letting his essay "The Negro Mind Reaches Out" anchor the book, Locke selected other pieces that attacked DuBois. DuBois had good cause not to consider Locke "a particularly close friend."[59]

Considering this antagonistic beginning, it was surprising that the animosity between the two schools only smoldered for twenty-two years. War finally broke out when the Locke School insisted on producing Arna Bontemps and Countee Cullen's *St. Louis Woman* (1946). The National Association for the Advancement of Colored People (NAACP) executive director Walter White commanded the DuBois camp. Langston Hughes led the Locke people. The specific issue was whether or not the African American struggle for equal opportunities should have to withstand, according to White, the portrayal in the play of "pimps, prostitutes, and gamblers with no redeeming characteristics":[60]

Even one role supposed to portray a decent person – that of a pious church-going woman. They represented her as having had several children, each by a different father without benefit of clergy. I had been shocked on reading the script to find every cliche and stereotype of the minstrel Negro included in it. My disapproval had angered a number of people.[61]

White launched private and public campaigns to stop *St. Louis Woman* from opening. Months before the play was to open, *Variety* carried a front-page piece on Lena Horne's refusal to perform the lead in the play because of pressure from the African American press. Suspecting his involvement, the Locke people charged White with hypocrisy. White claimed the Locke group had not condemned the play based on Lillian Smith's novel *Strange Fruit* (1945), which contained similar stereotypes, because his daughter Jane played the lead. *Variety* said that the charge "was strengthened by the fact that this was Miss White's first professional engagement, outside of some minor roles in stock."[62] White refuted the charge:

While I would have written *Strange Fruit* quite differently, . . . its story and motivation were vastly different from that of *St. Louis Woman*. Lillian Smith had written her tragic story of racial hate in Georgia as honestly as any author had ever put word to paper. Considerable as were its faults, it had an integrity and realism which were totally absent from *St. Louis Woman*. My enemies and critics, happy to find what they believed to be inconsistency between my attack on *St. Louis Woman* and my support of *Strange Fruit*, charged that Jane had been given the role only to silence criticism from me. It was a foul business, but I was very proud of the manner in which Jane withstood the attack, although Gladys [his wife] and I could see that she was deeply hurt.[63]

White solicited and received public condemnations from the producers-directors Abram Hill and Dick Campbell, along with the actor Frieda Washington. The Locke group countered with additional published speculation that White was avenging his son Walter, Jr., who had unsuccessfully auditioned for the starring role of Lil Augie in *St. Louis Woman*.[64] The Locke people further charged that Hill and Campbell were being hypocritical. Hill, they claimed, had earlier optioned the play for his own theatre in Harlem,[65] and Campbell had desperately sought the Della role for his wife, Muriel.[66] Furthermore, Frieda Washington had written Countee Cullen that *St. Louis Woman* was a "fine" play and that he should give the Della part to her sister Isabel.[67] White and Hughes fought the climactic battle in, of all places, a New York City taxicab:

I rode downtown with Walter and told him that I thought about their jumping on *St. Louis Woman*. The more I talked, the more I resented it, and when I looked at Walter he was red as a beet. Since there were other people in the cab, I perhaps should not have yowled so loud. He and Roy [Wilkins] both seemed like they had rather not been in it now. I said *Porgy*'s interminable crap game ran for years, and I never heard a word out of them. Roy said he did denounce it, but he was unknown in those days and nobody paid him any mind.[68]

The DuBois school lost this battle. Broadway loved *St. Louis Woman*. The importance of this bout far exceeded the merits of either group's case. Hughes, who strongly agreed with Locke's position on showing common folk, detected that whenever ordinary people and their problems popped up on stage, the theatre-going, middle-income African Americans "raised cane." There had been similar skepticism about his *Little Ham* (1936). Typical of the critical reaction to that work was the critic Darwin T. Turner's complaint that Hughes had simply "jumbled together . . . shoe shiners, beauticians, numbers runners, homosexuals, West Indians, followers of Father Divine, gangsters, [and] middle-class Negroes [who] cut, shoot, drink, make love, gossip, play numbers, and flirt, but rarely utter a significant thought."[69] Hughes disagreed, saying that *Little Ham*, like all of his plays, had a serious undertone.[70] Hughes thought the critics simply resented seeing on stage the lifestyles of low-income people. He wondered why there had not been similar complaints about Hill's *On Striver's Row* (1938), which showed an upwardly mobile Harlem family. That the daughter with a Radcliff education refused to marry the mama-selected "right" man was, to Hughes, as repugnant as Lil Augie and Della "jukin' it up." Hughes decided to highlight his distaste for such "uppity Negroes" in a series of articles for the *Chicago Defender* newspaper. By assuming the voice of the lovable, poor rascal Jesse B. Semple, Hughes satirized pretentious middle-income African Americans. That the articles became the source of both Alice Childress's *Just A Little Simple* (1953) and Hughes's musical *Simply Heavenly* (1957) said that others too frowned on racial hypocrisy. To drive home his point, Hughes staged the songs and styles of poor churchgoers. With his gospel musical hit *Black Nativity* (1961), he spotlighted his beloved ordinary people, dressed up in their church finery, shouting like "Kingdom come." For Hughes the fun part

was, of course, in his knowing that DuBois's supporters understood that they had to hold their tongues about the shouting sisters:
They would have "told off" any critical middle-income people
who dared to split their lips.

The final class of third-period plays, Inner Life versus Inner
Life, which probed both life and the afterlife, ultimately widened
the gap even further between the DuBois and Locke schools of
drama. Ironically, this class, however, offered these schools the
spiritual basis for an eventual union. Racism was not central to
questions posed by this class: Who am I? From where have I come?
What is life, and about what should it be? These queries emerged
from Locke's belief that:

The artistic problem of the Young Negro has not been so much that of
acquiring the outer mastery of form and technique as that of achieving an
inner mastery of mood and spirit. That accomplished, there has come the
happy release from self-consciousness, rhetoric, bombast, and the hampering habit of setting artistic values with primary regard for moral effect – all those pathetic over-compensations of a group inferiority
complex which our social dilemmas inflicted upon several unhappy
generations.[71]

In assigning such introspection to the drama in 1925 Locke obviously had the writer Jean Toomer in mind. Not only had Locke
seen early drafts of Toomer's *Cane* (1923), but he was Toomer's
patron: He had published in *The New Negro* two sections from
Cane, as well as two of Toomer's poems. In his collection *Plays of
Negro Life* (1927), Locke included Toomer's *Balo*, notwithstanding
Sterling Brown's belief that the piece was "more incident than
play."[72] Toomer, in *Balo*, ignored "moral effect" *and* standard
"form and technique." He instead pioneered in America the ideas
of the French dramatist Alfred Jarry's absurdist movement of the
late nineteenth century. *Balo* tells the story of a young man's search
for himself and Jesus in a dying cotton field in Georgia. Balo
struggles to reconcile his love for Jesus with his hatred of his white
neighbor, who, like Ubu in Jarry's *Ubu Roi* (1896), represents all

that Toomer deems "monstrous, irrational, inane, and ugly" in the South.[73] Acting out of both his loving and his loathing, Balo chants loudly to the white man: "White folks ain't no more'n niggers when they gets ter heaven." The white man reports this remark to Balo's parents, along with the judgment that Balo is "actin' like he crazy." The "craziness," however, signals that Balo has found Jesus also in the discovery of his own self-worth. That Balo comes under a spell from actually "seeing Jesus, the Light that came to Saul," summarizes brilliantly Toomer's belief that God was so much a part of *all* people that racism blasphemed God. *Balo* was important for addressing both the social issues of the DuBois school and the artistic imperatives of the Locke school. Toomer so packaged his theme and structure, however, that the DuBois school adherents felt themselves alienated from the play; they found its surrealism inaccessible. Locke admired the play because it showed the ability of African American drama to be "racial . . . purely for the sake of art."[74] Locke must have wondered, however, how this particular mood-and-spirit class of drama would in the future fulfill his assignment that drama "attain the full horizons of self and social criticism.[75] Ten years after his death in 1954, Locke was answered by Adrienne Kennedy in her play *Funny House of a Negro* (1964): With this play, the Inner Life versus Inner Life class matured. Kennedy used early and late absurdism in *Funny House* to tell the story of a mixed-race woman named Sarah, who, like Balo, is searching for her heritage. Like the dramatist Luigi Pirandello (1867–36), Kennedy made Sarah's questions about her lineage unanswerable, causing several of the play's "Herselves" (or possibilities) to present their own versions. This early absurdism showed that the Truth that was sought by both Balo and Sarah was relative and personal. Because Sarah could not find the "order, logic, and certainty" of her ancestry, she committed suicide. Kennedy asserted that Sarah, had she been able to rid herself of the need for rationality in an often silly world, would no longer have needed to *look* for her heritage, but simply could *be* it. Similar answers to questions about the meaning and purpose of life appeared in such traditionally structured morality plays as Langston Hughes's ever-popular *Tambourines to Glory* (1963) and Loften Mitchell's *The Cellar* (1952). These plays, like the absurdist ones, gave the Inner Life versus Inner Life class the distinction of being the only class that offered a metaphysical underpinning for an ultimate fusion of the two schools. In other words, racism abated when people genuinely knew, accepted, and respected their own self-worth and history, as well as those of others. Although the DuBois school might dismiss the dramatic form housing this message, its adherents could not question the validity of the premise.

A wall replaced the chasm between Art-Theatre and Protest drama during the fourth phase, which has become known as the Black Experience Theatre Period (1968–75). The heated, first-period debates and insults of DuBois and Locke again erupted into open warfare. Ed Bullins's withdrawal of his plays from performance at Black Panther Party rallies in San Francisco epitomized this hostility. The Panthers had embraced Bullins in 1965 because his short, poignant plays exposed the cutting edge of urban life. Such early Bullins dramas as *Clara's Ole Man* (1965) and *How Do You Do?* (1965) drew the crowds to the Panther rallies. Bullins's Art-Theatre plays, however, soon lost their usefulness to the Panthers: The plays were not revolutionary enough. As Locke had recommended, Bullins's plays showed African Americans as they were – shortcomings and all:

The Negro today scorns a craven and precarious survival at the price of seeming to be what he is not. He resents being spoken of as a social ward or minor, even by his own. He is through with those social nostrums and panaceas, the so-called "solutions" of his "problem," with which he and the country have been so liberally dosed in the past.[76]

Bullins fully subscribed to Locke's dictum, which became in 1965 the artistic base of Cultural Nationalism. This belief that African Americans could develop a nation – based on culture – within the American nation was opposed by the more politically revolutionary Black Panther Party. Bullins's plays were, therefore, at odds with

Panther beliefs. To underscore that this was a philosophical decision, Bullins changed the label on his plays from the popular one of "Black Revolutionary" to that of "Black Experience." This made clear that *his* plays represented "the *whole* experience of our being here in this land [emphasis added]" and not simply the political struggle.[77] Because Bullins used this label for six of the seventeen plays in the seminal black theatre issue of *The Drama Review* (Summer 1968), which he edited, the new name stuck. Bullins's stature helped to make permanent the change in name from Locke's Art-Theatre School to the Black Experience School. As if to emphasize that he was not tampering with Locke's theories, Bullins resurrected in his work the common folk. He defiantly put back on the stage what he called the "nigger street styles," who were the pimps, prostitutes, drunks, and addicts earlier seen in Hughes's *Little Ham*.[78] Bullins, too, pays homage to the heavy-partying, loud-talking and louder-dressing, low-income people who, for the most part, lived in the alleys, back streets, and the Projects of urban America. The only trouble was that this was the very group who, along with whites, was viewed by the revolutionary dramatists as "enemies of the people."

This, as well as other fourth-period changes in each class, exacerbated the friction between the schools. Whereas the DuBois Protest School called for armed insurrection in response to racism, New Inner Life versus Outer Life plays by the Locke people looked at race relations from a deeply personal perspective that sought to heal. Alice Childress's *Wedding Band* (1973), for example, encourages the audience to empathize with the play's two lovers, who happen to be of different races. What alarmed the DuBois school was that this theme showed the "regression" of Childress from her earlier, hard-hitting attack on white liberal racism in *Florence* (1950). Another such "back flip" is seen in the reconciliation in Samm-Art Williams's *Welcome to Black River* (1975). Set in North Carolina, Williams's play has a landowning white family accept its blood relationship to the neighboring African American sharecroppers. These white people, reasoned the DuBois school,

were probably some of the same ones who, during the second period, had lynched Thea in Edmonds's *Bad Man* (1934) and had
raped Annie in Richardson's *Compromise* (1926). Yet this reflected
what the Locke school saw as some improvement in race relations.
No more comforting to the DuBois people was their being portrayed in New Binding Relationships plays as a destructive force,
infecting both nuclear and extended families. "Revolutionaries"
appear as threats both to the nuclear family in Joseph A. Walker's
Tony Award-winning *The River Niger* (1973) and to the extended
family in Ed Bullins's *The Fabulous Miss Marie* (1971). As the
DuBois people viewed it, when the Locke school was not making
these outrageous charges against them, it was staging plays that
were excessively preoccupied with such "trivia" as dishonesty, women's power, and blind ambition. What particularly angered the
DuBois school was that "The System" honored the Locke people
for their "socially irrelevant pettiness." Not only, for example, did
Lonne Elder's *Ceremonies in Dark Old Men* (1969) and Phillip
Hayes Dean's *The Sty of the Blind Pig* (1971) each carry on at length
about a family's being harmed equally by dishonesty and by a shady
lover, but both plays also received Drama Desk awards. As far as
the DuBois school was concerned, the Locke people could have
their "silly awards," especially if Charles Gordone's *No Place to Be
Somebody* (1969) deserved the Pulitzer Prize. The significance of
this public brawling between the Locke and the DuBois supporters
was that for the first time Locke's people were not intimidated by
what Locke called "solutions to the Negro problem." Although
they did not turn their backs on the struggle of the sixties, the
Locke people felt no obligation to join the parade promoting "social nostrums and panaceas." It would have been easy enough, for
example, for Bullins to have appeased the Panthers in 1967 by
writing more revolutionary plays. It was not until 1970, however –
when he was good and ready – that he offered *Death List* and *The
Devil Catchers*. Bullins, as well as many other Locke people, simply
defied the "Kill Whitey" trend common to the DuBois people's
Black Revolutionary drama, which had evolved from Protest

drama. The New Binding Relationship class, then, showed a drama that was as street tough as its "Back Street" people.

To the DuBois school, the New Flow class plays of Locke's school were even worse than the plays of the New Binding Relationships class. In their efforts to make their work "delightfully rich transfusions of essential folk-arts," as Locke dictated, dramatists created mixed-media Flow plays with characters who were consummate antirevolutionaries. Melvin Van Peebles's *Ain't Supposed to Die a Natural Death* (1971) and *Don't Play Us Cheap* (1972) were, for the DuBois people, prime examples of plays that abused "Negro" women and spouted commercial revolution. An even better example was provided by Bullins who, in his *Street Sounds* (1970), spotlighted every frailty known to inner-city man or beast: Harlem politicians, dope sellers, black deejays, corner brothers, "mad dawgs," errand runners, thieves, liars, black critics, and so on. Bullins, like Locke, was "being racial purely for the sake of art." The DuBois people knew better, however. Bullins included sketches in *Street Sounds* that made fun of the "militants" and "revolutionaries" who bellowed as many nonsensical clichés as did an "electronic nigger." It became increasingly clear to the DuBois people that the dramatists of these Flow plays used Locke's recommended "flavor of language" as well as "flow of phrase, rhythm, and music" not "to make a distinctive contribution to theatre," but to put down Black Revolutionary drama. The DuBois people struck back. Their Black Revolutionary plays killed off the kinds of characters featured in Flow plays. At least two of Bullins's "Back Street" – type characters, for example, died from a revolutionary's bullet in every single Black Revolutionary play. Trouble was clearly brewing. It was the New Inner Life versus Inner Life class that kept private the tensions between the two schools. Even Bullins, undoubtedly the most versatile of the Locke people, abandoned his periodical use of profane language and situations to consider What is life, and about what should it be? In Bullins's *A Son, Come Home* (1968), which contained the same kind of lyrical and poetic-prose dialogue the Panthers had earlier booted off the stage, the son was not after political power, but was seeking his mother, as well as himself. The son finds his mother "saved," in a Father Divine–like "home of saints." The excellently crafted episodes delicately unveil the theme that "one can never go home again." With *A Son, Come Home*, Bullins showed the extent to which he had conquered not only what Locke had called "the outer mastery of form and technique," but also his "inner mastery of mood and spirit." Bullins perfected the form (*a*) by not treating episodes as building blocks of plays; (*b*) by not distinguishing episodes by the entrance, exit, or silence of a principal character; and (*c*) by not building the action to an appropriate climax and resolution through a conventional beginning, middle, and end. Instead, Bullins shortened his plays' beginnings and endings. He enlivened, extended, and circled the middles. Because television and film set his urban audiences' expectations regarding entertainment, Bullins developed snapshot episodes. The results were his surgically carved and brilliantly conceived thought-provoking plays. The importance of Bullins's Inner Life versus Inner Life plays, as well as of Adrienne Kennedy's *Cities in Bezique* (1969) and *A Rat's Mass* (1969), was that they forced even the revolutionaries to stop temporarily their "self-consciousness, rhetoric, and bombast." These plays demanded more from all people than "moral effects," which became only pretense. The plays forced their audiences to probe what it was that set them apart from the beasts.

The last period of Black Experience theatre, The Bridge (since 1975), was important because it mixed the ideas that flowed from the DuBois and the Locke schools. Its waters, although brackish, nourished compromises tendered by both sources. The DuBois people, who had lost the playwright Amiri Baraka to full-time political organizing, heeded Richard Wesley's call to lower the rhetoric as they reevaluated theories and strategies. Considerably more moderate plays were rushed on stage. The Locke people dropped some of its "Back Street" mermaids-and-sharks characterizations and plots, as well as its Black Revolutionary–bashing themes. Permanently altered classes of drama wound new ways. The Unified

Inner Life versus Outer Life class, for example, looked with more skepticism at the whites it had previously embraced, thereby pleasing the DuBois people. Three subclasses developed, the first of which was Historical Results. This subclass depicted the tragic outcome of racism. The African American historical play finally matured – thanks to urgings of the playwright Loften Mitchell and the critic Helen Armstead Johnson that more historical plays be written.[79] Of course, significant historical drama also predated this period. William Branch's *In Splendid Error* (1954), for example, revisited the Frederick Douglass–John Brown confrontation over moral duty and good judgment. Branch's *A Wreath for Udomo* (1961) synchronized the racial separatist movements in America and in South Africa.[80] Important, too, were the Ed Bullins and August Wilson cycles of plays on twentieth-century African American life. No playwright, however, so completely mastered the dramatization of real and imagined historical events as did Charles Fuller – notwithstanding Amiri Baraka's dunking him in the under current of being "the most reactionary sector of the black middle class."[81] Fuller used history to validate the African American's being "part and parcel of everything that goes on here."[82] Fuller's plays were more than just representations of historical events. They juxtaposed studies of overt and imagined racism with blatant and concealed intraracial discrimination. The motivation, inevitably, was a struggle over *place*, as well as claims to place. In his critically acclaimed *The Brownsville Raid* (1976) and his Pulitzer Prize–winning *A Soldier's Play* (1981), Fuller helped people better understand their natures. The same hatred and tunnel vision that motivated the white bigots in Brownsville, Texas, also plagued the African American who murdered Sgt. Vernon Waters in the later play. The same claims on place, in other words, changed the inquiry in both plays from *Who* did it to *What* was the murderer. Fuller showed these battles over rights involving rank, situation, or space as defining the African presence in America. He exposed the carefully designed and placed obstructions to African American advancement. The diverse stumbling blocks ranged from the

slaves' efforts to improve their lot in the seventeenth century in
Sally (1988) and *Prince* (1989) to the businessman Bruner's can-
didacy for political office in the twentieth century in *Burner's Frolic*
(1990). Fuller's reading of history was still optimistic: The Africans' enslavers would one day get their due, he said, just as surely
as the white liberal who had raped Sally was identified, years after
his deed, when the blind woman in *Jonquil* (1989) recognized
his voice.

Fuller's positivism influenced the development of the second
subclass, Biography, which was now different. Although Frederick
Douglass, Toussaint L'Ouverture, Sojourner Truth, and Harriet
Tubman appeared continually in African American drama, their
treatment now depicted new perspectives on them. Their DuBois-
era contributions, for example, took a back seat to their challenges
in such plays as *Frederick Douglass Now* (1989), a one-man multimedia piece; *Toussaint, Angel-Warrior* (1985) by Audley Haffenden;
A Woman Called Truth (1989) by Sandra Fenichel Asher; and *Hats:
A Tribute to Harriet Tubman* (1986), also a one-woman work. Even
the analyses of such modern idols as Mr. Justice Thurgood Marshall in Fred Pinkard's one-man play, *Thurgood Marshall: Justice*
(1987), summoned people to service, not to idolatry. Many of the
newer plays on the Reverend Dr. Martin Luther King, a model for
most African Americans, portrayed him as but a man – at times a
frightened and troubled one, but unrelenting in his fight against
racial and economic oppression. Typical of these plays was Ron
Milner's *Roads of the Mountaintop* (1986), the story of the internal
struggles of King and his family after he was awarded the Nobel
Peace Prize in 1964. These historical and biographical plays were
significant because they told of simple human beings – people like
everybody else – who were not afraid to do the unpopular deed on
behalf of the "downtrodden." This new attitude contributed to the
rise of the third subclass, Victims, which offered a surprisingly new
view. These people were "told off" when they tried to use their
misfortunes to justify their own hypocrisy and greed. These victims, too, needed the gun to be pointed at their scheming heads, as

shown in Gus Edwards's play about such a brother. Edwards's *Black Body Blues* (1978) warned African Americans not to let themselves become as prejudiced as some whites were. In the play, Fletcher, a drug pusher, kills the white family who had hired his brother Arthur as their servant. The tragedy was that these whites were not stereotypical bigots, but thoughtful people who genuinely cared about Arthur. The double tragedy was that Fletcher thought the killing would "free" Arthur. Like the bigoted white neighbor in Willis Richardson's *Compromise* and the white northerner in Alice Childress's *Florence*, the brother Fletcher needed to be whipped senseless, Edwards implied. The Victim plays demanded, then, that African Americans today devote themselves as passionately to changing African American thieves, drunks, addicts, and good-for-nothings as they do to pursuing racism. According to Fuller, choosing not to accept this challenge made African Americans "denigrate themselves and shame their parents."[83] The challenge, in other words, was a moral duty that was not for sale.

Even the plays in the Unified Binding Relationships class reflected during this final period the calmed waters between the DuBois and the Locke people. Black Experience dramatists stopped painting revolutionaries as family typhoons. More thoughtful questions were raised in subclasses concerning women, men, and values, as well as African heritage. Especially critical in the New Women Subclass were the discrepancies in the images of women. Dramatists ceased worrying about "the tremendous contradictions" in the African American mother, who, according to the critic Barbara Christian, both got "characterized as strong and [was] punished for being so."[84] Women who scrutinized their feelings, motivations, fathers, and careers were successors to Lena Younger in Lorraine Hansberry's *A Raisin in the Sun* (1959) and to Sophia in Errol John's *Moon on a Rainbow Shawl* (1962). The new women concluded that they needed to express their "particular and powerful love" for each other. In *Long Time Since Yesterday* (1988) by P. J. Gibson, for example, six sophisticated, college-educated women finally understand that they reject their capacity for feeling and loving because, as the poet Audre Lorde has stated, they permit others to devalue these traits.[85] At an impromptu reunion following the suicide of one of their number, the women, too, see their feelings as "our power, our ability to posit, to vision."[86] They resolve, therefore, that their *expressed* feelings will guide their life pursuits.[87] Such refreshing insights won public acceptance because, as Christian has pointed out, women, in increasing numbers, now controlled how their images were projected. Men, however, also drew more perspicacious women. Samm-Art Williams's *Woman from the Town* (1989), for example, shows a woman whose life is marked by the pain of family-and-hometown rejection because of her teenage pregnancy. While Williams exposes her pain and revenge wish, he also so balances them that the woman comes to understand the need to let them go, to not let them become ends in themselves.[88] This character, unlike Alberta Warren in Dean's *The Sty of the Blind Pig*, discerns that for her to control her life, she has to stop viewing herself as a victim; she cannot continue "celebrating her victimization."[89] This decision becomes the motif in the lives of women as they respond to male privilege in the home and the workplace. Women can attack male license in the home by reassessing father–daughter relationships, says *Here in My Father's House* (1989) by Jewel Brimage and others. Like Adele Parker in Elder's *Ceremonies in Dark Old Men*, the women in *Father's House* decide that they have to discard the "prolonged spiritual effort to reach the father, to be transformed into him, and to be his likeness, more son than daughter."[90] They want, instead, to know "how really to become their father's daughters . . . and how to emulate his judgment."[91] Understanding fully *his* means of "acquiring the wisdom to find one's way in the world" not only helps the woman better appreciate the complexity of her love for her father, but also aids her in assessing her own worth outside of the home.[92] Women can defy public perceptions, therefore, and compete in a white person's world of work, because their fathers, as well as other men at home, support their "liberation" from nuclear-family preoccupations –as depicted in the New Men subclass.

The representations of such supportive men emerged during this final period from the fourth-period's distorted pictures of men as dreamers, drunks, and "dick heads." Dramatists showed men developing more positive parenting strategies and more trusting friendships. The new father, for example, was in touch with every aspect of his children's growth and development. Unlike the hapless poet–house painter Johnny Williams in Joseph A. Walker's *The River Niger* (1973), these men did not entrust important decisions to poorly nurtured sons. Richard Wesley's *The Past Is the Past* (1989) and *Mommy Loves You* (1989) by Toni Ann Johnson demonstrated this point well. Wesley argued that a father "must break the cycle" of abandoning his children because of feeling that he was not "enough" – especially when what he wanted was "to give them the world." Just being "father," said Wesley, was more than enough. Johnson agreed. She further demanded that husband–wife "emotional dislocations," as the critic Paula Giddings called them, not strain father–daughter ties.[93] Fathers and daughters must not "act out their lives in the web of conventions," argued Barbara Christian, "which they may or may not believe in, may or may not feel at ease in, [or] may or may not help them to grow."[94] According to Wesley, fathers must replace these imposed protocols with endemic ones specific to their relationship. Whereas this benefited the children, it especially helped the father, as well as the fatherly. The benefits, as shown in *Training the Beast* (1989) by Frederick Glover, were that men learned to give of their knowledge and experience without imposing their successes, ambitions, or fears on young people. These men became more open and trusting, another characteristic of this fifth-period man. That there was a need for such men is apparent in *That Serious He-Man Ball* (1988) by Alonzo D. Lamont, Jr., where three close buddies, like the women in *Long Time Since Yesterday*, unleash their pent-up feelings about each other. That the emotions come out during a tough basketball game underscores the necessity for men to cease using aggression to express both anger and love. Lamont suggests that men invest less of their egos into appearances and things.

The New Values subclass deconstructed most earlier themes. Not until Richard Wesley's *The Talented Tenth* (1989) was there a significant follow-up to Lorraine Hansberry's introduction into Black Experience drama of the theme of class and heritage as principal constituents of African American life. Wesley's play has three well-off couples probe their estrangement from their previous values and former inner-city friends. These characters have moved from low-income to middle-income neighborhoods – areas that they believe better reflect their self-worth. They soon discover, however, that living in a new place does not change their feelings enough about themselves. They have compromised their self-esteem because their "outward appearance, rather than their inner qualities, became the measuring stick."[95] Even after adopting the new behavior patterns and tastes that came with their believing "that they *were* their appearance," Wesley's characters still feel like "pariahs."[96] Wesley attributes this to their having bought into a "destructive hierarchy" that, by its nature, has to have outcasts so "that [its] members could have someone to look down upon."[97] This satisfies people's need to feel superior. Although Wesley's people are assigned by their color to the misfit class, they try, nevertheless, to escape the category and protect themselves by owning "as much property as possible." They become, in some cases, greedy materialists.[98] Tragedy occurs when Wesley's characters discover that their suburban house, stuffed with expensive doohickeys, is but an alienating island-trap. Because these characters find themselves cut off from their history, as well as from their *real* selves, some decide to return "home." Wesley suggests that the spiritual odyssey demands not that they give up material comfort for a less affluent lifestyle, but that they go back to assist those who are trying to help themselves.

The playwrights Steve Carter and Duma Ndlovu agreed with Wesley. They suggested in the African Heritage subclass that this need for reestablishing ties among all economic classes applied as well to all African peoples. Carter's *Eden* (1976) depicts a sophisticated Caribbean family that looks down upon its neighbors, a

poor southern African American family. *Shelia's Day* (1990) by
Ndlovu celebrates the inextricable bonds that South African and
African American women discover. Both plays argue that African
peoples benefited from the African traditions of viewing life as an
experience rather than as a problem, of using error as a learning
tool, and of declaring commonality through an in-depth knowledge
about ancestors. Tradition, critic Audre Lorde has suggested,
helped people – especially uppity ones – to see that they must live
in "correspondence with the rest of the world as a whole."[99] Other
people's pains and problems belonged to all, as long as they shared
the same experiences. The task, then, was not to divorce oneself
from other's problems, but to ease them before they become one's
own. This change, according to Lorde, would rise "endemically
from experience fully lived and responded to . . . no matter how
bad or how painful living may be."[100] Carter's Caribbean family,
therefore, is incapable of dismissing its poorer neighbors from
mind because tradition forces the Caribbeans to confront the
other's pain or error. There are simply too many lessons to be
grasped.[101] *Shelia's Day* demonstrates that these lessons offer com-
monalities to peoples, regardless of time and space. The African
tradition of "Beg Pardon" is a useful example. Only healthy gains
would come to people who supplicated their "ancestors' pardon for
offenses committed against them during the year, intentional or
not," the critic and author Eugenia Collier has explained. People
"petitioned not only for themselves and their neighbors, but also
for relatives known and unknown scattered throughout the world.
Indeed the ancestors were nearly a tangible presence."[102] The pe-
titioning made functional the bonds between the African Americans and the South Africans in *Shelia's Day*, between the African
Americans and the Caribbeans in *Eden*, and between the low-
income and moderate-income African Americans in *The Talented
Tenth*. Not only did African tradition, in another example, help
Lena Younger in Hansberry's *A Raisin in the Sun* move to the
Chicago suburbs, but tradition also made her take her Southside
(read, African) roots with her. Tradition even helped her compre-

hend her need to be in suburbia and yet to return "home" regu-
larly – not to interfere with, but to help – in any way possible –
those determined to achieve a better balance between life's pains
and pleasures. This theme, as well as other traditional elements,
appears throughout the body of Binding Relationships plays because of the dramatists' new consciousness, gained through the
cross-fertilization of the DuBois and the Locke schools.

Severely curtailed since Bontemps's *St. Louis Woman* (1946), the
Flow class of plays made a strong return during the final period. It
was amazing that the DuBois school could have at all affected
these plays, governed by Locke's concept of "flows of rhythm, music, color, and imagery." Yet gone were the seductive women, the
"tee-vee" militants, the inner-city freaks, and the stinging insults.
Such a large number of New Consciousness plays supplanted the
older group that the Unified Flow class divided into Serious and
Musical subclasses. Whereas the Serious subclass was further separated into two kinds, Social and Personality, the Musical subclass
split into five types: Social, Historical, Personality, Romantic, and
Sacred/Gospel. The musicals answered Locke's 1926 question
about how best to "liberate" the African American "gifts of song
and dance and pantomime" from the "shambles of minstrelsy."[103]
The Social Musical, for example, probably was what DuBois had
in mind when in 1909 he asked Bob Cole to write protest musicals.
Without changing totally the formula for musicals, the Social Musical solved the contradictions in clarifying versus simplifying an
issue. Clarification was achieved by making plots tell balanced stories – in terms of fun and seriousness – of innocent protagonists
struggling with antagonists over issues. Young people battled sex
and violence on television or drug addiction in such works as *A
Place to Be Me* (1989) by Runako Jahi, *Momma Don't* (1990) by
Michael Matthews, and *Stop and Think* (1989) by Karmyn Lott.
Racial and social conditions antagonized people in Micki Grant's
Don't Bother Me I Can't Cope (1972) and Lott's *Stop and Think*.
Richard Wesley created the most original adversaries in his *The
Dream Team* (1989), a drama in which desegregation separates two

baseball-playing brothers, only one of whom goes to the newly integrated major leagues. The significance of these musicals is that their social consciousness deposes "fun and games." Audiences pondered the significance of delightfully packaged and clarified issues.

The Historical Musical, which not only told the stories of important events and places but also reflected the history of the genre itself, moved from streamlining to elucidating issues. The early musicals of this period, which chronicled the history of musical comedy, re-staged the works of the Early Musicals Period. There was no defining of issues in such works as Loften Mitchell's *Bubbling Brown Sugar* (1976), concept by Rosetta LeNoire, and Honi Coles and Bobby Short's *Black Broadway* (1980). The historical importance of *Bubbling Brown Sugar* was in its role as the first show to portray the history of African American music both on Broadway and in Harlem. *Bubbling Brown Sugar* even used veterans from the original shows, including Avon Long, Joseph Attles, and Josephine Premice. *Black Broadway* cast stars of the twenties and thirties in the same roles they had originated: Edith Wilson in *Plantation Revue* (1922), Elisabeth Welch in *Runnin' Wild* (1923); Adelaide Hall in *Blackbirds of 1928;* and John W. Bubbles as Sportin' Life in *Porgy and Bess* (1935). These re-creations sparkled from the addition of such contemporary stars as Bobby Short, Gregory Hines (*Eubie!* [1978]), and Nell Carter (*Ain't Misbehavin'* [1978], another historical revue). Vernel Bagneris's *One Mo' Time* (1979), which reconstructs the history of vaudeville in the twenties, changed these musicals, however. *One Mo' Time* evolved from a series of tunes by, among others, Ma Rainey, Bessie Smith, and Ethel Waters to a musical with its own vital theme: DuBois people's beliefs influenced Bagneris's post-opening decision to add episodes about the "difficult relationships between the black performers and the white theatre managers."[104] This trend to make the audience "work" also surfaced in such locale musicals as Mike Malone's *Breakfast in Harlem* (1988), *The Gospel of the Harlem Renaissance* (1990) by Titus Walker, and Bagneris's *Further Mo'* (1990). These revues and musicals emphasized both joys and hardships. *Further Mo'*, for example, set a joyful 1927 performance within the context of the impending destruction by fire of the Lyric Theater in New Orleans. Connie Ray's Off-Broadway hit, *Smoke on the Mountain* (1990), was no less a surprise with its satirizing of the misadventures of members of a Depression-era family as they traveled through the South. Once again the African American musical drama had become commercial enough for Broadway houses, the dramatists knowing full well what images to eschew and what beliefs to espouse.

Mixing tragedies and triumphs was also the trend in the Personality Musical, which celebrated the lives of entertainers and leaders. Some of the earlier musicals and revues of this period, however, were simply tributes. Ashton Springer's *Eubie!* (1978) and Donald McKayle's concept for *Sophisticated Ladies* (1981), for example, avoided the many hardships in the lives of Eubie Blake and Duke Ellington. Even in *Mood Indigo* (1981), Julian Swain shunned the blues in the lives of Fats Waller, Bessie Smith, Ma Rainey, Big Maybell, Eubie Blake, and Duke Ellington. Elmo Terry-Morgan, too, spotlighted only the talents of such international stars as Bessie Smith, Billie Holiday, Dinah Washington, Sarah Vaughn, and Lena Horne in *The Song of Sheba* (1988). *Williams and Walker* (1986), by Vincent D. Smith, the story of Bert Williams and George Walker, marked, however, the beginning of a move to balance the good and bad times of a person's life. *The Dark Star from Harlem* (1989), by Glynn Borders and Jan Tori Evans, although continuing this trend, gave more emphasis to the songs of Josephine Baker. Better balances emerged in depictions of the lives of Martin Luther King, in *I Have a Dream* (1989) by Josh Greenfeld, and of Mahalia Jackson, in *Truly Blessed* (1989) by Queen Esther Marrow. One interesting shift in emphasis has the tragic dominating the joyful in *Yesterdays* (1990) by Reenie Upchurch, which tells of the last two months of Billie Holiday's life. Set in a New York nightclub in May 1959, the play exhibits Holiday the victim:

Between performances of around a dozen of her best-known numbers, Holiday grows progressively tipsier and more combative as she free-associates autobiographical vignettes and rails at the police in the audience who are about to arrest her for drug possession. The many brutalizing experiences recounted include Holiday's rape at the age of ten, her later enslavement to drugs by a womanizing lover and numerous instances of humiliating racial discrimination.[105]

This portrayal, like those in the Social type, contradicts traditional music theatre convention, as can be seen in the tragic endings. Such violations appear even in two Romantic musicals: Lynn Ahrens's *Once on This Island* (1990) and *Count Your Blessings* (1990) by James M. Brown. Although the dramatists retained the traditional formula of having their two lovers pulled apart by fate, both books made social conditions the source of their characters' troubles. *Once on This Island*, for example, had "class and racial differences, rather than the sea, pull the star-crossed lovers asunder."[106] The musical – adapted from a novel by the African American from Trinidad, Rosa Guy – features a Caribbean peasant girl who longs for the son of a wealthy mulatto landowner. This plot underscores the DuBois school thinking that such differences had to go. *Count Your Blessings* similarly couches its call for social changes within the traditional love story. Here a young woman lawyer falls in love with her first client, a jailed street-wise rap artist. The reason for these two and similar adaptations of the musical was that African American dramatists feared their audiences would not believe in or accept a simple love story about a people who, after two centuries, were still plagued by the need to fight continually racism.

The Sacred/Gospel musical was the only type that escaped the influence of the DuBois school. The reason, of course, was the traditional uses of this music. Not only had Negro spirituals sustained an enslaved people, but they also had coded the comings and goings on the Underground Railroad. The spirituals, therefore, were subtle – not bombastic. Langston Hughes's integration of these spirituals into the first Sacred/Gospel musical, *Black*

Nativity (1961), canceled any social consciousness-raising. Hughes aimed to inspire people with the story of Jesus's birth in a poor neighborhood. This purpose, of course, suited the traditional functions of the spiritual and of gospel music in general. Gospel music originated as prayers to relieve personal tragedies. The songwriter Thomas Dorsey, for example, wrote one of the earliest gospel songs, "Precious Lord, Take My Hand," because he sought solace from the deaths of his wife and son. Not even the social theology of Martin Luther King had a place in such a private talk between a man and *his* God. Hughes's use of this music, along with the spiritual, combined private prayer with a subtle code. The initial sources of the plots are found in religion. Vinnette Carroll, for example, adapted Negro preachers' sermons in her *Trumpets of the Lord* (1963), which was from James Weldon Johnson's *God's Trombones* (1927), and she adapted the Book of Matthew for *Your Arms Too Short to Box with God* (1976). Ron Milner's *Don't Get God Started* (1987) stages a soul-stirring revival meeting. There are no protests about the social conditions that were causing people to abandon religion – even when Vy Higgenson and the Ted Kociolek–James Racheff team added secular lost faith–regained plots to the Sacred/Gospel musical. The fault lay with the young female characters who, in Kociolek and Racheff's *Abyssinia* (1988) and in Higgenson's *Mama I Want to Sing, Part I* (1982), *Let the Music Play Gospel* (1989), and *Mama I Want to Sing, Part II* (1990), stopped believing. The Sacred/Gospel musical, then, existed solely because producers sought to capitalize on the strong appeal of both gospel music and theatre. The works' popularity emerged with Hughes's *Black Nativity* (1961). Even had the director, Vinnette Carroll, not employed such gospel stars as the Reverend Alex Bradford and Marion Williams, *Black Nativity* would still have been an international hit.

Church people saw music as ministry, and it was not particularly surprising that people in record numbers attended the Sacred/Gospel musical: Higgenson's *Mama I Want to Sing, Part I* ran for almost a decade. This popularity – along with Higgenson's expert marketing skills – explains her development of the two sequels to *Mama, Part I.* (Do not be amazed if she – in the future – opens *Mama I'm Glad I Wanted to Sing.*) The Sacred/Gospel musical was so popular because it, like the works of the Early Musicals Period, made an art form out of what Locke called "a general resource of art." In other words, dramatists evolved "something technically distinctive" from the substance of race life. The Sacred/Gospel musical, therefore, will probably remain for a long time the most popular of the musicals.

Whereas the Serious subclass of Unified Flow plays in no way matched the popularity of the Musical subclass, the former was more important in terms of the development of African American theatre. The Personality and the Social types of the Serious subclass completed the job begun by Willis Richardson and Randolph Edmonds during the Early Serious Period (1923–38). The Personality play, interpreting the beliefs and achievements of the famous and the not-so-famous, had the modus operandi for successfully mixing Locke's and DuBois's theories. For the story of the anthropologist and folklorist Zora Neale Hurston, for example, the playwright Laurence Holder, in *Zora* (1989), had Hurston act like a Locke character in order to make DuBois points:

Can you imagine this cullud girl standing on 125th Street with a pair of calipers measuring the size of folks' heads? But the folk was all interested in this.
HEY! THE WHITE FOLKS SAY WE IS DUMB AND NOT EQUAL TO THEM 'CAUSE OUR HEADS IS SMALL AND OUR BRAINS IS TOO. SO COME ON UP HERE AND LET ME MEASURE YOUR BRAIN, HONEY. YES! AIN'T IT THE TRUTH! WHAT WILL THOSE PEOPLE THINK OF NEXT?
Yes! The colored folks was interested all right. They wanted to know the truth, and they weren't disappointed neither. Them niggers got big old heads.[107]

The significance of this return to Langston Hughes's method was that important beliefs and people gained popularity with audiences of the eighties. Whereas Hurston's racial and feminist ideas were new to many, other individuals were already such cultural icons that attempts to distill their many accomplishments were risky. Alice Childress was brave to attempt – and fortunate to capture – the brilliance of comedian Jackie "Moms" Mabley in Childress's *MOMS* (1989). Other Serious Personality playwrights stuck with their own members, friends, and neighbors. Tony Award–winning actress Trazana Beverley shows such a gathering in her autobiographical one-woman play, *The Spirit Moves* (1984); so do Gus Edwards's look at Harlem life in *Lifetimes* (1990); Shelly Garrett's *Beauty Shop* (1989), a comedy about a typical beauty salon; and Barbara Roberts and Robert Meiksins's *Juke Joint Jammin'* (1990), a one-woman show about the spirit of Chicago women of 1938.

These representations of what Locke called "the idioms and timbres" of African American life differed substantially from George C. Wolfe's postmodernist Serious Flow pieces: *Colored Museum* (1986), a satire about the "reprocessing of those old, stereotypical images"; *Spunk* (1989), vignettes inspired by three Zora Neale Hurston short stories; and *Jelly's Last Jam* (1992), a "cultural earthquake" on the paradoxical life of composer and pianist Ferdinand Le Menthe ("Jelly Roll") Morton.[108] Wolfe's new form resembled Hughes's form in *Don't You Want to Be Free?* in that both combined music, dance, song, poetry, and prose-poetry into an episodic structure. Wolfe's form, however, was without a story line. The Wolfe form, like Bertolt Brecht's Alienation Effect, forced the audience to think about the various truths that the characters were confronting about themselves. In order not to lose his audience in *Spunk*, Wolfe said that he kept people guessing "from moment to moment . . . and by beat by beat by beat . . . about where they – and the characters – would end up.[109] What Wolfe wanted spectators to think about in *Jelly's Last Jam* was that the middle-class, light-skinned Morton suffered from "the defining tragedy of this country – he was a racist" – toward ordinary dark-skinned blacks.[110] Wolfe honed this complex personality down to recognizable proportions, which he so well packaged with song, dance, and spectacle that critics and spectators raved about *Jelly*, as well as about Wolfe's other plays.

The same acceptance Wolfe received did not initially greet Phillip Hayes Dean's portrait of singer-actor-activist Paul Robeson. Dean's *Robeson* (1978), which starred James Earl Jones, evoked controversy. Two groups organized, one to deplore the show, the other to deplore the deploring. The former, the National Ad Hoc Committee to End Crimes against Paul Robeson, called the play "a pernicious perversion of the essence of Paul Robeson."[11] Paul Robeson, Jr., the leader of the committee, said that the play trivialized Robeson and made his basic character unrecognizable. The son believed that Robeson "resembled the false image that has been created by the white Establishment" and that the play, therefore, was "an insult to my father's memory."[12] Supporting Robeson's position were choreographer Alvin Ailey, author James Baldwin, Harvard professor Derrick Bell, Georgia state senator Julian Bond, poet Gwendolyn Brooks, director Vinnette Carroll, Coretta Scott King, playwright Lonne Elder III, and Representative Charles B. Rangel, among many others. The group carefully aimed its charge away from James Earl Jones, whose acting, the committee stated, "elevated the portrait to sympathetic and commanding levels."[13] The committee believed, however, that "it was precisely here that the greatest danger lay. For we in the Black community have repeatedly seen the gains among us reduced from REVOLUTIONARY heroic dimensions to manageable, sentimentalized size. If they cannot be co-opted in life, it is simple enough to tailor their images in death."[14] Paul Robeson, Jr., claimed that the play answered the 1951 call of the U.S. Foreign Service for a negative play about his father:

USIE [the United States International Information and Educational Exchange Program] in the Gold Coast, and I suspect everywhere else in Africa, badly needs a thorough-going, sympathetic and regretful, but straight-talking treatment of the whole Robeson episode. . . . It must detail Robeson's spiritual alienation from his country and from the bulk of his own people – how he looked hopefully to Moscow, as of course many

people of good-will did at one time, as the champion of a new, more hu-
mane social order; but how he has since, apparently in his blind bitterness, missed or ignored all the evil signs which have turned almost all the
rest away. . . . It must go on to detail his almost pitiful (for so robust and
seemingly dignified a person) accommodation to the Communist line,
whatever in its unscrupulous opportunism it required of him. And it must
treat this, and his related attitudes, as the illness of the mind and heart
that in fact they seem to be, rather than the ruthless schemings of one
intent on rising to personal power in the planned world revolution; but an
illness which is not easily recognized, yet contagious, and thus a deadly
danger.''[15]

The pro-play group thought that this twenty-seven-year-old cable simply reflected America's guilt about its racism and its paranoia about Communists. Dean, the group believed, was not a State
Department pawn, but a writer exercising the freedom to create,
free from all censorship. Censorship was an especially sensitive issue to this group of thirty-three prominent members of the Dramatists Guild, among whom were Ed Bullins, Edward Albee, and
Arthur Miller. In its "Statement on Group Censure of Plays," the
guild, in fact, deplored "attempts to influence critics and audiences against a play."[16] The National Ad Hoc Committee, however, prevailed: After only forty-five performances on Broadway,
Robeson closed. Yet the guild won as well because Joseph Papp,
producer of the New York Shakespeare Festival, reopened *Robeson*
on a bill with Ntozake Shange's *For Colored Girls Who Have Considered Suicide / When the Rainbow is Enuf* (1976). Papp, as well as
others, viewed the reopening as a victory over censorship.

The double bill of *Robeson* and *For Colored Girls* represented a
major shift in African American theatre. Just as *Robeson* made public the private humanity of an icon, *For Colored Girls* aired the private intraracial struggles among men and women. Shange's
"choreopoem" celebrates not only being African American and
being a woman but also being an African American assertive
woman: "Now you cant have me less i give me away." Shange's
tragic picture of the black man gone from insensitive and irrespon-

sible to mad was unlike any that had ever been seen in African American theatre. The colors in the painting glare so much, therefore, that they hurt the brain:

lady in red
he [beau willy brown] kicked the screen outta the window /
& held the kids offa the sill / you gonna marry me / yeh, i'll
marry ya / anything / but bring the children back in the
house / he looked from where the kids were hangin from the
fifth story / at alla the people screamin at him / & he started
sweating again / say to alla the neighbors / you gonna marry me /

i stood by beau in the window / with naomi reachin for me / &
kwame screamin mommy mommy from the fifth story / but i cd
only whisper / & he dropped em
. . . .
i waz cold / i waz burnin up / a child
& endlessly weavin garments for the moon wit my tears
i found god in myself
& i loved her / i loved her fiercely'[17]

The portrayal of this role won for the actor Trazana Beverley the Tony Award, and the play earned Ntozake Shange an Obie, along with the wrath of men. The men did not deny the images and the issues, but they did resent Shange's "airing her complaints for white people's enjoyment." Nevertheless, men began to think more seriously about their beliefs and attitudes regarding women and their actions toward them. Although important as the catalyst for changes in gender relationships, the play was even more striking for its historical significance in African American theatre. *For Colored Girls* represented a major shift in the fifth-period (since 1972) innovation in the Inner Life versus Inner Life class of the Black Arts School. The play complied with Alain Locke's call for Public Indictments – intended in 1927 to *dramatize* searing denunciations of whites for political and economic oppression. These fully developed plays were to replace DuBois's "moralizing" Protest drama. Shange's publicly "telling off" of certain African American

men complied with Locke's wish and DuBois protest, thus reform-
ing and unifying the DuBois and the Locke views about publicly
accusing people in order to get them to change.

Elements of this redefined major component of the Inner Life
versus Inner Life class were seen earlier in Leslie Lee's *The First
Breeze of Summer* (1975). Most other writers, however, abandoned
the intense introspection of the Inner Life versus Inner Life class
after 1972, except, of course, for Adrienne Kennedy, whose adaptations of *Electra* (1980) and *Orestes* (1980) were the bright spots.
After these, however, even Kennedy tired of writing about Inner –
and most other – Life. Nevertheless, the director George H. Bass
inspired her to write *Black Children's Day*, a play about the history
of African Americans in Rhode Island, for Bass's Rites and Reason Theatre at Brown University in Providence, Rhode Island.
Bass used his theatre, which the playwright P. J. Gibson called "an
artistic and scholarly think tank, a growth center," in order to commission original works that dramatized historical and social events
and issues.[118] Not only did Kennedy and Gibson write for Bass,
but also J. e. Franklin, Shirley Ann Williams, Andrea Harrison,
Phillip Hayes Dean, Ray Aranha, OyamO, Elmo Terry Morgan,
Ed Bullins, and Ossie Davis. Many of them wrote Public Indictments as severe as Shange's play and as full of human frailty – despite being about legends – as Dean's *Robeson*. This showed less
racial sensitivity and insecurity on the part of not only African
American drama but also some of the people themselves. Of interest was that although African American men never admitted to
Shange's charges – as late as 1990, the play was still being called
"an internecine canard" about men's and women's relationships –
the public eventually accepted *Robeson*. The play, as well as its star
Avery Brooks, received rave reviews during its 1990 revival – without the benefit of any committees.

Significantly, in the initial controversy over *Robeson*, not only did
African Americans show that they recognized the power of a stage
image to shape public attitudes and policies, but the African Americans – for the very first time – also organized nationally to alter

an image. Powerful African Americans, coming not only from the arts and letters but also from law, politics, civil rights, education, the media, medicine, and even religion, lent to African American theatre a previously denied credence and stature. That Paul Robeson – whose importance most outside of the African American community still cannot fathom – was the subject undoubtedly drew together this distinguished group. Nevertheless, the very existence of the committee showed that the community had the potential for making African American theatre so influential that the African Grove Theatre experience could never again happen. Still unresolved, however, was the legitimate question about censorship: Who endows anyone with the right to determine for others their best interests? Even had Phillip Hayes Dean been complying with the State Department's request to defame and disgrace Robeson, did any group have the right to close the show? Should the group simply have exposed the conspiracy? Although these questions raised by the Dramatists Guild, were germane to the very notion of a democratic society one must appreciate the Robeson committee's wish to delay the discussion until after the perceived danger had passed.

The Social type of the Serious subclass was even more important than the Personality plays in terms of healing entirely the rift between the Locke and the DuBois schools. This mending was significant because the union permitted each school to remain distinct. The Social dramatists, unlike Richardson and Edmonds, did not balance elements from both schools in their work. The playwrights, instead, developed totally new Locke structures and idioms for the DuBois themes. Not only did the plays combine both schools, but they also successfully mixed dramatic classes. Their plots and characters qualified the plays to be in the Unified Binding Relationships class. All of playwright August Wilson's works, for example, show members of nuclear, extended, and assembled families under such common social pressures that, as Locke puts it, "they are emotionally welded." The ways that Wilson arranges his plots and uses his idioms, however, are so musical that the plays belong more to the Unified Flow class. The question is, How does Wilson convert vortical Binding Relationships situations into Flow plays? Wilson obviously develops his plays like musical ensembles and compositions, and his use of music as a Greek chorus to give the drama structure, to comment on the action, and to reveal the theme are so innovative that they warrant close study. Wilson's extensive utilization of music to structure the *prologos* (beginnings of scenes), *stasima* (middles), and *exodos*, or *epilogos* (ends) answers Locke's 1926 call for a completely new mold for African American theatre. The mold would be a serious play in which music accomplishes what traditionally is accorded words – even, for example, exposing antecedent action. Instead of using words to introduce principal characters, or to alert the audience as to what sort of play to expect, Wilson employs *prologos* music. This unprecedented use of music in serious African American plays to introduce principal characters is at its best in Wilson's *The Piano Lesson* (1987), the story of an African American "family's struggle to remember and yet overcome the brutal legacy of slavery."[19] Wilson has a railroad cook, Doaker, sing his past with "Gonna leave Jackson Mississippi." The song is important not only for giving background information on Doaker, who irons his pants as he recalls train stops, but also for revealing the independence of the man who will referee the battle between his nephew, Boy Willie, and his niece, Berniece, over whether the family-heirloom piano is to be sold. The chance Wilson takes, of course, is that the audience might be so taken with the music that it misses the lyrics, along with, more importantly, the measure of the man.

Chance taking, however, has been Wilson's specialty, as can be seen in his employing music – or the lack of music – to alert the audience to the nature of the play. The irony of this situation is that most exposition in most serious plays – even in those with music – occurs without music. Wilson, however, has made this *prologos* lack-of-music exposition essential. His objective for the brief episode in which there is a call for music that is not there is to let the audience know in the case of *Two Trains Running* (1990) that it is the story of

African Americans who lose political games because the poor have no say about making up the rules:

WOLF: Here . . . Put that in the jukebox. (*He hands RISA two quarters.*)
RISA: It's broke.
WOLF: I thought it was just fixed. Memphis, I thought you was gonna get you a new juke box.
MEMPHIS: I told Zanelli to bring me a new one. That what he say he gonna do. He been saying that for the last year.[120]

Zanelli's not being compelled to bring the jukebox is the metaphor on which the entire play spins. The lack-of-music technique, then, helped Wilson inform audiences that the rule-maker Zanelli, like all of society's other Zanellis, could bring whatever he wanted to whenever he wanted to because African Americans had "no say so" in who brought them what, or when. Even more astounding than his economizing of exposition was Wilson's use of *prologos* music to call attention to the actions of important character, to heighten the whole action of the play, and to render more dramatic the end of the play. Foreshadowing to call attention to important people in the play appears in conjurer Bynum's singing of the title song in *Joe Turner's Come and Gone* (1986), Wilson's story of characters in search of others and of themselves. Wilson needed to let the audience know that the mysterious wanderer, Herald Loomis, loses his wife and his freedom when he is captured by the bounty hunter, Joe Turner. Wilson calls attention to roots-man Bynum's knowledge of Loomis's past and his future:

BYNUM: (*Singing.*)
    They tell me Joe Turner's come and gone
    Ohhh Lordy
    They tell me Joe Turner's come and gone
    Ohhh Lordy
    Got my man and gone
    He come with forty links of chain
    Ohhh Lordy
LOOMIS: Why you singing that song? Why you singing about Joe Turner?

BYNUM: I'm just singing to entertain myself. . . .

. . . .

LOOMIS: I don't like you singing that song, mister![21]

With this foreshadowing, not only does Wilson highlight the importance of the song itself, but he also makes considerably more dramatic the end of Loomis's searches for his wife and his new self.

The musical auguring of a specific character's fate expands to the foretelling of the full action of the play in *Fences* (1985), the story of Troy Maxson's dilemma in trying to come to grips with his too rapidly and radically changing world. Wilson heightens the changes that all the characters undergo by giving a song to Rose, Troy's devoted, irreligious wife. In the play, Rose changes not only into a careless wife but also into an unforgiving woman who is obsessively religious. Wilson calls attention to this imminent change by having the still irreligious and forgiving Rose sing the title song: "Jesus, be a fence all around me every day / Jesus, I want you to protect me as I travel on my way."[22] More surprising than Wilson's using music to foretell the full action of the play is his employing music to telegraph the end of *Fences*. To avoid helping the audience actually predict the details of that end, Wilson gives the "telegram" to a mentally impaired person. This encourages audiences to dismiss the character's wisdom. Wilson has Troy's death presaged by Gabriel, Troy's steel-plate-in-the-head younger brother, a war veteran, who wears a trumpet around his waist:

TROY: Go on in the house and get you something to eat now.
GABRIEL: I got to go sell my plums. I done sold some tomatoes. Got me two quarters. Wanna see? (*He shows TROY his quarters.*) I'm gonna save them and buy me a new horn so St. Peter can hear me when it's time to open the gates. (*Gabriel stops suddenly. Listens.*) Hear that? That's the hellhounds. I got to chase them out of here. Go on get out of here! Get out! (*Gabriel exist signing.*)
Better get ready for the judgment
Better get ready for the judgment
My Lord is coming down.

The irony piles on as Troy and Rose worry about Gabriel's well-being. The importance of the use of *prologos* music for background and upcoming information lies in the music's ability to delight as it informs with an immense economy. A song, Wilson shows, can say so much more so much more beautifully than can dialogue.

Wilson's *stasima* music – music within scenes – seduces, celebrates, and laments. The seduction songs function to court mates, to build tension, and to motivate action. These mating songs, as sung either by such "proficient" guitarists as Jeremy in *Joe Turner's Come and Gone* or by nonsingers such as Sterling in *Two Trains Running*, always get the men their women:

STERLING: I figure me and you get us a nice little old place . . . ain't you tired of sleeping by yourself? I am.
RISA: Naw, I'm just fine taking care of me.
STERLING: You ain't got to take care of you . . . let me do that. I'll take care of you real good. (*Sings*) Wake up, Pretty Mama
See what I got for you
I got everything
Set your poor heart at ease
I got everything for you, woman.
I got a list of things as long as my right arm.[123]

Although Risa rejects the offer this time, Sterling knows that the song will do its job. This typical use for a seduction song makes Wilson's use of the song as a structural device even more interesting. In *The Piano Lesson*, for example, he employs the song to build dramatic tension. He carefully creates the tension between Boy Willie and his sister Berniece over whether Boy Willie can sell the piano. Wilson even has them threaten each other with pistols. In his preparation for the obligatory showdown scene, Wilson makes the audience wait only for Lymon to return with a rope so that Boy Willie can move the piano, which will cause Berniece to shoot her brother. When the rope arrives, however, Wilson extends the tension by having family friend Wining Boy sing a steamy song: "Tell me how long / Is I got to wait / Can I kiss you now / Or must I hesitate."[124] Although the song is enjoyable, the audience wants it finished so that Boy Willie and Berniece can "have it out." Wilson also weaves song into the structure of *Ma Rainey's Black Bottom* (1984), his play about white people's treatment of African Americans as commodities causes African Americans to treat each other as frustration-escape valves. Wilson makes the title seduction song, "Ma Rainey's Black Bottom," the symbol of both the inner- and the intraracial conflicts. The announced conflict is over which version of the title song will be recorded by the legendary blues singer. Wilson gives the trumpet player Levee, the youngest member of Ma Rainey's group, the task of tearing down Ma's old "jug music" rendition to make room for his new "jazzed-up" version. The resultant tension binds and shapes the play's episodes, as new and old styles of the education song metaphorize subplots and themes. Wilson expertly uses the song to motivate most of the characters' actions, including the climactic murder of the pianist Toledo by Levee: It is the white producer's first encouragement and then rejection of Levee's artistic insurrection that cause Levee to kill Toledo simply for stepping on Levee's shoes. Significantly Wilson uses these seduction songs not only so that one character can tempt another but also so that the author can seduce the audience.

The celebrating, lamenting, and rebalancing of Wilson's other *stasima* music, as well as of his *exodos* music, are very important because they serve both traditional and unusual functions. One appreciates Memphis's singing his joy in *Two Trains Running* after he receives a surprising twenty-five-thousand-dollar settlement from the city for his condemned restaurant. Wilson amuses by having Risa play Aretha Franklin's "Take A Look" on the newly fixed jukebox in celebration of her success in getting Sterling to seduce her. What draws attention most, however, is Wilson's daring in having music in *Joe Turner's Come and Gone* incite the major crisis. His objective is to motivate Loomis to reveal his hopes and fears in a manner that is consistent with his mysterious ways:

SETH: Ho, Bynum!
BYNUM: What you hollering at me for? I ain't doing nothing.
SETH: Come on, we gonna Juba.
BYNUM: Yo know me, I'm always ready to Juba.
SETH: Well, come on, then. (*SETH pulls out a harmonica and blows a few notes.*)

. . . .
BYNUM: Alright. Let's Juba down! (*The Juba is reminiscent of the Ring Shouts of the African slaves. It is a call and response dance. BYNUM sits at the table and drums. He calls the dance as others clap hands, shuffle and stomp around the table. It should be as African as possible, with the performers working themselves up into a near frenzy. The words can be improvised, but should income some mention of the Holy Ghost. In the middle of the dance HERALD LOOMIS enters.*)
LOOMIS: (*In a rage.*) Stop it! Stop it!*[125]

Music – not a pitched battle of words between the protagonist and the antagonist – unleashes Loomis's furies, causing him to speak in tongues and dance around the kitchen. Music brings the Holy Ghost, which throws Loomis to the floor and terrorizes him with its visage. Even in *The Piano Lesson* it is music – the music of the pleading, the summarizing, and the developing lament songs –that drives Sutter's Ghost from Berniece's house. Wilson lends to Berniece's singing pleas to her ancestors ("I want you to help me") such power that music saves pianos and sanities both. Not only does Wilson show the violent strength of music, he also displays its delicacy, as in *Fences*, where Troy's lamentable lullaby persuades his wife, Rose, to take in his "outside" daughter: "Please, Mr. Engineer let a man ride the line / I ain't got no ticket please let me ride the blinds." Wilson best displays the power of music, however, when he uses it as epilogues to long and emotional monologues. In *Ma Rainey's Black Bottom*, for example, Wilson has Levee deliver the painful story of his father's being hanged and set afire for killing some of the white men who had raped Levee's mother:

My daddy wasn't spooked up by the white man. No sir! And that taught me how to handle them. I seen my daddy go up and grin in this cracker's face . . . smile in his face and sell him his land. All the while he's planning how he's gonna get him and what he's gonna do to him. That taught me how to handle them. So you all just back up and leave Levee alone about the white man. I can smile and say yessir to whoever I please. I got time coming to me. You all just leave Levee alone about the white man.*[126]

Most playwrights would have "gone to black" after such a powerful speech. Wilson, however, has so much faith in music's ability to simplify and illuminate that he has bassist Slow Drag close the scene with an *epilogos* song: "If I had my way / If I had my way / If I had my way / I would tear this old building down." Wilson even tops this effect with his use of the "Blue Song" in *Fences*. He utilizes this song not only for seduction, solace, foreshadowing, and healing but also for plot development. Wilson has Troy playfully and briefly seduce Rose as Troy introduces the song: "Hear it ring! Hear it ring! / I had a dog his name was Blue / You know Blue was mighty true." After Rose divorces Troy emotionally, Wilson has Troy sit on the steps, drink from a pint bottle, and sing the song – now a song of solace – and Troy adds, significantly, "Blue trees a possum in a hollow log / You know from that he was a good old dog." Shortly thereafter, the song foreshadows the fight between Troy and his son Cory with the additional lines: "Old Blue died and I dig his grave / Let him down with a golden chain." Then, just before Troy's funeral, Wilson has Cory, now a Marine, and his seven-year-old sister sing the full song, making it a dirge for their father: "Go on Blue, you good dog you / Go on Blue, you good dog you."

The importance of the *stasima* and *epilogos* songs is that although they are but guests in wordplay, the songs have dominant roles. This is by no means an accident. Wilson so conspires with music that in his development of structure and theme his plays resemble musical ensembles. Even Wilson's frequent director and collaborator, the august Lloyd Richards, has said that he handles Wilson's plays "as though they were music. I direct them with rhythms and just how that play in itself moves, both physically and vocally."[127] In fact, Wilson turns characters into rhythm and front-line sections.[128] In *Two Trains Running*, for example, a jazz septet tells stories about the struggles of people, as Wilson puts it, to "live life with dignity, to celebrate and accept responsibility for their presence in the world."[129] The group's leader, Memphis, who owns a soon-to-be-demolished Pittsburgh restaurant, plays trumpet. He clarions the runs of the life and death trains. Risa, Memphis's cook and waitress, plays piano to keep in rhythmic moral order her disorder-loving patrons. Risa's lover, the ex-convict Sterling, is on tenor sax because he turns going-against-the-grain into *the* grain. Hambone, Risa's dear friend, wails the soulful alto sax because he is wronged – he is known and longed for only after he is gone. Undertaker West, Risa's number one customer, blows the trombone because it moans the mournings of his customers. Joining Risa in the rhythm section on drums is Holloway, who knows and unrelentingly tells histories; and on bass is Wolf, who makes up "runs" as he runs numbers. Each player voices unison and harmonic tales about not being paid for sets because of loopholes. These tales, however, are not the story. It is the structure of these character's scenes, which, as the critic Nelson George has pointed out, "evolve into operatic monologues in which a speaker . . . riffs in enchanted phrases. Most other action stops as a single character steps up and solos."[30] The principal soloists are Memphis, Holloway, and Sterling. Memphis plays the head of the composition, introducing the melodic themes of the troubles of life (numbers, wives, separations, and finances). Holloway hollers about death, salvation, and channel (Aunt Ester is his medium). Sterling, fresh from prison, grinds out new and revolutionary rhythms. Supporting these leads with "Amens" (or riffs) is each member of the ensemble. Their language is the rural southern idiom, its repeated phrases strengthening ideational images, which, as Richards has pointed out, creates unusual images out of usual things[31]:

HOLLOWAY: West got tired of seeing niggers. Niggers dying from pneumonia. Niggers dying from tuberculosis. Niggers getting shot. Niggers getting stabbed to death with ice picks. Babies dying. Old ladies dying. His wife dying. That's the only thing West ever loved. His wife. She the only thing he understood. After she died West had nothing to live for but money.[32]

Each image in Holloway's speech miniaturizes the theme, which comes full-blown from the arranged, honed, and stylized DuBoisian issues about economic development, political control, and strategic planning in the African American community. Wilson metes out these issues to each of his principal soloists. Holloway blares the need to patronize African American businesses so that the money does not so soon "find that hole" that funnels "it to the white man." Echoing this Holloway solo are Boy Willie in *The Piano Lesson*, Seth in *Joe Turner's Come and Gone*, and Toledo in *Ma Rainey's Black Bottom*. Aunt Ester, the unseen mystical force in *Two Trains Running*, sends out the word that an African American "shouldn't play no game you don't help make up the rules." She transmits this wisdom not through the play's mainstays, but through Sterling, who still wears the prison issue in which he heard the new thinking from the Malcolm X followers in the penitentiary. It is Memphis who demands that the African American community begin comprehensive planning and follow through and that it stop running from rally to rally.

Wilson demanded that these lessons from history be learned and applied, and he received awards for taking the trouble to sing this need: the Pulitzer Prize for *Fences* (1987) and *The Piano Lesson* (1990); the Tony Award for *Fences* (1987); the New York Drama Critics' Circle Award for *Ma Rainey's Black Bottom* (1984), *Fences* (1987), *Joe Turner's Come and Gone* (1988), and *The Piano Lesson* (1990); and the Drama Desk Award for *Fences* (1987) and *The Piano Lesson* (1990). Wilson's importance to African American theatre is not only that of a single dramatist who consistently writes prize-winning plays but also that of a playwright whose works invariably combine the two schools of thought in African American theatre. Richardson and Edmonds pioneered the mixing technique, Hughes advanced it, and several playwrights periodically employed it. Wilson, however, perfected it. His decadent stories about often clowning people were the kind of plot DuBois had feared would feed traditional prejudices. Wilson tells these "lusty" histories successfully, however, because he uses them as cultural tools to gain political rights. Wilson's characters, however, are not DuBois's exemplary models and historical figures. They are, instead, the "open and free" characters of Locke expressing DuBois's frustrated hopes. Wilson's themes, like those of DuBois, espouse positions on racism, politics, and economics. Yet Wilson attempts to prick African American consciences – not white ones. The themes, therefore, are not the sentimentalized protests that Locke so abhorred, but the "enlightened" indictments that Locke promoted. Wilson even combines both men's precepts about dialogue in his plays. His language is as "literate and thought-provoking" as the best of the Protest dramatists. Yet the grammar and style of the language are those of ordinary people, embellished by music, poetry, and dance. The Wilson dramaturgy, however, is more than the sum total of DuBois and Locke. Wilson's own laws govern his balanced, interesting, and detached depictions of Truth and Beauty. His characters and situations are believable because they are so well-grounded in the truth of the African American experience. He uses that truth, however, to show also what the world could be.

The most recent trend in Black Experience drama has returned to the one-act play of the Early Serious Drama Period (1923–38). Dramatists offer pithy and "easily producible" plays with "not more than five characters."[33] The playwrights' principal aim is to reach the audiences in community and educational theatres. Their messages reflect African traditions and are designed to help African Americans see more clearly their moral, political, and economic rights and responsibilities. Because the focus is on African American concerns, few of the new plays address the Inner Life versus Outer Life issues first raised by Willis Richardson and Randolph Edmonds. The new dramatists have absorbed and accepted the significant unresponsiveness of whites to Langston Hughes's call in *Don't You Want to Be Free?* (1938) for a united struggle against racism; to Douglas Turner Ward's satire, in *Day of Absence* (1966), using humor to help people recognize their dependence; and to Alice Childress's warning in *Florence* (1950) that hypocrisy must end. This "new breed," as the producer Woodie King, Jr., has called these writers, even suspects of being only

wishful thinking Alice Childress's and Samm-Art Williams's
fourth-period celebrations of America's oneness.[134] Charles Fuller's historical full-length plays of the fifth period, therefore, have
been, for these writers, the principal representations of Locke's
view that drama, without moralizing, could challenge and indict.
Typical of this tendency in the new Unified Binding Relationships
plays are Elois Beasley's *The Fallen Angel* (1988) and Pearl Cleage's
Hospice (1983). Beasley tells the comic story of a woman, KC, who
marries – and loves – a homosexual man. Her extramarital affair
with a blackmailing cab driver leads KC to plot his murder with
her friend Kathryn, who helps her to realize that she must let go of
both her murder plot and her husband. The importance of this sophisticated play is that it indicts "morally improper" piety, abor-
tion, and fruitless love. With her play *Hospice*, Cleage adds self-
deception to this list. She tells the story of the reconciliation
between a "cancer-ridden" mother, Alice, and her pregnant
daughter, Jenny. The need for propitiation was caused by Alice's
deserting her then ten-year-old daughter to spend most of her
forty-seven years writing poetry in Paris. After baring their souls,
both women understand the other's need to be herself. Furthermore, each admires the other's determination not to let anyone
subvert her interests by placing her in the "black box." Crafted as
carefully as Richardson's and Edmonds's dramas, these plays represent a shift from the fifth-period's ethical analysis of the relationships of people to one another and to the community.
Dramatists now were focusing on the individual "in terms of his
own ideas of what is brave or cowardly, generous or selfish, and
right or wrong."[135]
    Although these plays share the third-period concerns about
family tensions, the treatments reflect tremendous changes. No
longer does a mother, as Sophia does in Errol John's *Moon on A
Rainbow Shawl* (1962), demand that her daughter (Esther) con-
form. Instead, in *The Fallen Angel* the mother Alice explains her
earlier rebellion to her accommodationist daughter. That this
daughter refuses to judge her mother completes the shift in tone

and theme between Binding Relationships plays of the third and the final periods. Unchanged, however, is the African tradition of extended family, which gains prominence during the fifth period. KC and Kathryn in *Fallen Angel* are as much a family as are the sawmill and turpentine workers in, respectively, Edmonds's *The Bad Man* (1934) and Smith and Morell's *Turpentine* (1936). Kathryn's forcing KC to face the truth about her husband reflects the mill workers' finally seeing the truth about Thea. Whereas thirty-six years between the fourth period and the present did not alter the bonds among members, the span does reflect a change from fourth-period concerns to more recent worries about the harmful esoteric impacts on both the nuclear and the extended family. The new dramatists assumed that family members could withstand the dishonesty decried in Lonne Elder's *Ceremonies in Dark Old Men* (1969) and Phillip Hayes Dean's *The Sty of the Blind Pig* (1971). The ethical concerns supplanted moral ones. Morality, for the new dramatists, was increasingly subjective and nonjudgmental. This represented a radical change, which was not the case with the latest trends in the Flow class. By its very nature, the Musical subclass maintained principally the structure of Bob Cole's *A Trip to Coontown* (1898). The newer musicals were considerably less gaudy, of course, even if they were not particularly as enlightening as DuBois had wished. Although the stereotypes of Arna Bontemps and Countee Cullen's *St. Louis Woman* (1946) of the third period were no longer a problem, other difficulties existed. The imbalances between spectacle and theme, which had plagued *Shuffle Along* (1921) and *Hot Chocolate* (1929), still haunted *Ain't Supposed to Die a Natural Death* (1971) and *Mama I Want to Sing, Part II* (1990).

The fifth-period corrections in the Social, Historical, and Personality types made the musicals as socially relevant as the Serious Flow play, especially after Ed Bullins changed them in the fourth period. Whereas the dramatized lifestyle was still a "Back Street" one, Bullins's messages were clearer. Bullins, in one of his latest plays, *Salaam, Huey Newton, Salaam* (1990), for example, makes unmistakable his theme: Get off and stay away from crack. He dramatizes Marvin X's last encounter with Huey P. Newton before Newton's murder on August 22, 1989.[136] As Marvin, Huey, and Young Brother smoke crack together, they reminisce about people and events during the sixties. Young Brother, trying to establish his own importance, interrupts with the compliment: "Yeah, Huey, I really respect you." Young Brother's refrain, ironically, calls Huey's attention to his present disgrace. Marvin and Huey agree that crack is their worst enemy and that they must beat their habits. Huey's murder soon thereafter motivates Marvin to start his tough rehabilitation. The play ends with Marvin's salute to Huey: "Rise, my people. Rise from the projects, rise from the hills, rise and reclaim our souls. A warrior has fallen." This tribute occasions a significant covenant: "But we must continue until victory. But the greatest battle is to win our own souls. And for that reminder, I thank you, Huey. Salaam, Huey, salaam." In its stark simplicity and elegiac language the play is as touching and enlightening as Bullins's earlier *A Son, Come Home* (1969). That play's importance was that it could tell many tragic stories without being melodramatic or maudlin. The language is as rich, musical, and colorful as that in August Wilson's full-length plays. By returning the newer Unified Flow class closer to its origins, Bullins mirrored the latest tendency in the most recent New Inner Life versus Inner Life class. Morality plays and dream plays reappeared. Each subclass, however, was different. J. D. Hall's morality play *G/E* (1988), for example, combines Hughes's moral viewpoint in *Tambourines to Glory* (1963) with the absurdist elements in Jean Toomer's *Balo* (1924). There is an outlandish struggle in the play between the superego (G) and the libido (E), allegedly over space, lifestyle, and value system. The real conflict, however, is over The Mind. Tired of the piety of "G," "E" tempts him by smoking crack cocaine from "the pipe," by reading a pornographic section from a novel, and by making love to an inflated life-size doll. "G" rejects the temptations. He washes his hands and reads aloud the Twenty-third Psalm. At the conclusion, "E" simply waits for the next cycle of temptations. Unlike Toomer, Hall does not assign a particular race to either character (or quality). Language, however, makes them both African Americans who, like Sarah in Adrienne Kennedy's *Funny House of a Negro* (1964), are searching for themselves. Instead of committing suicide as Sarah does, however, "E," like Essie Belle Johnson in Hughes's *Tambourines*, prays for his sinning partner. Whereas Hall does not use Kennedy's perfectly rendered time lapses, he matches her in spectacle and outrageousness.

Bill Harris's dream play, *Every Goodbye Ain't Gone* (1988) does utilize effectively Kennedy's time-lapse technique. Harris follows the traditional dream-play convention of reshaping "reality according to [the author's] own subjective vision."[37] Like the Swedish dramatist August Strindberg, Harris seeks "meaning in an incomprehensible universe, trying to reconcile the most disparate elements of lust and love, body and spirit, filth and beauty."[38] Harris, however, alters the formula. Although he shifts time and place, he does not dismiss logical sequence. One easily follows his play, therefore, which "takes place largely in the mind and memory of Frank, an orphan in a storm, waiting for a bus." A serviceman, Frank meets and marries Rula, an independent and captivating nightclub singer. She refuses, however, to grant him his wish that she give up the road. Singing is her life, and she soon becomes desperate: "I just need him to tell me it's all right. Just take me and hold me and tell me it's OK, babe." Without Frank, Rula attempts suicide. After rushing to her side, he finds her well. Notwithstanding her pleas for him to stay and go back on the road with her, Frank says goodbye. The significance of this play is in its reversal of Ntozake Shange's fifth-period public-indictment innovation in *For Colored Girls Who Have Considered Suicide / When the Rainbow is Enuf* (1976). Frank commits none of Shange's indictable offenses. Rula's attempted suicide results from her own failure to recognize her "rainbow."

The most fascinating aspect of the evolution of the Black Experience School was its unpredictability. It was not enough that Alain Locke had begun his Art-Theatre by throwing out the seeds that began this school. These germs were, of course, the Noah stereotypes peopling the musicals of the Early Musicals Period (1898–1923). Locke had also to take on DuBois, the man who prepared the soil for Locke's kernels. Locke shared DuBois's contempt for the images and the musicals, but Locke showed equal distaste for the ideas of DuBois. The whole "Inner Life" versus "Outer Life" fuss, although enlightening, was essentially Locke's pulling down of that which DuBois had built to advance his political goals. One might think that the playwrights of periods of Early Serious Drama (1923–38) and the early part of Experimentation and Diversification (1938–68) – especially Langston Hughes – could have persuaded Locke that his differences with DuBois were reconcilable. This did not happen, however. Locke rested only after he had literally driven DuBois from the theatre in 1938. Locke, therefore, relished and embellished the pronounced differences between the two schools, which were in full bloom with the later diversified plays of the fifties and sixties. The plays, especially those by African American academies, had absolutely nothing in common with DuBois's Protest School. One might expect this distancing trend, amplified by the tumult of "Back Street" Black Experience Drama (1968–75), to continue, especially with the reins being held by Ed Bullins, Mr. Deconstruction himself. Bullins's name-changing ceremony served appropriate notice to the DuBois people that his expulsion from their San Francisco ranks would be costly for them. Bullins recognized that the Black Panthers' attempt to make peace with him by naming him their minister of culture was just their way of cashing in on his New York City success in 1968 with the three one-act plays, *A Son, Come Home, The Electronic Nigger,* and *Clara's Ole Man,* which they had earlier dismissed as nonrevolutionary. The Panthers–Bullins feud – as well as the dispute between Langston Hughes and Walter white – revisited intellectually and emotionally the personal and philosophical differences of Locke and DuBois. African American drama, logic dictates, should have continued to speed in these contradictory directions for decades, but things changed. One of Bullins's own students, of all people, healed the rift. Richard Wesley's outcry for less noise and more thought so lowered the heat that the Locke and the DuBois schools, although remaining distinct, came to understand the importance of each to the other's well-being as well as to the theatre. This movement matched in interest and significance changes in the works that came out of Locke's own school, from sketchy musical routines to well-developed plays and from plays that were consciously apolitical to those of August Wilson with their DuBoisian themes. It was as if Time showed how correct Locke's and DuBois's theories had been, not only for the twenties and thirties but also for the eighties and nineties. In other words, African Americans needed the "flatteries" and "drawing rooms" of the earlier period (to borrow from the poet Sterling Brown), as much as they needed the accurate "representations" and real "homes" in the later decades.[39] A knowledge of history reveals the earlier needs. By challenging those who would profit from or grin at Manuel Noah's devilish political cartoons of African Americans, DuBois was able to comfort African Americans as much as he pained racists. DuBois fired important ammunition in 1913 at those intent on denying full citizenship to African Americans. Locke's later demand that DuBois cease his fire spoke not poorly of either man, but in recognition of DuBois's success. With his Protest school, DuBois had relieved the Locke generation somewhat from a sole preoccupation with an eternal struggle.

2

The Black Arts School of Drama

Some younger Negro writers say, "What is the use of your fighting and complaining? Do the great thing and the reward is there." And many colored people are all too eager to follow this advice; especially those who are weary of the eternal struggle along the color line, who are afraid to fight and to whom the money of philanthropists and the alluring publicity are subtle and deadly bribes. To them I say that the Beauty of Truth and Freedom which shall some day be our heritage is not in our hands yet, and that we ourselves must not fail to realize.

William E. B. DuBois

STRANGE as it might sound, William E. B. DuBois had more in common aesthetically with Sheriff Mordecai Manuel Noah than DuBois had with Alain Locke. Every one of Noah's plays, which were as stiff and as dreadful as DuBois's own, had politics in mind. Yet had Noah had to function during the DuBois Era of Protest Drama (1913–32), the first of five periods of the Black Arts School, he would have been plagued by conniption. Before dying, however, he would have published the nastiest editorials possible. The fun Noah did make of William Brown's African Company would have been nothing compared to what he would have said about DuBois's pageant, *The Star of Ethiopia* (1913), which had African peoples inventing everything from

78

fire to the Sabbath. DuBois's every effort to forge a Pan-African perspective, to fashion community links, and to develop drama classifications would certainly have been lampooned. DuBois, however, might have ignored Noah, just as he was able to ignore the white liberal members of the board of directors of the National Association for the Advancement of Colored People (NAACP). The board was determined not to allow DuBois to "promote himself" with *The Star of Ethiopia* as a part of the NAACP's exhibit for the 1913 National Emancipation Exposition in New York City. To put on his pageant, DuBois had to raise his own money, one-twelfth of which he himself contributed,[1] and hire his own staff.[2]

Three hundred fifty actors performed *The Star of Ethiopia* over seven days for thirty thousand people. Audiences saw Africans making iron in the first of six scenes, building the Egyptian civilization in scene two, building their own great empires in scene three, and "selling out" to Europeans in scene four:

The Mohammedans force their slaves forward as European traders enter. Other Negroes, with captives, enter. The Mohammedans take gold in barter. The Negroes refuse gold, but are seduced by beads and drink. Chains rattle. Christian missionaries enter, but the slave trade increases. The missionary wails. The missionary's wail grows fainter and fainter until all is a scene of carnage and captivity with whip and chain and only a frantic priest, staggering beneath a cross crowned with blood thorns, wandering to and fro in dumb despair.[3]

Redemption comes in scenes five and six, where, among other adventures, the seaman Alonzo pilots for Columbus and the adventurer Dorantes discovers New Mexico. Then, in these scenes, come the "heroic" struggles for freedom: the Maroons', the Haitians', Crispus Attucks's, George Lisle's, and, of course, Nat Turner's. The pageant ends with a blast:

A single voice sings "O Freedom." A soprano chorus takes it up.
The Boy Scouts march in.
Full brasses take up "O Freedom."
Little children enter, and among them symbolic figures of the Laborer,

the Artisan, the Servant of Men, the Merchant, the Inventor, the Musician, the Actor, the Teacher, Law, Medicine and the Ministry, the All-Mother, formerly the Veiled Woman, now unveiled in her chariot with her dancing brood, and the bust of Lincoln at her side. With burst of music and blast of trumpets, the pageant ends.[4]

Noah would not have stopped laughing. He would have found comic also *The Washington Bee*'s notion that the pageant was the biggest thing in the drama that Washington, D.C., had yet seen:

[It] is a serious effort by our most distinguished scholar to use the drama in a large form to teach the history of our origin, to stimulate the study of history of the peoples from whom we have sprung, to ennoble our youth and to furnish our people with high ideals, hopes and inspiration. The influence of the drama on the life of a people is admitted by all writers on the subject to be very great. Not all our men and women of dramatic talent allow low vaudeville and semi-smutty skits to set the taste of our people for amusement.[5]

Noah would not have missed the insult. Nor could Locke miss the slight in the *Bee*'s referring to DuBois as "our most distinguished scholar" and thus ignoring Locke's honor in being Harvard's first African American Rhodes Scholar.

Locke had to be amused when in 1916 the DuBois people asked him, their silent nemesis, to assist them in turning theatre into a political weapon. The NAACP vice-president Archibald H. Grimke invited Locke to help judge a play-writing contest, sponsored by the Committee on the Drama of the Washington, D.C. branch of the organization. Locke wanted no part of this protesting crew, but he discovered that the committee planned to produce the winning play. Locke saw the significance of the NAACP's being a theatre producer: Herein lay the possibility of developing the truly "Negro theatre" that he longed to launch. All he needed was to persuade these Protest-theatre people to adopt his Art-Theatre principles. He accepted Grimke's invitation, only to be quite disappointed on play-selection night. The majority of the committee wanted to choose a protest play. When he and the Howard University director of drama Montgomery Gregory failed to persuade the group to select a folk play, Locke attempted to get the committee to postpone selecting a winner. To give himself some wiggle room, Locke tried to have the group adopt "the idea of the Negro theatre, as distinguished from the idea of race drama."[6] The committee quarreled far into the night. Locke finished his argument with a flourish: "One play no more makes a theatre than one swallow a summer."[7] The committee chose the swallow: Angelina Grimke's protest play *Rachel* (1916). Locke immediately fired off a letter of resignation to Ambassador Grimke (Angelina's father):

[There was] an utter incompatibility of point of view – something more than a mere difference of opinion – indeed an abysmal lack of common meeting ground between myself and the majority of the members. . . . It was my impression that the Committee was free to discuss the matter [of developing a theatre] as itself a problem, and that, without preconception of hampering instructions, it was to consider how best to further race drama. I expected to have an open and carefully planned competition which would include other types of race or folk play . . . along with the problem play.[8]

Grimke accepted Locke's resignation. The committee produced *Rachel*, making it the first play by an African American woman to be publicly performed.

With his defeat over the contest, Locke was, for the time being, smothered; he had no fiscal sponsor. Locke spent this period watching – sympathetically – how the DuBois writers used theatre to connect African peoples to every important development in America and the rest of the world.[9] This demonstrated for the first time in world theatre that African Americans were not only jesters or victims. DuBois expanded and consolidated his power base, proving himself to be a first-class politician. Locke probably noticed how in *The Star of Ethiopia* DuBois had glossed over the large role Christians had played in the slave trade. DuBois knew only too well how Christian missionaries had cooperated with slavers. Yet he still showed the missionaries wailing over the "scene of carnage and captivity." DuBois's decision not to offend the church was a political choice. It resulted in an invitation in 1916 to perform his pageant at the Centennial General Conference of the African Methodist Episcopal Church in Philadelphia. Although he was not religious, DuBois was very grateful for this important support. He added scenes to the pageant that featured the "religious develop-ment of the Negro and the twelve apostles of Negro Christianity (de Luna, Victoria, Hosier, Allen, Jones, Leile Chavis, Carey, Nat Turner, Vesey, Varick, Gloucester, and Payne)."[10]

So many writers followed DuBois's lead that three classes of Protest drama developed: The Revelation class used drama to "re-veal the Negro to the white world," as DuBois put it, "as a human, feeling thing."[11] The Contribution class highlighted African Amer-ican benefactions by showing that "the Negro was connected with almost every event in American history." The Conscience class pricked white consciences for the purpose of getting liberals to join the struggle for equality of opportunity.[12] These classes flourished. Most discouraging to Locke must have been that even such highly respected Washington writers as Thelma Myrtle Duncan and May Miller wrote these plays. Locke expected more from Duncan (au-thor of *Sacrifice,* 1930) and Miller (*Riding the Goat,* 1929) than to think that they could change white people's attitudes toward Afri-can Americans simply by revealing to the whites one-dimensional characters named Dependable and Devoted. What was the point, for example, of Duncan's writing a play about a character, Roy, who forfeits his good name and his college scholarship in order to pro-tect the reputation of a friend, Billy, who steals a chemistry exam-ination? Even more disheartening to Locke was Miller, who was already a highly respected poet. To Locke, she was risking her own reputation with *Riding the Goat,* in which the character Ruth Chap-man risks her reputation in order to save an "uppity" physician from being ousted from a lodge and ruined financially. DuBois no doubt thought that such revelations of goodness were important "not for the sake of an ethical sanction, but as the one true method of gaining sympathy and human interest."[13]

Although Locke must have thought that both authors had wasted their talents on such sentimentality, he did appreciate the Contribution class of Protest drama with its aim of making African Americans aware, as DuBois said, that from Africa "arose one of the earliest, if not the earliest, of self-protecting civilizations, [which] grew so mightily that it still furnishes superlatives to thinking and speaking men."[4] Locke, too, called this civilization our "legacy," our "ancestral culture," functioning as both an "emotional inheritance" and a "deep-seated aesthetic endowment."[5] Both men, then, wanted to see theatre during the twenties and thirties imprint Africa's contributions on the mind of African Americans, who generally had felt estranged from – and, in many cases, ashamed of – things African. Locke and DuBois applauded such Contribution class plays as *Ethiopia at the Bar of Justice* (1924) by Edward J. McCoo, which depicts Ethiopia as the cradle of civilization, and *The Light of the Women* (1930) by Frances Gunner, which highlights the pivotal roles played by women throughout history. Locke's problem with these plays was their virtual language, which subscribed to DuBois's notion that dialogue should provoke thought, not recognition. Locke believed it was distracting to have King Jamesian prose and poetry in Maude Cuney-Hare's *Antar of Araby* (1929), a romance that extols the black-skinned warrior Antar for defeating the Persians to win the heart of his beloved Abla: "The lovely virgin has pierced my heart with an arrow of a glance for which there is no cure. She moves and I should say it was the Tamarisk that waves its branches to the southern breeze."[6]

DuBois dismissed Locke's concern that such dialogue deceived because it made African Americans seem to be what they were not. DuBois believed that "color," not language, was the issue. DuBois said that by confusing this, Locke was leading young writers to believe that "all would be well" if they simply "kept quiet" and wrote well.[7] The tragic result of such notions, DuBois concluded, was that these writers let whites off the hook. According to DuBois, "surprising number of white people" thought that a few African Americans getting published was going to stop "agitation of the

Negro question."[18] DuBois wanted to make certain that such "agitation" would continue, and he forced whites into the struggle by having them suffer along with the characters through the internal aftermath of the lynching and rape depicted respectively in Grimke's *Rachel* and John Matheus's *Ti Yette* (1929). May Miller's *Graven Images* (1929), one of the best plays of the period, was just what Bible-toting southerners needed: God punishes Moses's sister Miriam for defaming the Ethiopian Eliezer. The DuBois Era was significant, then, because it compelled African American dramatists to address the political and socioeconomic issues of race. To ensure a plentiful supply of such plays, DuBois set up playwriting contests. He instructed competitors "to write honestly about ordinary decent colored people -- not beggars, scoundrels, and prostitutes."[19] DuBois received hundreds of scripts, many of which he published in his *Crisis* magazine. To make certain that the plays were widely produced, he established the Krigwa Players, a national little-theatre network. His contests not only provided these little theatres with one-act plays, but the contests also motivated other magazine editors to follow suit. In this context, DuBois, although a sociologist, was almost as important to the development of African American theatre as Mr. Brown.

The importance of the second period of the Black Arts School, the Era of Warnings in Protest Drama (1932–51), was that during it, DuBois's aims were abandoned in favor of "scaring up" racial equality, of originating structural innovation, and of setting the succeeding theme. Four classes of Scare plays developed: Communism, Murder, Labor Strike, and Hypocrisy. Langston Hughes's Communism-menace play *Scottsboro, Limited* (1932), which celebrated the infamous 1931 case, was among the best. Its political significance lay in Hughes's telescoping the impending electrocution of eight young African Americans convicted of rape into the broader political and economic issues of citizen apathy, women's rights, and worker exploitation. Hughes's purpose in raising the passivism question was to mobilize African Americans. He told them that the only thing "more shameful than the South killing the boys was that twelve million Negroes" permitted it.[20] Hughes demanded that African Americans *and* whites raise "such a howl – and I don't mean a polite howl, either – that the doors of Kilby Prison shake until every one of the boys is out."[21] He recommended that African American newspapers publish the official court records so that people could see "to what absurd farces an Alabama court could descend."[22] Hughes's aim in addressing the women's rights problem was both to connect and to repudiate racism and sexism – almost forty years before the feminist movement of the seventies. He understood that economics linked racism and sexism. He pointed out that African Americans could not possibly expect "Southern gentlemen" to give equality of opportunity to African Americans when the southern power brokers did not provide such equality to their own women. If these "gentlemen" had given decent wages to the two alleged victims, the women would not have needed to "hop a freight" to Chattanooga and prostitute themselves.[23] The fight against discrimination, for Hughes, demanded that *all* in "the South rise up in press and pulpit, home and school, Senate Chambers and Rotary Clubs, and petition the freedom of the dumb young blacks – so indiscreet as to travel unwittingly, on the same freight train with two white prostitutes."[24]

This stunning appeal mirrors such first-period Conscience works as *Ti Yette* and *The Star of Ethiopia.* What distinguishes *Scottsboro* from those plays is Hughes's experiment with what he calls a "jazz verse" form. Seven years before introducing expressionism into African American theatre with his *Don't You Want to Be Free?* (1938), Hughes inaugurated movement and voice as structural devices. He required the actors to simulate being on a train by swaying. With "jingling rhymes and driving rhythms," he counterpointed the African Americans' "deep" pitches and tones against the "shrill and staccato" voices of the white racists. The play ends with these bassos and tenors harmonizing the chant "Fight! Fight! Fight! Fight!" The boys smash the electric chair. Then comes Hughes's electric jolt: The cast sings the "Internationale" as the Communist flag rises. This scene underscores Hughes's belief that some young African Americans had been forced to view Communism as the only constructive alternative to racism. Hughes did not promote or endorse Communism, notwithstanding Amiri Baraka's view that *Scottsboro* was a "Marxist-oriented revolutionary model."[25] Although Hughes knew Marx, he not only continually disavowed Communism but also believed that theatre had "no limits on worriation when it got mixed up with the LEFT."[26] He understood, however, that people labeled him a Communist because he had visited and spoken admiringly of the Soviet Union.[27] Hughes said that the only way to stop the labels was for him to write only about "roses and moonlight."[28] Hughes used the "Internationale" and the Soviet flag because, like Theodore Ward in his *Big White Fog* (1938), he wanted to shock Americans into living up to the Constitution.

Such jolts, Locke undoubtedly believed, delighted more the author than they enlightened – or frightened – any racist. The Locke school, nevertheless, suffered through Hughes, as well as through Ward's *Big White Fog*, as a well-intended lament that racism would turn well-meaning African Americans into Communist murderers. The Locke people contended that this approach reduced African Americans to just the impulse-driven creatures that Noah had painted. It was almost hilarious, according to the Locke school, for Ward, in the *Big White Fog*, to burden Victor Mason with his son's fate because he rejected the revelation, conscience, and contribution ways of his father(s). Even more comic was the notion that racial bigots might care, especially when they had already yawned at Hughes's terror tactic in *Mulatto* (1935), where a bi-racial son murders his white father.[29] In fact, such plays worked no voodoo even on African Americans: J. Augustus Smith and Peter Morell's Labor Strike-scare play *Turpentine* (1936) sparked not a single boycott for worker benefits. Only the mill workers *in the play* got raises because of boycotts. The real workers, like the folk hero John Henry in Theodore Browne's *Natural Man* (1941), worked themselves to death. DuBois, of course, expected no such direct results from drama. He wanted drama only to raise consciousness.

Even if *Turpentine* increased not a single salary, DuBois appreciated the historical importance of the play: It recommended economics as a political tool twenty years before the Montgomery, Alabama, bus boycott. Recommendations aside, nothing changed. This lack of change caused Theodore Ward to employ the "white liberals' hypocrisy" theme in his *Our Lan'* (1946). The Locke people probably hoped that Ward realized that this traditional theme in African American literature was but a guilt sledgehammer. The DuBois people however, marveled, at Ward's play about the Reconstruction Era: Ward had northern white liberals give freed slaves a plantation previously owned by southerners. By making northern and southern whites later conspire to return the land to the original owners for political expediency, Ward ended this second period of the Protest school by saying that white liberals played both sides of the race issue.

Although William Wells Brown had introduced in *Escape, or, A Leap for Freedom* the theme of the white liberal hypocrisy eighty-eight years before Theodore Ward, Ward's expert use of this theme had a tremendous impact on the younger dramatists of the third period. They picked up this theme and, for a quarter century, played it in such an assured way that they seemed to be itching for a fight. When, for example, William Branch rode into New York town astride his *A Medal for Willie* (1951), people sensed "something was up." The Locke people and the white liberals tipped their hats, but little did they suspect that this college-educated dramatist was in the vanguard of the Attack Era (1951–65), the Golden Age of Protest drama. Branch was a sure shot. He emptied The Contributions and Warnings Saloon of complaint plots, worn structures, and Sheriff Noah's deputy characters. Branch's roughnecks blasted white liberals and Locke's ranchers, and his lead attack unbuckled the saddled fury of African Americans over the segregated military. Branch tells the story of Mrs. Jackson, a mother who throws away the Distinguished Service Cross awarded her son posthumously for bravery in Korea. Angry about racism in America, Mrs. Jackson fumes that the United States – not Korea – should be the battleground for democracy. Branch pours the woman's bitterness into an elaborate structure. Instead of employing the usual well-made-play formula, he devises a seven-scene design with a scene-setting prologue and an epilogue that alternately addresses and ignores the audience. This design worked, thanks to area lighting. Thus years before Ed Bullins, Branch stared down all rules of dramatic structure by ignoring them: He introduced new characters and different issues in each scene, except in the climactic seventh. For the characters in his new piece, Branch scooped up a handful of Noah's and Locke's friends – pantry maidens, racists, military heroes, politicians, educators, and mammies – and issued most of them from the usual mold. For his mammy, Mrs. Jackson, however, he added a twist. Although he had made her appear typical of Noah's Contented Slave stereotype, proud to have given her only son "for her country," he had the wrong ceremony words issue from this "tired and wilted" woman: "Yes, Willie's dead and gone now, and I'm proud he was brave and helped save somebody else 'fore he got killed. But I can't help thinkin' Willie died fightin' in the wrong place. (*Quietly intense.*) *Willie shoulda had that machine gun over here!*"[30] This image shocked the audience more than Hughes's unfurling of a Communist flag. What made Mrs. Jackson's truth spilling so painful was its complementing theme: Eliminate racism by eliminating racists. Branch's theme lassoed Locke's people to the white liberals and the bigots. Branch implied that anyone not willing to line up behind Mrs. Jackson should be branded a contended slave.

The Branch posse of playwrights not only whooped up its agreement, but it also sophisticated Protest drama. In her *Trouble in Mind* (1955), Alice Childress gift wraps the old complaint about the recycled roles given African American actresses. Childress selects the ancient – but new to African American drama – technique of putting a play within a play. Her choice of technique fits her story well: In *Trouble in Mind,* the character Wiletta Mayer, an actor, complains to her white liberal director because she resents the way an African American woman is made to seem an idiot in the play being rehearsed, "Chaos in Belleville." This play-within-a-play has a suspicious mother who sends her fugitive son for "safekeeping" to a southern sheriff, knowing that the boy will be going to his certain death. Wiletta refuses to play the stereotype as written. The director, unrelenting and fuming because Wiletta has called him a racist, dismisses the cast.[31] The importance of this Childress piece is its demonstration that Protest drama need not sacrifice theme for new technique. Childress makes the play-within-a-play innovation work by using the director's refusal to change the scene in the inner play as the inciting action in *Trouble*. Even more importantly, Childress shows the often hidden toughness of the African American woman: Wiletta does not blink; she demands that African American theatre people understand that negative images projected by actors in dramatic roles actually do shape public perception and policies. Theatre people, therefore, have to boycott foolish characterizations. Their failure to do so, Childress says, means that African Americans and white liberals are cohabitants in the same blame space.

The crown jewel of Protest drama was Loften Mitchell's *A Land Beyond the River* (1957), which expanded the concept of the traditional Protest play. Mitchell added to the familiar plot, theme, character, and structure his specially designed Negro spirituals, along with such alien – yet enabling – devices as natural and artificial sounds. The play's well-known plot represents the real events surrounding one of the cases that led to the U.S. Supreme Court's 1954 decision declaring segregation in the public schools unconstitutional: "The case involves a rural area called Clarendon County, South Carolina. A group of farming folks, led by the Reverend Dr. Joseph A. Delaine, agitated for bus transportation for Negro children to rural schools."[32] In an attempt to raise money for the farmers, Mitchell tells their story in *Land Beyond the River*: Reverend Cloud, a white liberal, imposes himself on the African American community. Reverend Layne, who leads the community, welcomes Cloud as a negotiator. When Cloud discovers, however, that the lawsuit occasions other demands for full citizenship, he tries to bribe Layne to sell out his people. That Reverend Layne rejects the offer is as much Mitchell's testimonial to the African American clergy's righteousness as it is an indictment of the white clergy's immorality. In arguing that white liberal ministers have to understand they can have no real voice in African American policy making, Mitchell obeys the Protest theatre convention that characters personify issues.

What distinguishes *A Land Beyond the River* are Mitchell's specially designed spirituals and sounds. He could have been August Wilson's mentor in the use of *stasiman* music to foreshadow events and to develop themes. Mitchell augurs the town's losing its integration suit, for example, but offering repeated looks at "troubles" in various spirituals. When Reverend Layne tires of being principal, preacher, and general repairer, he sings "Nobody Knows the Troubles I've Seen." "Troubles" are a work song in "I'm Going to Tell God All My Troubles When I Get Home," providing rhythm for a farmer's repair of the run-down school. Troubles in "Oh Freedom!" rally the townspeople to sue for integrated schools, and "I'm So Glad Trouble Don't Last Always" is balm for the bone-tired Ruby. These Negro spirituals enliven the drama and magnify the theme. Even more exciting, though, is Mitchell's use of howling wind, thunder, lightning, and rain to prophesy doom:

Through the darkness the sound of the howling wind is heard.)

MARY: (*Steps out on porch.*) Ummm. It's a black night, ain't it? Clouds over yonder look like they gonna bust loose any minute.

BILL: Yeah. Listen to that wind, will you? There's something heavy and powerful out yonder, pushing down against the trees – like something wants to tear them loose and there ain't nothing in the world can stop it.[33]

Although the history of world drama was replete with such uses of the elements, this scene inaugurated nature as symbol in African American Protest drama. An even more striking first, however, was Mitchell's use of sound as a character:

(The wind rises as the lights go down. A roar of thunder crashes through the night. The lights pick up Layne and Duff on the road. Repeated

*crashes of thunder are heard, followed by streaks of lightning. Layne
trips, nearly falls. Duff grabs hold of him. Repeated crashes of thunder
are heard, followed by streaks of lightning.*)

DUFF: Reverend – you all right? You reckon we oughta go back?

LAYNE: No! No, we can't go back!

DUFF: This storm is something fierce!

LAYNE: Let it be fierce, Duff! It can't stop us. (*Turns, yells out at the
storm.*) Cry out, O God, in your anguish! Send the thunder to jar us
awake! (*Thunder roars.*) Send more and more and more! And lightning
to light our way! (*Thunder roars, lightning flashes.*) Your voice will be
heard, and the rain shall make us clean! (*Another roar of thunder.*) The
right is with us, Duff! We won't be stopped! We won't![34]

Not only does Mitchell have Reverend Layne, like Shakespeare's
King Lear and Othello, cry out to nature, but he also makes syn-
thetic sounds symbolize the white racists. After the audience learns
to associate slamming car doors and roaring car motors with
whites, Mitchell converts these sounds into such palpable pres-
ences that the African American characters, upon hearing them,
freeze. To vary and color his sound characters, Mitchell adds wild
screams and jeers, as well as gunfire and mocking laughter. The
sound of gunfire becomes a tension-building device, as the initially
distant sound of shots draws nearer, four times escalating the
alarmed reactions. According to Mitchell, this emphasis on sound
for "character illumination" compensated for the well-known facts
of his plot.[35] Mitchell thus added a seminal element to Protest
drama, which, because of the familiarity of plot, had previously relied on preaching to engage the audience. In fact, it had been on
this sermonizing (or "sentimental moralizing," as Locke called it)
that Protest drama had thrived. The plays had been but treaties
using highly recognizable stereotypes, plots, and themes. Mitchell's addition of spirituals and sound characters permanently
changed the nature of Protest drama.

Of particular importance, these changes encouraged other no-
table word-oriented authors of the period – writers like James
Baldwin and Amiri Baraka – to tamper with the fixed formula.
Baldwin, whose *Blues for Mr. Charlie* (1964) was more theatre essay

than play, made stereotyped characters relive the well-known facts of the murder in Mississippi of Chicago teenager Emmett Till. Baldwin made observations about the white liberals involved as well as about sex as the underlying factor in racist relationships. The significance of Baldwin's play, however, is that it refreshes a familiar tale and introduces a new insight. Baldwin's plot invigorates because of the predicament in which he places his white, liberal, southern newspaper editor Parnell. Baldwin makes Parnell's childhood friend, Lyle, the confessed murderer of Richard, a teenage repatriate from "the North," who has flaunted his disrespect of southern tradition by flirting with a local white woman. At the murderer's trial, Parnell refuses to testify against Lyle. Baldwin made Parnell's refusal unusual by giving Parnell a "friendship" with Richard's family and making him lust after Richard's girlfriend, Juanita. Through Parnell's dilemma Baldwin offers the theory that the white liberal felt no deep-seated loyalty either to African Americans or to whites: Panell looked down on the white bigot because, as a liberal, he believed himself superior to the bigot. The liberal accepted African Americans only because he expected them to want to emulate him. The white liberal, in other words, was standing up not for what was right, but for himself as right. This self-as-paradigm concept manifested itself not only in racism but also in relationships. Baldwin demonstrates, for example, that racism resulted from white people's fear of and attraction to the sexuality of African Americans. He presents multiple examples: Lyle's wife, Jo, believes that she will be "no more good for nobody" if she is raped by an African American. She fantasizes and lies, however, about Richard's grabbing her hand and pushing himself up against her "real close and hard – and, oh, he was just like an animal, I could – smell him!" Lyle, who kills "niggers" for sport, murders Old Bill in order to continue to sleep with Bill's wife. Baldwin, however, regarded the problem as far more complicated than the allure–repulsion syndrome. He has all his characters blame sex for their troubles: Richard thinks that he becomes addicted to heroin because he hates sleeping with white women.

Parnell's unrequited love for a young African American girl – and for Juanita – softens his backbone. Meridian bemoans his not having acted on his love for Juanita as a cure for the mess. Jo blames Lyle's not giving her enough sex for her lusting after the preacher. Lyle opposes race mixing because it will lead to some "big buck nigger lying up next to Josephine." Sex was not only the cause but also the tool of racism and instability.

Baldwin, furthermore, makes sex the weapon of choice in all the play's battles. Victory is sexual conquest: For example, Parnell is admired by the white bigots because he "tom-cats" around all night with women who try to "saddle" him. Richard celebrates having knocked down Lyle by declaring that if he could get into the "drawers" of Lyle's wife, she, too, would know he is "master." The getting of enough sex defines happiness: Lyle attributes Susan's looking as ripe as a peach to the fact that her husband, Ralph, "ain't been slack" in his "duty." For Baldwin, all troubles have sexual signatures: Not only do the whites "castrate" Parnell for standing with the "darkies," but the whites' God "castrates" African Americans. The supreme insult – the one that finally causes Lyle to shoot Richard – is Richard's bragging that he knows in the biblical sense, white women better than does Lyle. Baldwin's plot, then, raises an important question: Why did Baldwin assemble these stereotyped characters to make his quite ordinary observations? One possible answer is critic Calvin C. Hernton's suggestion that Baldwin might be showing not only that "sexual guilt and paranoia were intricate aspects of racism in America" but also that no justice existed for African Americans in the South.[36] Baldwin probably did not have Hernton's ideas as his principal influence because such beliefs had been prominent features of the African American drama landscape since William Wells Brown had introduced them in 1858. Most dramatists, in fact, had represented the beliefs considerably better than Baldwin. He was, in any case, simply a too-strinkingly original writer to rehash the obvious. Baldwin had to be up to something else. One answer might be that he was warning African Americans to stop their bluffing: Expect no help from anybody, he said. Fight your own battles. If you lose, blame yourself. Richard, whom Baldwin cut from Noah's Brute Nigger stereotype, carries this fresh notion. Baldwin has him break *all* rules: Everything that Richard says and does to Lyle pushes toward a showdown. Notwithstanding Hernton's objections, *Village Voice* critic Michael Smith is correct in his judgment that Richard asks to be murdered. When the bloodshed time comes, however, Richard goes – without a struggle – to his certain death:

PAPA D.: He played his record. Lyle Britten never moved from the door. And they just stood there, the two of them looking at each other. When the record was just about over, the boy come to the bar – he swallowed down the last of his drink.

RICHARD: What do I owe you, Papa D.?

PAPA D.: Oh, you pay me tomorrow. I'm closed now.

RICHARD: What do I owe you, Papa D.? I'm not sure I can pay you tomorrow.

PAPA D.: Give me two dollars.

RICHARD: Here you go. Good night, Papa D. I'm ready, Charlie. (*Exits.*)[37]

This is so out of character for such a street dude as Richard that Wiletta, in Childress's *Trouble in Mind,* would have justifiably boycotted Baldwin for not having armed Richard. Baldwin shoves Richard even further out of character by having Richard – facing a weapon – castrate Lyle, acting between the two shots that finally kill Richard. Baldwin needs no defense, however, because his point is that Lyle's murder is Richard's suicide. By not being prepared "to back up his talk," Richard – and African Americans – enticed death. Richard's bluffing of Lyle, Baldwin shows, is as lethal as Meridian's trusting Parnell. Parnell, along with other white liberals, is so useless, Baldwin is saying, that Parnell should be avoided – not to punish him, but to save the African American. The importance of this Baldwin play is, then, its introduction of Malcolm X's early revolutionary philosophy to African American theatre. This brilliant word play became the prototype for those who would remake American life. The theme of *Blues,* in other words, totally transformed these dramatists and their beliefs. Amiri Baraka, for example, has admitted that *Blues* inspired him:

It was one of the great theater experiences of my life. A deeply touching "dangerous" play for Jimmy, it not only questioned nonviolence, it had a gutsy – but doomed – black hero and his father go at each other's values, echoing the class struggle that raged between Dr. King and Malcolm X. . . . It was an extremely powerful work, so powerful I believe that the bourgeois (mainly white) critics at that point read Jimmy out of the big-time US literary scene. He had gone too far. And as critical as I had been before of Jimmy and what I perceived as his stance of avoiding reality and confrontation, now I was elated and almost raised up off the ground by this powerful play.[38]

Baraka was so influenced by Baldwin, in fact, that Baraka trumpeted Baldwin's theme in all of his own Protest plays. In *Dutchman* (1964), which opened one month after *Blues*, Baraka makes the bluffer not a bragging adolescent but a bohemian intellectual. The result, however, is the same: although tempted to slaughter Lula, the Ivy Leaguer Clay initially appeals to her. Clay later warns Lula that he is capable of "turning his back on sanity" and murdering her. Clay finally attacks Lula, slapping *"her as hard as he can across the mouth. Lula's head bangs against the back of the seat. When she raises it again, Clay slaps her again."*[39] Clay dies, however, because he has no clearly analyzed plan for his salvation. In *The Toilet* (1965), *The Slave* (1965), *Experimental Death Unit #1* (1965), and *J-E-L-L-O* (1965), Baraka repeats Baldwin's theme that burning all bridges to white liberals is the first step toward liberation. Severing connections is not, however, a particularly easy task. Baraka, in *The Slave*, spells out the expected painful costs: Walker kills his mulatto daughters. The pain connotes, of course, that some previous associations with white liberals were satisfactory. Just as Walker and a white liberal had once had a happy marriage, so too had the African American and the white liberal once been happy together. White liberal playwrights, for example, had produced a distinguished body of empathetic works from *The Nigger* (1909) by

Edward Sheldon, the story of a "white" man's discovery that he is African American, to David Feldshuh's *Miss Evers' Boys* (1989), based on the infamous Tuskegee Study of the effects of syphilis in African American men. There were such representative works as Eugene O'Neill's *All God's Chillun Got Wings* (1923) and Paul Green's *In Abraham's Bosom* (1926), which acknowledge the African American people's humanity; John Wexley's *They Shall Not Die* (1934), which erases inequities in the legal system; Arnaud D'Usseau and James Gow's *Deep Are the Roots* (1945), which gives war veterans their well-earned due; and Martin Duberman's *In White America* (1963), which displays the African American's historical struggle against racism. Even though these plays were noble efforts, Baraka, along with the young playwrights, insisted that the plays and their authors be summarily dismissed. In 1965 Baraka embarked on finding an ideology for his planned new drama. Theatre was to join poetry and music in becoming the cultural arm of the Black Liberation Movement.

The most important aspect of the fourth period of Black Arts theatre, the Era of Black Revolutionary Drama (1965–72), is that Baraka, after painstakingly studying Yoruba culture and the Nation of Islam, discovered and imposed an ideology on the drama. He chose *Kawaida*, the philosopher Ron Karenga's ideology of culture that proposed to build a nation based on a common value system. The ramifications of Baraka's replacing DuBoisian philosophy with *Kawaida* were so fundamental that "protest," which implied control by the other, vanished from the name of the school. This meant that playwrights no longer represented appeals to share power, but depicted seizures of power. This shift in focus frightened not only whites but also Locke's people, who attacked the notion that plays could be "collective, committed, and functional."[40] The Locke people found totally unacceptable Baraka's explanation that collectivism meant that the plays came "from the collective experience of Black people and spoke from their collective consciousness."[41] The Locke school argued that African Americans were "not a monolith." To assume that there was or could be a "collective consciousness" was, therefore, a priori nonsense. The Locke people attacked as well Baraka's belief that plays were capable of "committing" and "stimulating" people to make "revolutionary changes" in the socioeconomic policies that controlled their lives.[42] The Locke people argued that theatre could only reflect – not change – life. The Locke school was so defensive, of course, because it realized that it would lose status if Baraka were to succeed in making viewers "commit totally to building a new nation."[43] Thus Baraka was a danger to the Locke school because Black Revolutionary drama deconstructed both Outer Life *and* Inner Life. The Locke people wondered: Just who did this Howard University dropout, Greenwich Village beatnik-poet, and darling of the guilt-ridden white liberal literati think he was to come charging into "our" theatre and try to tear down everything?

The Locke people wasted no time in picking apart every phrase uttered by Baraka, who gave them plenty of pickings. He transposed each of the seven principles (or *Nguzo Saba*) of Karenga's *Kawaida* doctrine into drama: *Umoja* (Unity), *Kujichagulia* (Self-Determination), *Ujima* (Collective Work and Responsibility), *Ujamaa* (Cooperative Economics), *Nia* (Purpose), *Kuumba* (Creativity), and *Imani* (Faith). The Locke people detested Karenga's use of Swahili, which they thought had failed to mystify a doctrine that a later disaffected Baraka called a jumble of "borrowed ideas from Elijah Muhammad, Nkrumah, Fanon, Toure, Nyerere, Garvey, Malcolm . . . Mao and even Lenin and Stalin and Marx."[44] The Black Revolutionary dramatists, enjoying the Locke people's discomfort, wrote hundreds of short plays, or "skits," as they were called by the Locke school. Baraka's effort to revolutionize the masses by teaching them, through drama, each of *Kawaida* seven principles produced seven classes of plays. The *Umoja* (Unity) plays, for example, instructed about the need for and means of maintaining unity in the family and the community. Baraka's use of this principle, however, highlights early differences between him and Karenga. Early *Kawaida* gave "male chauvinism a revolutionary legitimacy" as Baraka in 1967 saw it practiced by Karenga's organization (US) in California, the group on which Karenga tried out his communal beliefs.[45] Baraka's "revisionist" interpretation of *Kawaida*, on the other hand, encouraged women to "stand with us shoulder to shoulder against black people's enemies."[46]

The plays by the black revolutionary dramatists followed Baraka's line. Ron Zuber's poetic *Three X Love* (1972), for example, saw men and women "Pushing together for truth. Pulling / Together for unity. We together displaying our adulthoods / With dignity, respect, and understanding. With love as / Black as a shadow, moving with our every step. The shadow / Of one spirit dancing close to the sun."[47] Such close "revolutionary" unions between the sexes were needed because the Locke people had thrown every "decent" person into the battle against these "fools." Parents, grandparents, and older folk in general forbade children to "join that bunch." The Baraka people, however, continued to develop plays that encouraged the children and cautioned the parents. In Ben Caldwell's *Family Portrait, or My Son the Black Nationalist* (1967), for example, a son leaves home after he tires of hearing his parents' "same-old same-old" that African Americans need to prove themselves worthy of "living with white people." Not all parents, however, were so hardheaded. When the older generations in William Wellington Mackey's *Behold! Cometh the Vanderkellans* (1971) hear the liberation doctrine, they change. Most people stayed put, however, prompting authors of *Umoja* plays to employ the same death-scare tactics used earlier by Hughes in *Mulatto*. Whereas Baraka's *Arm Yrself or Harm Yrself* (1967) only alerted the older folk to the fact that this was more than a war of words, Marvin X's *Flowers for the Trashman* (1968) and *Take Care of Business* (1968), as well as Jimmy Garrett's *And We Own the Night* (1968), showed them that young revolutionaries were willing to kill – even their own mothers. Baraka defended depictions such as that of Johnny's matricide in *And We Own the Night:* There were

some things about negro life – and I use that term very consciously – that need to be put on these Negroes so that they'll stop acting like they do. They need to see that boy shootin' his mama down, with her blond wig on. It might change them – that will shake them, that will scare them to death.[48]

The Baraka people used these same terror tactics to forge unity in the community. Most plays showed that communal solidarity depended on stopping the homicides and suicides that were rampant, as seen in Tom Dent's *Ritual Murder* (1967). Equally critical was the elimination of socioeconomic-class differences. Carlton Molette and Barbara Molette's *Rosalie Pritchette* (1971) argues the class issue by depicting a bridge-playing African American woman who puts down Movement members until she herself is victimized by white racists. These racists, claims Clarence Young III's *Perry's Mission* (1970), come to the community to cause disunity. The *Umoja* plays guarded against such guerilla adventures within both the family and the community. It did not take long, however, for the Locke people to realize that all of this unity business was at their expense.

The costs became even more evident in the *Kujichagulia* (Self-Determination) plays. This second class of drama returned to Baldwin's and Baraka's admonitions to African Americans to sever all of their ties to whites. Baraka added in his plays the benefits of the cut-off, that is, healthier concepts of self and race. Because the Locke school's relationships with whites were mutually beneficial, the Locke people had no intention whatsoever of cutting their contacts. To force the issue, therefore, the DuBois school painted whites in their worst colors. The playwrights resorted to myth and history. Baraka accuses whites of living up to their beastly origins in his play *A Black Mass* (1965), which is based on the Nation of Islam myth of the Creation. This myth establishes African Americans as the Original People. The play shows white people to be mere scientific aberrations resulting from a lapse of mind over spirit. The significance of this delightful play is that its spectacle captures the imagination as much as its theme displaces the slave mentality. In other words, being The First dashes all possibility of being inferior, and slavery then becomes the grudge act of spiteful children. As spelled out by Baraka in *Slave Ship* (1967), slavery not only was

genocide but also parricide.[49] Baraka's method of handing down
this verdict became clear in a comparison of his *The Death of Malcolm X* (1966) with a similar play, *El Hajj Malik* (1968), by the
Locke school dramatist N. R. Davidson. Davidson's play chroni-
cles Malcolm's life by sticking closely to the events in Alex Haley's
The Autobiography of Malcolm X. Furthermore, Davidson capitalizes
on every opportunity to entertain the audience with music and
dance. Baraka, on the other hand, uses the story of Malcolm's life
to accuse whites of conspiring to assassinate Malcolm. Baraka proposed, in other words, to use everything at his disposal to "accuse
and attack anything that can be accused and attacked."[50] His purpose was to force the audience-victims to call up the "wisdom and
strength in their own minds and bodies."[51] This purpose simultaneously degraded white liberals and some middle-income Locke
people. A passage from *Slave Ship* showed Baraka's hand:

PREACHER: Yasss, we understand . . . the problem. And personally, I
think some agreement can be reached. We will be non-violent . . . to
the last . . . because we understand the dignity of pruty mcbonk and
the greasy ghost. . . . And penguins would do the same. I have a
trauma that the gold sewers wont integrate. Present fink. I have an en-
ema . . . a trauma, on the coaster with our wife bird-crap. (*One of the
black men, out of the darkness, comes and sits before the tom a wrapped-up
bloody corpse of the dead burned baby, as if they had just taken the body from
a blown-up church. He places the corpse in front of Preacher. Preacher stops.
Looks up at "person" he's tomming before, then, with his foot, tries to push
baby's body behind him, grinning and jeffing all the time, showing teeth and
being "dignified."*)
PREACHER: Unnnerr . . . as I was sayin' . . . Mas' un . . . Mister
Tastyslop . . . We Kneegrows are ready to integrate . . . the blippy
rump of stomach bat has corrinked a lip to push the thimble. Yass.
Yass. Yass.[52]

Such insults were so insufferable that the Locke people vowed
revenge. They could only plan and seethe at the moment, however,
because of the popularity of both the play and the Movement. The
troubles of the Locke school escalated, as the third class of plays,

Ujima (Collective Work and Responsibility), fueled the proverbial fire. This class of drama went right after the Locke group's jugular vein, that is, their supposed values: their obsessions with external appearance, with economic class, and with rugged individualism. The *Ujima* plays downgraded outer images and elevated internal peace by posing "questions of what we will be or what we will do."[53] Sonia Sanchez's *Sister Son/ji* (1969), for example, tries desperately to assess the impact that historical events, personal decisions, and rites-of-passage had on one woman's life. According to the DuBois people, such inner probing distinguishes them from the Locke people, who would waste time just finding the right mask to wear. Alice Childress's *Wine in the Wilderness* (1969) tears away these layers of skin – and soul – whiteners. She forces a pretentious artist, Bill, to submit to the beauty and wisdom of a maid named Tomorrow-Marie, or Tommy for short. After discovering that Bill has been lying to her in order to get her to pose so that he can paint her as a wino, Tommy gives him a "knock down and drag out." She makes up with Bill the next day:

I don't stay mad, it's here today and gone tomorrow. I'm sorry your feelin's got hurt, . . . but when I'm hurt I turn and hurt back. Somewhere, in the middle of last night, I thought the old me was gone, . . . lost forever, and gladly. But today was flippin' time, so back I flipped. Now it's "turn the other check" time. If I can go through life other-cheekin' the white folk, . . . guess yall can be other-cheeked too. But I'm goin' back to the nitty-gritty crowd, where the talk is we-ness and us-ness. I hate to do it, but I have to thank you cause I'm walkin' out with much more than I brought in.[54]

Childress's asking such Locke-type characters as Bill to stop masquerading injures them as much as Baraka's calling them "Knee-grows." She adds insult to injury by having Tommy "taste" and reject the Locke people's egocentric lifestyle, returning instead to her "we-ness and us-ness" crowd.

Tommy's decision followed the advice in Salimu's *Growin' into Blackness* (1969) and Roger Furman's *The Long Black Block* (1971).

These plays told young people to combine their resources so that they could reject the individualism cherished by Locke. This same advice defined the limited number of plays in the *Ujamaa* (Cooperative Economics) class. These plays explained the concept of profit sharing in community-owned shopping and financial organizations. The plays, however, fell quite short of their purpose. Dramatists neglected to illustrate either the techniques for or the advantages in investing money in cooperative food stores, buying shares in cultural organizations, or setting up educational endowments. The writers depicted, instead, the need to watch out for the commercial piracy of talent and businesses. These plays included OyamO's *His First Step* (1968) and Ben Caldwell's *The King of Soul, or The Devil and Otis Redding* (1967). Baraka warned in *Junkies Are Full of (SHHH . . .)* (1972) that the first order of cooperative economics was to rid the community of the white-controlled drug business. These *Ujamaa* plays still did not quite "fit the bill." There needed to be fewer plays offering negative examples such as the forty-year-old shoeshine "boy" in Arthur Graham's *The Last Shine* (1969), who, to his horror, finds himself replaced by a machine. With a greater number of depictions of positive business circumstances, the *Ujamaa* plays and the theatre organizations that presented them might not have folded so soon after the grants dried up.

"Wars" broke out during the fifth class of Black Revolutionary drama. The conflicts in the *Nia* (Purpose) plays concerned problems with delivery systems for goods and services. The DuBois people saw – or "manufactured," as the Locke school said – so many difficulties that they wrote four subclasses of these plays: Criminal Justice, Values, Government, and Education. The Criminal Justice subclass accused police and correctional officers of targeting African Americans for brutality, of covering up complaints from African Americans, of compelling African American police to be especially inhumane toward their own people, and of corrupting and raping prisoners. The most often repeated charge during this period concerned police brutality. The most interesting claim was

Ben Caldwell's. In his 1968 *Riot Sale, or Dollar Psyche Fake Out,* Caldwell accused the police of orchestrating their brutalization through a system designed for genocide. Some police officers themselves later verified Caldwell's claim. This 1972 confirmation by Edward Palmer, co-founder of the Afro-American Patrolman's League of Chicago, however, did not shake the Locke people's faith in the authorities.[55] Not even the notorious Rodney King beating in 1991 by the Los Angeles police – nineteen years after Palmer's allegation – managed to persuade many in the Locke school that the police viewed all African Americans as "criminal elements."[56] It took an admission by the white president of the National Chiefs of Police, Chief Dennis Martin, to convince them that racism was rampant in many police departments.[57] Martin even substantiated Palmer's claim that "policy in the police department was to cover up complaints, especially against white policemen, for acts against black people."[58] A former Los Angeles police officer, Charles Johnson, an African American, verified the truth of Baraka's complaint in *Police* (1968) that African American officers were especially vicious toward their own people. Palmer earlier attributed this fact to the police officer's need to "prove to the establishment that he was not 'one of those.' This proof-by-combat caused him to overreact."[59] The DuBois school's solution to this police crime, except for that which is presented in Peter De Anda's *Ladies in Waiting* (1968), was to kill the police. Typical were Lonne Elder's *Charades on East 4th Street* (1972) and Ted Shine's *Contribution* (1969). The former depicts the ritual murder of police, whereas the latter has an apparently warm and kind woman poison an overbearing sheriff. OyamO's *The Breakout* (1968) even recommends the murder of police informers, since the police would poison the squealers anyway when their "snitching" was no longer needed. The significance of the Criminal Justice subclass, then, was in its reminder to the Locke school that blind faith in the police and the criminal-justice system invited trouble.

It was this trust, in fact, that the Values subclass of *Nia* plays aimed to destroy. These plays posited that whites had no values worth imitating (Baraka's *Home on the Range* [1966]) and that white values led to infighting and low self-esteem (Ben Caldwell's *All White Caste* [1969]). In *Home on the Range* Baraka places an African American criminal in a suburban white home. He makes the television-watching white family speak a language foreign to the criminal, as well as to his friends, who join him in a wild party. Instead of throwing the intruders out, the whites party with them until the whites fall out among themselves. The criminal discovers that the whites are not people at all, but "evil ghosts without substance." The whites cover their emptiness, Caldwell's *All White Caste* shows, by either depriving or seducing African Americans. The seduction sparks fights among the African Americans, not only for the whites' economic leftovers but also for the right to be like the whites. The resulting self-hatred by a "confused" people, says Baraka's *Great Goodness of Life* (1966), causes such a lost of self-esteem that even fathers betrayed their sons for the promise of privilege among the whites. Baraka's first answer to this values crisis is to use the same scare tactics as used by Hughes against whites during the second period. This time, however, Baraka levels the death threat at the Locke people. Revolutionary soldiers in Baraka's *Experimental Death Unit #1* (1964) kill a Locke school-type African American woman, along with two sex-seeking whites. Two years later, however, in *Madheart* (1966), Baraka has a young revolutionary spare the life of his mother and sister, who both wish to be white. When he is asked if there is any hope for converting his family, the revolutionary character applies Karenga's revised belief that women must "refuse to be flesh and object, and had to demand a full and fulfilling role and relevance in both love and struggle."[60] This Values subclass is important because it shows the prominence granted the struggle for the minds of young African Americans by the Locke and DuBois schools. The DuBois school worried about not having the young join Locke's people in assimilating and integrating. It feared too that young people would struggle for racial and social parity only for the purpose of entering the same socioeconomic class as whites.[61]

The third group of *Nia* plays, the Government subclass, accuses the authorities of committing genocide against African Americans, of frustrating people with bureaucratic redtape, and of invading people's privacy. Ben Caldwell's *Top Secret, or a Few Million after B.C.* (1968) argues that the government's birth- and population-control programs were plots. *Top Secret* rejects the political scientist Ronald Walters's conclusions that birth control had not necessarily reduced the African American population and that genocidal implications did not emerge when one sector of the population is limited disproportionately.[62] *Top Secret* contends, instead, that the government was trying desperately to control growth in the number of African Americans so that authorities could more easily kill them all. Caldwell further charges in his *Run Around* (1968), that politicians employed bloated bureaucracies and complex guidelines not only to strangle assistance programs but also to frustrate recipients and so limit their numbers. Low-income applicants, according to Caldwell, fell prey to endless forms that floated from office to office. As a result, people gave up, but the government could still keep tabs on them. In his *The Job* (1966), Caldwell depicts how such forms invaded people's privacy, and how low-income people could combat the intrusion: One bureaucrat – a white woman – so angers a musician applying for assistance by asking him impertinent questions about his music and his private life that he beats her with his saxophone.

Such humor, however, is missing in the final subclass of *Nia* plays, Education. These plays led to open conflict between the DuBois and the Locke schools, when the plays humiliated Locke school educators by calling them "niggers in the window."[63] Ron Milner's *The Monster* (1969) portrays revolutionary students murdering "niggerologists," as the law school educator Thomas Todd has labeled those "out front" African Americans who wield only the symbols of power. Milner's students would want nothing to do with the psychiatrist Alvin Poussaint's recommendation that DuBois school students and Locke school administrators negotiate the latter's "special dilemma" of being the "nigger in the middle."[64]

Marvin X's *The Black Bird* (1969) supports the students' hardline position. His play argues that the Locke adherents socialized children to be "niggers" by using white "clowns, fairies, elves, and angels, as well as Peter Pan, Little Red Riding Hood, and that grand matriarch, Mother Goose."[65] *Black Bird* depicts A Brother undoing the Locke people's brainwashing. He tells his sisters the story of a black bird that is nearly killed because it refuses to leave its master's burning house.

The continual public insults hastened the inevitable clash. As with the Langston Hughes–Walter White war of 1946, New York City was the battleground. Poet Askia Muhammad Toure replaced White as head of the DuBois people. Producer-director Bob Macbeth led the Locke school faction. Macbeth started the "War of 'Sixty-nine." The artistic director of the New Lafayette Theatre Macbeth believed that his theatre needed "to have a say about this Revolutionary thing," as well as about those "Harlem revolutionary cowboys."[66] He asked Ed Bullins to write a "real" play. Macbeth knew that to set Bullins loose on the revolutionaries invited trouble – especially with the playwright's scores to settle with the revolutionaries from the early Black Panther days in San Francisco. Macbeth had nothing but contempt for most of the "podium-revolutionaries," as he called them. They angered Macbeth because of their hypocrisy: He saw the "revolutionaries stuffing their noses with cocaine" before pouncing onto the stage to stir up armed insurrection, and he welcomed Bullins's having a go at these "cowboys." Bullins wrote *We Righteous Bombers* (1969) in three weeks. It is a political satire that tells the story of the deaths of some would-be revolutionaries. The deaths result from the government's capitalizing on the young people's idealism about war, on their faulty analyses of their political problems, and on their poor plans for battle. Bullins borrowed not only from Albert Camus's *The Just Assassins* (1949) but also from plays by Jean Genet and Jean Paul Sartre. To drive home the parody, Bullins uses the nom de plume Kingsley B. Bass, Jr., a concoction from Kingfish, one of the characters in the "Amos and Andy" television show: "Kingsley" from the first syllable of "Kingfish," and "Bass" from the "fish."[67]

Bombers became a hit. It won the Harriet Webster Updike Theater Award for literary excellence. To Bullins's and Macbeth's surprise, the play was taken as a serious statement by the hundreds who filled the theatre for each performance. The "Harlem cowboys," however, found cause enough for a showdown with Macbeth: "With their weapons showing underneath their dashikis," Macbeth recalled, they demanded that Macbeth close the show or have his theatre "burned down again."[68] Macbeth suggested, instead, that the theatre, along with the revolutionaries, co-sponsor a symposium on *Bombers*. The revolutionaries readily agreed. The significance of the symposium was that it updated the DuBois–Locke debates of the twenties. The poet and playwright Marvin X moderated. The writers Askia Muhammad Touré and Ernie Mkalimoto opposed the play. Robert Macbeth, the critic Larry Neal, and Amiri Baraka supported it. The pro-play team, which might be considered representative of the Locke school, was a strange crew. Baraka was philosophically allied with the DuBois team, whose positions the playwright had not only articulated but also popularized. He sided with the affirmative group simply because of his close friendship with Ed Bullins. The fact that Baraka was even in the New Lafayette Theatre was newsworthy because he did not like Macbeth. Macbeth had continually refused to produce any of Baraka's plays at the New Lafayette, believing "that they had no substance. They were not even plays."[69] While Baraka was defending his friend, therefore, he seldom missed an opportunity to knock down Macbeth's arguments, which, ironically, also defended Bullins. These interior fireworks made this symposium as interesting as it was important.

Following Mkalimoto's opening broadside against the play ("It is a super-nigger fantasy"), Touré shaped the debate with four points. The first was the DuBoisian argument that art should be not for art's sake, but for the people's sake. Touré contended that Bullins played art's-sake games with the "developing community mind" and that he placed "art above the revolutionary needs of his people. This crushed the collective spirit of the Black community."[70] Toure particularly resented Bullins's portrayals of "the revolutionary Black sister as a neurotic, loose slut rather than the queen she really is." Toure then tried to stack the panel by inviting his colleagues, April Spriggs and Helba Kgositsile, to join the group, a move rejected by Macbeth. The uproar caused by the director's refusal to admit the women was finally quieted when he placed two chairs up front for them. Spriggs and Kgositsile refused to join the discussion. Toure continued with his second point: Bullins did not make his "intentions clear":

Is this play intended by the author to be a serious portrayal of the lives of certain Black activists; is it meant to be a satire on the lives of certain death-worshiping, gun-happy groups in the struggle; or is the play truly a satire of fools bent upon getting a lot of Black people killed with their adolescent bravado? The playwright fails to distinguish between the fool and a true revolutionary, so that his audience can make a true distinction between the positive and negative examples.

Tour's third point was that Bullins projected the wrong image. The revolutionaries looked like

vacillating, schizophrenic "bombers," . . . while the Grand Prefect Smith is portrayed as cool, calm, supremely confident commander, consistent in his beliefs, positive in his aim of victory over the Black rebels, seemingly endowed with an invicible will and fighting spirit, outwitting the "bombers" at every turn, a master of disguise and deceit, eternally cleaver and resourceful.

Toure's final point was that he resented that the play was a "hymn to death – to death as escapism." It succeeded, he claimed, in "giving the impression that Black revolutionaries were wedded to death, rather than to affirming life."

Responding to Toure's first point about the roles of art and the writer, Larry Neal stated that artists have two functions: They can provide negative examples to teach what not to be; or they can provide direction; or they can do both at the same time. It is surprising that Toure let Neal get away with this position for Toure railed against middle-class playwrights whose negative examples overwhelmed the "positive directions." Neal knew that the "both" business was pure sophistry. Perhaps Toure would have pounced on Neal had Baraka not so curiously changed the debate subject to form – his softening-up attack on Macbeth. Baraka declared that form was the biggest problem in the piece. To illustrate, he played the contemporary gospel song "Oh, Happy Day." Critic Neal led the assault with a diatribe about content and form that showed him to be simultaneously for and against Macbeth as much as he was personally opposed to Toure: The problem with the play was form, not content. It was a problem "where you can't express the total meaning of what the author is saying because he's using a form that is dead. You know, that West kind of intellectual formalization." Neal succeeded in reshaping the debate, moving it away from Toure's concerns about content and toward the uniting ground of anti-Western form. What is interesting is that Baraka immediately leapt to a defense of Bullins:

I guess that most of us know that Ed Bullins is probably one of our most powerful playwrights, no matter what anybody says. [Applause] And the materials that he's dealing with generally are the materials that we have to begin with now. This is the material – the stuff that a lot of people are talking about in *Muhammed Speaks* and the *National Guardian* and on the sidewalks. These materials are the things that playwrights have to deal with. . . . [The materials] have to be recreated so that we can take a close look at them – at their theories, at their lives and so forth. And I think that's what Bullins was doing. I think first of all that those of us who really, strongly disagree with the play should write a play in reply.

To keep the hot light off of Bullins and on Macbeth, Baraka launched an attack against the "violent integrationists" who had brought whites back into the liberation movement. The audience shouted its "Amens," probably not recognizing that the "violent integrationist" attack was on Toure and the "form" on Macbeth, whose preference for plays with Western dramatic form was quite well known. Neal's bringing up the point and Baraka's seconding it seemed orchestrated to put Macbeth on the defensive. He fell for the bait:

One of the things Ed and I knew when we attempted the play is that Western form is really ragged. The Western play form is just very hard, and it doesn't serve our purposes. We have done four plays. And we'll probably do a couple more of what are commonly called plays because – well, we'll have to get that out of our system, I guess. But, then, at some point or another, the form will change. . . . LeRoi is right: there are things that you must experience. . . . But the form is limited.

This concession apparently prompted Toure to keep Macbeth on the ropes. After reiterating that projecting negative images for "a particular purpose" only creates a damaging confusion, Toure vented his frustrations:

TOURE: . . . I think Brother Macbeth pointed out that he wanted people to make remarks and come out and say various things [during the performance of plays]. Am I correct Brother Macbeth? Yes, well, Brother Ernie and I and other brothers did make remarks and we kind of got vamped on. Like we weren't being polite and cultured enough – in the drawing room sense of the word.
MACBETH: In my theatre?
TOURE: In your theatre, Brother Macbeth, in your theatre. That's right.
MACBETH: People have been talking back to plays here since we opened. Ain't nobody ever got stopped.
TOURE: I'm not speaking of you.
MACBETH: But you're suggesting that you got put down by the theatre because –
TOURE: No, not by the theatre. No . . . this is not concerning you. . . . That's all I have to say about that, Brother Neal.

This was Toure's payback not only to Macbeth, but also to Neal for having rather nastily interrupted one of Toure's more eloquent comments about the play's crushing the spirit of the people:

NEAL: My spirit ain't crushed, man.

TOURE: Also, another thing –
NEAL: Let me interrupt you a minute. Is anybody's spirit crushed because of this play?
VOICES: No, No. No.
NEAL: I mean, really. Go ahead. Finish reading.
TOURE: I'm not reading.
NEAL: I mean speaking. I'm sorry.
TOURE: Also, someone – I think Brother Macbeth –
NEAL: I just had to explode. I'm sorry.
TOURE: Yeah.
NEAL: I got the spirit, right here.

This prompted the second of Neal's diffused and confused elucidations about everything, including confusion. Baraka ended the debate with one final swipe at Macbeth, who had said earlier that the really important thing was that the audience determine how it felt about the characters and ideas: "What is important," according to Macbeth, "is that you respond, that you feel things, that you hate what the characters say and what they stand for." Baraka said that he was not for "a whole lot of vague feelings":

Like I feel something. I don't know what it is. What we have to do at this point in our lives . . . is try to say it like a big poster. . . . A play it seems to me, a work of art, should talk to you. What is being said should be clear, like, "Get off the sidewalk." But done with a great deal of artistry and feeling.

The most interesting point about this "war" was how Baraka made it so much less black and white than the dispute between DuBois and Locke or the cab scene between Walter White and Langston Hughes. Despite the myriad of hidden agendas, Baraka succeeded in avenging his having been shut out of the New Lafayette, in defending his friend, and in dismissing his friend's play. This symposium and *Bombers* itself were important in that both forced the DuBois people to reexamine their beliefs and strategies. The Movement by 1969 was replete with the early sloganeering designed to motivate people to join the struggle. The problem, as both the play and the syposium showed, was that the struggle was both means and end. The revolutionaries, therefore, expended valuable time and energy feeding feedings. This was what Baldwin warned about in *Blues for Mr. Charlie* through Richard, who had no plans for taking his friends and neighbors beyond the shock of snubbing tradition. Baldwin and Bullins asked, What is your plan?

The significance of the sixth class of Black Revolutionary drama, *Kuumba* (Creativity), was that it best answered the questions about the relationship between form and content. This mixed-media theatre was almost void of controversy, except for Larry Neal's contention that Ron Karenga was "ignorant" about the blues:

Doesn't [Karenga] know that the blues are the fundamental source of *all* relevant Black music? Ask Leon Thomas or Pharaoh Saunders. *A cultural revolution that does not include and absorb blues and feelings and modes of sound will surely fail.* The blues sound is the blackest part of the Black man's voice; this sound is the essence of our existence here in this land of the beasts. Further, the blues are the creation of a collective sensibility."[71]

Neal was responding here to Karenga's belief that the blues taught "resignation." Most Black Revolutionary playwrights, consequently, avoided the blues, as well as most other music. Baraka's use of Albert Ayler's improvised background music for *Home on the Range* (1966) and of Archie Shepp's music in *Slave Ship* (1969) were but examples of Baraka's "revisionist tendencies." Neal applauded Baraka's music. Neal even called for revocation of the ban on musicals, which were stigmatized still because of the Early Musicals Period of the Black Experience School. Neal held that "revolutionary musicals" could best "absorb and assimilate the dynamic culture now pulsating through Black America . . . including the sound of James Brown, Junior Walker, and Smokey Robinson."[72] The critic Peter Bailey offered a compromise: If revolutionary playwrights wanted to continue eschewing musicals, then the dramatists could at least include a few songs in their plays by turning to Isaac Hayes, Aretha, Nina Simone, or Curtis Mayfield for songs with revolutionary lyrics. Poor attendance at the revolutionary plays prompted debate over the place of music in revolutionary drama. At one point during the early seventies, revolutionary dramatists were "preaching to the choir," except in the South, where groups of poets developed a new form of revolutionary theater called poetry shows. These shows added theatricality, music, and dance to poetry readings. The BLKARTSOUTH Poets and the Sudan Poets of Houston specialized in these shows. The BLKARTSOUTH Poets' drama-poetry piece *The Turn of the Century: A Set for Our Rising* (1971) became a hit. The Sudan Poets even incorporated slides and folk songs into their shows. Furthermore, groups outside of the South (e.g., The Last Poets of New York and the Organization of Black American Culture [OBAC] in Chicago) adopted these shows. Music, then, despite Karenga, aided the *Kuumba* plays to beautify lives and communities and thus fulfill the purpose Karenga assigned to this sixth principle.

The final class of Black Revolutionary drama, *Imani* (Faith), used spiritual pieces to undermine and replace the churches. The revolutionaries wanted to subvert churches because the Locke people ran them and because, as Baraka put it, the churches "covered truth rather than reveal it."[73] The *Imani* plays, therefore, revealed the "covered" truth: Not only had the Christian church pillaged Africa's minerals, treasures, and peoples, but the church also had provided the theological rationale for the physical, mental, and economic slavery of Africans in America. Ben Caldwell's *Mission Accomplished* (1968), for example, shows Christian missionaries subverting African religions and customs in order to loot the continent's minerals and treasures. The missionaries exchange Bibles for riches. Caldwell recommended that people be as skeptical as he made his African king:

INTERPRETER: He [the king] said his senses warn him that you [the Catholic priest] are evil and your god must be evil. . . . The man of the good god does not lie, and steal, and kill for gain. All the universe is his provision, by his being a natural part of it! . . . He said they are in need of no salvation. He said his people have visible, beautiful souls that do not need saving. He said no man, among his people, wants everlasting life![74]

The priest forces "everlasting life" upon the king, nevertheless, before knocking him out and robbing him. Caldwell's satire is important for dramatizing Pan-Africanist Edward Blyden's 1887 warning that Africans must be wary of those who bear gifts. The theft of their goods prefaced the enslavement of African peoples. The first subclass of *Imani* plays, Sabotage, therefore, undermined the church because of its heritage of, as Hayward Henry, Jr., put it, excusing slavery in America.[75] The DuBois school welcomed the Last Poets' *Epitaph to a Coagulated Trinity* (1968) because it questioned why the church had refused, in the sixteenth century, to declare slavery a sin. Why had it winked at merchants who converted Christian dogma into slogans about "saving the heathens from a pagan land"? This looking the other way, said Henry, "to this day" causes the most devout of white Christians to exhibit few signs that they "have moved from their historic incapacity to deal humanely with blacks."[76] Even the Locke people involved with the church shaded their eyes from this Christian tradition.

Some ministers, as shown in many *Imani* plays, emulated the early white missionaries by stealing the present-day worshippers' minds. Ministers, in other words, exchanged money and thought for graphic retellings of biblical tales. Ironically, the tales, which the ministers expertly enacted only for their telling emotions, were meant originally to condemn the sins of slavery and racism. These ministers, Ben Caldwell's *Prayer Meeting, or The First Militant Minister* (1967) maintains, were merely agents of the status quo. Caldwell agreed with the writer Calvin Bromlee Marshall III's belief that many ministers blasphemed Jesus Christ by not painting vivid pictures of Him battling the oppressive and dehumanizing conditions of His day.[77] *Prayer Meeting*, therefore, advocates converting African American ministers into revolutionaries – accomplished in the play by having a thief fool a down-home preacher into thinking that the thief is God. "God" commands the minister to put aside his Bible, pick up his weapon, and defend revolution-aries. The significance of this satirical morality play was that it taught Black Nationalist theology: "If the message of Christ frees men to exist for the rejects, the outcasts, and the downtrodden," said Hayward Henry, "then the message of Black Revolution is the message of Christ himself."[78]

The DuBois school assailed the Locke church people for de-stroying people's faith in themselves. The school proposed a "New Spirituality," the second *Imani* subclass, which started people thinking about a human being's purpose in life, about freeing themselves from the desire for material possessions, and about connecting human energies with those of nature.[79] The DuBois school wrote plays that recommended a complete reordering not only of values and priorities but also of religion bureaucracies. The school made the needs of the needy paramount in this new "church." Among the greatest of these needs, the DuBois people believed, was the one to restore the faith of the poor in their own abilities, as well as in their individual godliness. These were the "fortunes" that the Locke people had stolen, said the DuBois school. The thefts had occurred with the indoctrination that "God takes care of His own." This belief set up people like the boy in Ronald Drayton's *Notes from a Savage God* (1968) to pray for help, as he sits for three days without food in a filthy rooming house. When, of course, no nourishment comes – because God expects people to do for themselves in their own heavens – the boy blames God. The boy robs himself even of the possibility of salvation, ac-cording to the Locke people's own dogma, with blasphemy: "God is dead." The real tragedy, as the DuBois school saw it, was that the hungry boy had lost his faith in his ability to feed himself. The costs of such self-desecration were exorbitant, not just for the alienated boy, but for all innocent people. Drayton's *Nocturne on the Rhine* (1968) presents the tally in terms of a correspondingly high number of physical and spiritual deaths. *Nocturne* tells the story of a person, called simply The Thief, who robs banks to help build a community hospital. He kills a guard during one robbery and re-

ceives the death penalty. The Thief, nevertheless, refuses to repent. He dismisses the priest who comes to him to administer the
last rites because the Thief feels that his intentions are his abso-
lution. Thus this simple morality play exemplifies how the material
could free people from their obsessive materialism. Whereas the
Locke people easily dismissed the theme as but the repackaged
Word of God, the DuBois school intended more. The message
moved heaven from Heaven to a "room in a filthy rooming house."
The theme, more importantly, made saviors out of everybody. One
needed no longer to go to Christian ministers, such as the one in
Baraka's *The Baptism* (1964), for prayer and baptism. As Baraka
shows in this allegory of the Passion, ministers ministered confus-
ingly. The play's ministers thought it trivial that Boy wanted to be
saved from a homosexual (Satan). Boy, therefore, must pray for,
baptize, and save himself. If Boy cannot save himself, then it is up
to Drayton's Thief or Baraka's motorcycle-riding Messenger –
symbols of the common people – to save him.

Whereas the Locke people found this absurdist "New Spirituality" difficult, because it welcomed abuse from the greedy, from
the hypocritical, and from the egomaniacal, the DuBois school
viewed the New Spirituality as sacred, because it met Blyden's cri-
terion for religion: It must value the abilities of African Americans
and encourage their excellence and assertiveness.[80] To spread this
New Spirituality, Baraka in 1968 created rituals. He first developed the pantomime "Insurrection and Misplaced Love," which
showed African Americans in control of the world, as well as of
themselves.[81] Baraka added to the ritual form chants and miniri-
tuals, which he thought of as "skits where we try to get to a kind of
unconscious future language. We try to recreate that kind of emotional tone that exists in the Black church, but put a different content in it, a content that has to do with things which we can't
completely understand yet. Like ritual-historical theatre."[82] Rituals, in fact, became the backbone of the *Imani* plays, thanks to
Robert Macbeth. Macbeth's *A Black Ritual* (1969) was the first
full-blown *Imani* ritual and contained such chants as: "Black gods

and spirits of my fallen / fathers; make my Black arms strong, my / back straight and my Black bursting heart / mighty . . . MIGHTY . . . to withstand and conquer this monster." The chants were accompanied by slides ("Pictures of white men with dogs. There are twenty-five to thirty pictures that are repeated over and over.")[83] The deeply spiritual chants moved the final stage of Black Revolutionary theatre closer to the forms, orders, and expectations of the traditional African American church. The rituals of Val Gray Ward's Kuumba Workshop in Chicago, in fact, were church:

Actors are dispersed among the audience. As "preacher," Ward sermonizes, the actors pop up, "testifying" with some relevant poem or epigram or excerpt from the works of Black authors, new or famous. The audience reacts with fervor, and it is not uncommon for some inspired brother or sister to leap up, issuing forth a spontaneous "testimony." Tension and release. And some sing. Significantly, Kuumba has had no permanent base of operation. For a while, the group operated out of Mrs. Ward's home, then they found temporary sanctuary in St. James Methodist Church.[84]

Black Revolutionary drama, therefore, remained throughout the fourth period an effort to change African Americans and to revitalize Western theatre "by attacking the intellectual and ideological premises of Western civilization." The plays themselves gradually changed from shocking to sacred,[85] and the Locke church people drew easier – if shorter – breaths.

Playwright Richard Wesley was the peacemaker between the DuBois and Locke schools. He uncaged roof-top pigeons with his play *The Black Terror* (1971). Seen by the warring DuBois and Locke people, the birds sang Wesley's song to stop fighting until all do a "painstaking and self-deflating political analysis of the situation."[86] People listened. Wesley transformed the final period of Black *Revolutionary* drama (since 1972) into the more peace-seeking Black Arts School. The change signified a new purpose and a new dramaturgy. The purpose was to advocate close analysis;

without it, all efforts to improve African American life would be fruitless. The dramaturgy shifted to accommodate the Wesley notion that theatre best assisted in reevaluation by turning down rhetoric and humanizing characters, thereby giving audiences harder and clearer choices. Dramatists readily took to Wesley's new direction, because they – and the audiences – were weary of the limitations of "honky baiting."[87] Audiences were equally bored with the "cussing and lamenting without enough hoping and perceiving."[88] There was no interference from Baraka, because by 1972 he had become a full-time political organizer. He had renounced *Kawaida*, furthermore, and had adopted Marxism.[89] Consequently, most dramatists rejected him.

In addition, the dramatists made significant changes in each of the seven classes of drama. In the New *Umoja* plays, for example, more humor, less ideology, and a different technique appeared in the efforts to build unity in the family and in the race. Typical of these plays was *Pepper* (1972), by Willie B. Shipman, where a family carefully rehearses the answers it needs to adopt a child from an agency, only to have the husband and the grandfather get everything wrong. Plays about ideological problems and class divisions changed to plays about personal problems between generations, as indicated by *Warn the Wicked* (1973) by Bill Harris and *In Both Hands* (1973) by Annetta G. Jefferson. Even the plays of political analysis of the struggle employed different techniques, such as Ted Lange's use of the avant-garde in his *A Foul Movement* (1973). New *Umoja* plays, then, became more developed, engaging, and entertaining. Although the New *Kujichagulia* plays still encouraged self-evaluation and race concept through history, the plays became more analytical, inclusive, and varied. Even in the biographical plays about such revolutionary heroes as Fred Hampton (Eugene Perkins's *Fred* [1974]) and George Jackson at Soledad Prison (*Place for the Manchild* [1972] by Young Hughly), audiences did not simply hear volumes about oppression. People experienced, instead, analyses of events leading up to the Hampton murder. They saw the family relationships that helped people to survive. Such analyses included sensitive portraits of women, who were no longer sex objects who longed to be white. Dramatists presented, instead, compassionate and heroic representations of women in such works as Margo Barnett's *Black Is a Beautiful Woman* (1974) and Tony Cox's *Man's Best Friend* (1974) and *Portraits of Woman* (1974). Audiences got more varied treatments of known historical data. Historical pageants, for example, could better engage audiences, not only because of their slides and live music but also because of the inclusion of more local history and color. *Stay Strong for the Harvest* (1976) by the Urban Theater of Houston, therefore, extended from Africa to the American Southwest, focusing on Native and African American alliances and on the Maroon settlements. The broader analyses, extensions, and inclusions of the second class of plays were present also in the New *Ujima* plays. The themes of plays about characters who were working out diverse personal dilemmas shifted from accusing whites of victimizing people to investigating rural–urban problems, forced retirements, and interpersonal relationships. In *Chi-Star* (1973) by the Reverend Spencer Jackson, for example, a country boy who comes to the city analyzes just why he has so much trouble adapting to urban living. *Madam Odum* (1973) by Louis Rivers, like Thomas Pawley's *The Tumult and the Shouting* (1969), studies the effects of an educational policy that forces a college professor to retire. The professor's struggle to maintain her beliefs, along with her position, is a microcosm of the African American's political effort. Such inquiries again expanded the roles of women. *Don't Call Me Man* (1973) by Howard Moore answered Larry Neal's call for Movement plays to have more music (or "vectors of Black cultural life," as he put it).[90] Not only did Moore tell the story of a jazz singer's efforts to make her man respect her, but the Billie Holiday Theater persuaded the jazz singer Betty Carter to make her acting debut.

Dramatists still shied from plays about the building and maintaining of stores, shops, and other businesses. Thus there were no productions of *Ujamaa* plays. There was also an 86 percent decrease in the number of *Nia* plays attacking social, political, and economic systems. Typical of the few New *Nia* plays produced were *S.T.R.E.S.S.* (1973) by Vance Smith, which shows the police using decoys to apprehend street robbers, and *Home Grown War* (1974) by Lawrence Kabaka, which tells the story of a young revolutionary murdered by the police. There was, however, an 86 percent increase in the number of New *Kuumba* musicals, led by Hazel Bryant's *Makin' It* (1972) (with Gertrude Grenidge and Walter Miles), *Sheba* (1972) (with Jimmy Justice), and *Every Man a Roach* (1972). Other musicals dealt with the search for identity, urban life, history, and family problems. In *O-Ree-O* (1972) by William Walker (with Otis Dancy), a young person uses his African American consciousness to find himself. *Changes* (1973) by Motojicho (with Valeria Smith) presents snapshots of urban life, including generational family problems, police brutality, and unemployment. C. Bernard Jackson's *Earthquake* (1973) is a multiethnic montage of experiences common to Los Angeles. History is the subject of *$600 and a Mule* (1973) by Lester Wilson, whose highlight is its "sensuous dance" portrayals of George Jackson and Angela Davis. *The Spirit of Christmas* (1973) by Irvin Gaye tells the story of the transformation undergone by a wealthy entrepreneur after the kidnapping of his daughter. Among the New *Kuumba* innovations was *Multi-Media Cultural Odyssey* (1972) by Bartuss Experience of Cleveland, a blend of rock music, drama, film, poetry, and song.

Even more numerous than the New *Kuumba* musicals were the New *Imani* rituals and religious plays. Instead of focusing on African Americans as victims, the Black Arts School rituals explored their self-development, as initiated by the National Black Theater's *The Revival* (1972). A combination of music, dance, drama, and rapping, the Rituals subclass used traditions from the church to argue that without love for one another, African Americans were unable to help those still plagued by corruption and despair. The National Black Theater presented also its *Soul Journey Into Truth* (1975), which added chants, as well as audience participation, to the usual music and dance. The Kuumba Workshop of Chicago performed its *Destruction or Unity* (1972), which calls on the community to unite or die. The appearance of religious New *Imani* plays was the most astounding development in Black Arts theatre.

Unlike the plays of the Era of Black Revolutionary Drama, the New *Imani* plays, with the exception of Eugene Perkins's *God Is Black But He's Dead* (1974), affirmed faith in God. Most of these plays, like *Black Jesus* by Alfred Brenner, analyzed Christianity by placing it within the context of urban America. In *Jesus Christ – Lawd Today* (1971), for example, Glenda Dickerson makes Jesus a Malcolm X-like character leading poor African Americans. Jesus admonishes all races to live by His principles. Jesus dies, appropriately enough, by hanging. The play ends, however, on a positive note, with the song "Reach Out and Touch Somebody's Hand." In *Nigger Heaven* by the Black Fire Theatre of Birmingham, Alabama, gospel music and dance paint a positive picture of heaven from an African American perspective. *Yes, Lord* (1973) by Douglas Johnson also features gospel, poetry, and dance. Several theatre companies revived earlier plays, including Langston Hughes's *Gospel Glory: A Passion Play* (1961).[91] Not only did Black Arts theatre make its peace with the church, but some perceptive theatre people proposed emulation. In 1972 the first southern regional conference of African American theatres and cultural groups submitted that theatres, aiming for greater financial and community support, should develop a *church-like structure*. Theatres should enlist long-term commitments of support from individuals, and they should call on the multiplicity of talents available in the community.[92] Had African American theatres adopted such policies, then theatre, like the church, would have become a more stable and vibrant community institution.

The recent Black Arts plays are concise and cogent works with very little rhetoric. These quite sophisticated plays straddle classes. Amiri Baraka's *Song* (1989), for example, calls for family unity (*Umoja*) and for responsive government (*Nia*). Suzan-Lori Parks's *The Death of the Last Black Man in the Whole Entire World* (1990) mixes *Kujichagulia* and *Umoja*. P. J. Gibson's *Konvergence* (1989) adds *Ujima* to *Nia*. Ben Caldwell's *Birth of a Blues!* (1989) joins *Ujamaa* and *Kuumba*. *Nia* and *Imani* are found in such representative works as Daniel W. Owens's *The Box* (1989) and the New York Urban Bush Women's *Praise House*. There is far more to these recent Black Arts plays, however, than mixing of classes. The plays close completely the historic schism between the Black Experience and the Black Arts schools. Whereas Baraka's *Song,* for example, is as revolutionary as his *Slave Ship, Song* conforms completely to the tenets of Locke's Art-Theatre School. How Baraka, as well as the others, accomplished this deserves close study.

Song allegorizes the story of a writer, the Old Man, or Professor Woogie, who earlier has pushed out of his life his wife and their two sons, Blue Hot and Blue Cool. When POST MAN – also known as Mr. Boogie, or Death – comes to take Professor Woogie, the professor's discarded family pays him a surprise birthday visit, which puts off Death. The significance of this apparently simple "song" is its updating of audiences on what, in 1990, was new with Baraka – after a quarter century in the theatre. On the one hand, there was nothing particularly new about the themes in *Song.* Professor Woogie is the Court Royal figure from Baraka's earlier *Great Goodness of Life* (1966). In that play the brutal government bureau that Court Royal has permitted to murder his son now comes to claim the father. He was "past usefulness to the users," who abused him "as long as we could with disinterest."[93] Baraka, in other words, is just as hard on governmental agencies in *Song* ("the Bureau of Most Concern") as he was on the criminal-justice system in *Great Goodness.* Even Baraka's secondary theme – the healing of family rifts – mirrors one he used before, in his *Madheart* (1966). In this play Black Man decides not to give up on his "devil-worshipping" family: "They're my flesh. I'll do what I can. We'll both try. All of us, black people."[94] Nor was there anything particularly new in *Song* about Baraka's use of spectacle. It would have been, admittedly, quite difficult for even his furtive mind to find a way to equal the sight of Court Royal's court-appointed attorney:

A bald-headed smiling house slave in a wrinkled dirty tuxedo crawls across the stage; he has a wire attached to his back leading offstage. A huge key in the side of his head. We hear the motors "animating" his body groaning like tremendous weights. He grins, and slobbers, turning his head slowly from side to side. He grins. He makes little quivering sounds.[95]

Nothing tops this image in *Song*, not even Baraka's materializing of Signifying Monkey and of Br'er Rabbit: "OLD MAN *waves the papers, rustles them, and in a crackle, a MONKEY appears. A chimpanzee with boater hat, and dressed up. He carries a cane, a boutonniere in the lapel of his blue blazer. He has white linen pants.*" Br'er Rabbit is equally well decked out: "*OLD MAN crackles the papers, waves them some more. A RABBIT appears. In designer jeans, a jacket. A large RABBIT, with dark glasses, smoking a reefer.*" These traditional characters, however, did add to Baraka's continued use of mysterious anonymity to characterize evil. Thus the VOICE OF THE JUDGE in *Great Goodness* becomes in *Song* POST MAN, a cold-blooded Grim Reaper. Baraka was, however, trying something new with his naming of characters. The names taken from African American traditions (Br'er Rabbit, Signifying Monkey, "blue hot," and "blue cool") not only typified traits, as was the case with most other Barakaian characters, but the names themselves represented issues: OLD (Boogie) MAN is POST (Woogie) MAN. But even this naming was not the most fascinating new aspect of Baraka's writing. His language was that. Baraka, first, lifted his ban on profanity. He had announced the ban in a 1968 interview: Asked if he thought that the profanity in his plays gave people reason to "reject Black," Baraka had answered, "Yes" and that he believed that this was especially true about "the amount of bad language in his early work." He explained that he had recorded what he had heard and seen. He was, in other words, "a camera to show people what they are." He added, however, that he was "past" the profanity, because he now saw "the need in raising" people, which required that he use "language a little differently."[96] Baraka's profanity in *Song*, therefore, raises questions about the purpose of this play. If Baraka rejected vulgarity in 1968 because he proposed "raising" people, then did his return to swearing in *Song* mean that he had abandoned drama as a consciousness-raising tool? The question in no way implies the impropriety of his "bad language," because, in fact, it neither shocks nor detracts. This was not because the profanity was so familiar, but because the profanity naturally fit the rhythm and the sense of what he called his "Conqueror's Language."[97]

Baraka was working as early as 1968 on the complex grammar and style of this new language, which reached maturity in *Song* as an "emotional language." It was this language that tied the play to both schools. The language contains Bullins's "Back Street" vernacular ("MONKEY: What's up with y'all?"), and there are, of course, the requisite dozens ("MONKEY: Dude can't even talk straight. . . . Talk just like his mother. She cdn't talk neither. Mama babble like a drug addict too"). There is more to it, however, than recognizable street tongues. It is also carefully orchestrated sounds, rhymes, silences, and rhythms. The meticulously selected sounds, for example, evoke specific emotions:

OLD MAN: . . . All this talk and surreal fantasy. A nut dressed like a postman with some symbolic bullshit jargon – Jesus – You're some nut from the street. Some frustrated poet or something. Wants to bore people at bars showing their poems or something. Your name is probably Alphonso or something dumb.

These sounds, like sonar, detect and pinpoint OLD MAN's deepest anger. Short and hard syllables, punctuated by shrill and cutting "esez," not only reveal but also stir up rage. Added to these scientifically chosen sounds are such in-line rhymes as "Your employers are my annoyers," or

POST MAN: You filled up spaces with faces, you clogged up drafts with laughs but, in the last resort, GOOMBYE! Your house, already past, is called by us, "The Last Resort."

Constituting the opposite sound extremity of the axis are silences, which fill important areas within the sphere:

POST MAN: I'm a new mailman. I'm the mailman you couldn't know 'cause I started after you died.

OLD MAN (*stands looking at the POST MAN then, [at] the audience – head cocks to the side – looking him up and down; he takes a couple back steps*): OK, you said all that, now you can leave.

Rhythm, of course, gives voice to silence. Baraka's beats are those in African American music. Words, then, are merely "notations," as well as "nodes" of pulse and feelings:

OLD MAN: No Mail? (*Pondering.*) I ain't dead. I could get junk mail. I could get circulars and posters and coupons and give-aways. There's plenty mail I could get. I could get mail marked "Resident" or "Present Occupant." Wouldn't even nobody have to know me as me.

Although pleasing, this combination of rhythm, in-line rhyme, silence, and sound is not the whole story. The most interesting aspect of the Conqueror's Language is its contradictory presentation of concepts. The belief that Africans were the Original People, for example, becomes a paradox: "The first negroes were not colored. The first negroes were white people!" Such ironies make perfect sense even before one understands fully their meaning. The sense, then, comes as much from ear-pleasing utterances as from the thoughts symbolized by the syllables. Baraka, therefore, has hit upon something quite important. Because this Conqueror's Language now clothes his already well-honed techniques of developing dramatic structure, characterization, and theme, Baraka is set apart. What *Song* shows that is new about Baraka is his place now among the very best of the playwrights in world theatre.

Although P. J. Gibson's *Konvergence* (1989) is as hard-hitting as the Protest plays during the Golden Era, the Attack Era (1951–65), she aims her blows at those breaking the bonds of Locke's Binding Relationships class of plays during the Experimentation and Diversification Period (1938–68) of the Art-Theatre School. The result is a Protest play about relationships between men and women. Gibson tells the story of an estranged couple, Nanyel and Derek, who meet after a one-year trial separation. Gibson argues that women such as Nanyel watched silently as their husbands became "another chocolate-covered android of the system."[98] When a wife did intervene, she would too often be told off:

DEREK: Look, Nani, I don't need a lecture from you, especially over an issue that's dead and over with.

NANYEL: You are the issue. Are you dead and over with? How can you continue to believe you can help others until you come to understand you've got to help yourself? Some politician you are. In fact, some man.

Gibson avenges Derek's putting politics before the well-being of his wife by having Nanyel reject her husband's plea to take him back. This play is important because neither class nor race influences Nanyel's decision. Instead, her rejection of Derek stems from her recognition that two bright people who had "set out to make a change" in their community failed because they had not begun by transforming themselves. Consequently, they gave away too much of themselves, "too much of our truth."

This kind of cognizance also characterizes Ben Caldwell's *Birth of a Blues!* (1989). In it Caldwell continues the warnings found in his plays of the Era of Black Revolutionary Drama (1965–72), in which he cautions about the white exploitation of talented African Americans, as seen earlier in his own *The King of Soul, or The Devil and Otis Redding* (1967) and in OyamO's *His First Step* (1968). *Blues*, which is Caldwell's best satire, reveals the history of the African American blues singer Baddest Black Blues Boy Ever Been Born King. Interviewed by a "young white reporter," BBBBEBB King relates how whites had capitalized on a genuine American folk art. White businessmen had promised King millions, which they made but also kept for themselves. They gave King crumbs, along with "beautiful white girls." These entrepreneurs end up owning "one of the biggest record companies in the world." Like other *Ujamaa* plays, and like the blues itself, *Blues* has no happy ending. A wiser – but broke – King has only his memories of "a whole lotta good times."[99] He moans and hollers the blues on a street corner, as he huddles against a strong wind. Based on this outcome,

Ron Karenga's position that the blues promoted acquiescence gained credence. Larry Neal's notion that the blues offered hope was digestible in light of *Blues* only if taken with the assumption that BBBBEBB King soon would approach Mr. Music Entrepreneur for back pay and payback. Because Caldwell chose not to show this confrontation, *Blues*, of course, did not alter the New *Ujamaa* class.

Equally unvaried were the New *Kuumba* plays. These latest multimedia works, like the musicals of the Black Experience School, continued to question identity, urban life, family, and history. The principal difference between the musicals of the two schools surfaced in *Down on Beale Street* (1988) by Levi Frazier, Jr., with music by Howard Robertson, Jr. This typical revue highlights the denizens and the good times of such Beale Street spots as the Palace Theatre in Memphis. Frazier guides an aspiring blues singer through the lives of such figures of the thirties, forties, and fifties as Ida Cox, B. B. King, W. C. Handy, vocalist Anita Tucker, choreographer Annie Jean Barnett, and dancer Babe Barlow.[100] This revue, however, is more than just another "hokey, carnival-spirited" good time. Frazier, who is the artistic director and the co-founder, with Deborah Frazier, of the Blues City Cultural Center for the Performing and Visual Arts in Memphis (1979–), includes large segments about the "cultural exploitation and the value of black institutions."[101] This revue, therefore, follows the precedent set by Hazel Bryant's musicals of the Black Experience Theatre Period (1968–75). The significance of all of these musicals-with-messages is that they finally achieve what DuBois was seeking when he asked Cole in 1909 to write protest musical comedies for Broadway.

Of all the recent plays and performance pieces that unite the Locke and DuBois schools, Daniel W. Owens's *The Box* (1989) and the New York Urban Bush Women's *Praise House* best represent those works that wipe clean the schools' structural and thematic differences. *The Box* (1989), for example, demonstrated to Black Arts dramatists that they did not have to avoid surrealism in "street drama." Traditionally, these new *Nia* dramatists had avoided surrealism because the typical street person had little time and less patience for deciphering symbolism. In *The Box*, however, Owens throws three young people from different socioeconomic classes into a time-lapse box containing their common ancestry – symbolized by the "ragged, grey-haired" Ole Man. This would be no problem for busy people. The trouble begins when Owens proves the young people's "oneness." He has the humming Ole Man take the youths back to slavery-time auction blocks, breedings, and castrations. By juxtaposing past, present, and future time and action, Owens reveals his theme: The African Americans' exit from their box (i.e., their situation) depends on their uniting, as well as on their applying the lessons of history. This theme challenged the foundations of the fifth-period conflicts between the Locke and the DuBois people over values and education. The times were too desperate, said Owens, for such labels as "nigger in the window" or "niggerologist." (The Voice of the Slavemaster in *The Box* tells the three young people that they "in a moment . . . will be dead.")[102] Owens reiterated that the struggle to "restore our people to their traditional greatness" begins with stopping African Americans from fighting among themselves and against their histories.[103] Because Owens's young people do not heed his call, their history slips out of the box during one of their fights. Caught in the past, they are hanged for leading a slave uprising in Virginia. Owens, like Gibson, added a radical concept to the revolutionaries' customary exhortation, "Change now." "Yourself" was affixed to the slogan by this representative of the brash new crop of well-educated African American playwrights. Enlightened busy people, said the latest New *Nia* plays, had no plans to replace white pettifoggers with African American shysters.

Equally different patterns and theses occur in *Praise House*, a ritual by the New York Urban Bush Women, a collective of women artists:

[*Praise House*] pays tribute to a group of American folk artists, alternately called "visionaries," "outside artists," or "innocent surrealists." Without any formal training or any apparent educational background from which to draw historical imagery, these largely unrecognized painters and crafts-people – Minnie Evans, Sister Gertrude Morgan, James Hampton and others – produced compelling mystical art.[104]

The play's director, Jawole Willa Jo Zollar, used this art to choreograph dances, to design visual elements, and to commission plays. The centerpiece of *Praise House* is Angela DeBord's verse drama inspired by a James Hampton painting. Hannah, a young girl, sees "visions" that call her out to play "on the back of the cows." Her grandmother, who recalls the pain of ancestral African visions, stops Hannah. She needs Hannah's help. The grandmother's gift of seeing visions has revealed that it is Granny's time to "cross de ribber." Hannah witnesses Granny's crossing, her bargaining her way through the Pearly Gates with her peach cobbler recipe, and her high-stepping her way around heaven with the gospel choir.[105] The importance of this praise-ritual is not only that it celebrates the works of living, unknown, and self-educated artists but also that it displays how the retention of African tradition shapes African American beliefs and attitudes. The Urban Bush Women asked only that African Americans follow the ancestral "visions" that came from their African hearts and minds. Expect this "listening to the heart" to be hard work, warned Director Zollar, because the "reward" will be only the work itself.[106]

Suzan-Lori Parks's *The Death of the Last Black Man in the Whole Entire World* (1990) fuses the two schools of drama by pouring a hardcore DuBois theme (the sense of self and of race as seen through history) into a Locke form (something akin to ritualistic absurdism). The slight plot metaphorizes the history of African Americans, personified in Major Gamble – or is it Gamble Major? Not even the "Voice on thuh Tee V" seems to know. One knows, however, that Gamble is a thirty-eight-year-old "spearhead in the Civil Rights movement . . . [who, although] born a slave, . . . [teaches] himself the rudiments of education." Europeans capture, enslave, ship, breed, rape, auction, and lynch him. Parks's substitution of realism for absurdism makes the play difficult to categorize. It has an African American content and theme, along with an absurdist structure and a ritualistic treatment. The content shows Parks's complete grasp of the southern African American idioms, lifestyles, and obsessions. She chose an early language ("Who gived birth tud this I wonder who") that is distinct from the old Negro dialect in that Parks's language refuses to make fun of itself:

Yesterday today next summer tomorrow just uh moment uhgoh in 1317 dieded thuh last black man in thuh whole entire world. Un! Oh. Don't be uhlarmed. Do not be afeared. It was painless. Uh painless passin. He falls twenty-three floors to his death. 23 floors from uh passin ship from space tuh splat on thuh pavement. He have uh head he been keepin under thuh tee V. On his bottom pantry shelf. He have uh head that hurts. Don't fit right. Put it on tuh go tuh thuh store and it pinched him when he walks his thoughts don't got room. Why dieded he hunh? Where he gonna go now that he done dieded? Where he gonna go tuh wash his hands.[107]

Parks, unlike Baraka, did not so much invent a language as accurately record one. She evidently had spent much time listening to African Americans who spoke a rural, nineteenth-century African Americanese. "Dieded," "afeared," "painless passin,' and "splat" are dead giveaways. The one possible change might be "whole *wide* world" for "whole entire world." Her language choice refreshed, as did the way in which she used the southern lifestyle: Cold compresses, buried rings, and strangled hens made clear her message. Parks further revealed the lifestyle by sticking her feet under many a southern table. She served up such staples as watermelon, fried drumstick, cornbread, and ham, accompanied by black-eyed peas, greens, and prunes. One eased this meal down, of course, with lots of grease and lots of pork.

Parks's striking originality was in her naming of characters after these traditional foods. African American theatre had never seen "the likes of it," to borrow another phrase from the Old Folks. Frances Gunner, of course, during the DuBois Era of Protest Drama (1913–32), had given birth to such characters as spirit of Service, Beauty, and Truth. Edward McCoo, too, had had Negro Church "bless out" Opposition. Parks went the furthest, however, by parading before the public, in broad daylight, such "figures" as Black Man with Watermelon (Gamble) and Black Woman with Fried Drumstick (Gamble's wife). Parks gave them an extended family (or chorus) of food stuffs, historical figures, places, and conditions. She used this grits-and-gravy ensemble to rattle brains with her reading of history, as it was informed by the historians John H. Jackson, Dr. Yosef ben-Jochannan, and Chancellor Williams. Parks's theme, like that of Caldwell in *Mission Accomplished* (1968), was that Europeans had stolen not only Africa's people, mines, and minds but also Africa's history. Europeans, in fact, had told Africans in the diaspora that African history began with Europe's "discovery" of Africa. Parks admonished African peoples to learn truth-history and to learn "to write it down."

This content and theme were not, however, Parks's signature. Rather, it was her mix of absurdist structure and ritualistic treatment that distinguished her work. Parks divided *The Death of the Last Black Man* into seven sections (an overture along with six "panels"). The significance of this division lay in the unique function of each part. The sections were not meant to outline history in cause-and-effect sequences, but in associational episodes. The Overture, for example, introduces the play's theme, subthemes, and characters. The remainder of the play is divided into three Black Man–Black Women "duets" and three "choruses." The duets carry the main plot line, which unravels in succeeding panels the story of Black Man's capture, attempted lynching, escape, recapture, lynching, and rebirth. Parks uses the duets to personalize the terrorism of a lynching:

BLACK WOMAN: Your days work aint like any others day work: you bring your tree branch home. Let me loosen thuh tie let me loosen thuh neck-lace let me loosen up thuh noose that stringed him up let me leave thuh tree branch be.

. . . .

BLACK MAN: Put me on uh platform tuh wait for uh train. Uh who who uh who who uh where ya gonna gon now – . Platform hitched with horses/steeds. Steeds runned off n left me there swingin.

. . . .

BLACK MAN: Swingin from front tuh back uhgain. Back tuh-back tuh
that was how I be wentin. Chin on my chest hangin down in restin eyes
each on eyee in my 2 feets. . . . It was difficult tuh breathe. Toes un-
crossin then crossin for luck. It was difficult tuh breathe.[108]

Whereas the depiction of such horrors began in 1916 with Angelina Grimke, Parks adds her special commentary. She compares
this atrocity to that of modern, legal lynchings (i.e., capital punish-
ment), which her Black Man also braves:

BLACK MAN: Thuh straps they have on me are leathern. See thuh cord
waggin full with uh jump-juice try me tuh wiggle from thuh waggin but
belt leathern straps: width thickly. One round each forearm. Forearm
mine? 2 cross thy chest. Chest is mine: and it explodin. One for my left
hand fingers left strapted too. Right was done thuh same. Jump-juice
meets me-mine juices. I do uh slow soft shoe like on water. Town crier
cries uh moan. Felt my nappy head to frizzly. Town follows thuh crier
in uh sorta sing-uhlong-song.[109]

These personal narratives make accessible the many subthemes
Parks raises through the choruses. The choruses are rituals. These
repeated sounds, sayings, and visions not only carry Parks's admonition to write down the history, but they also flash highlights of
that history. Most notable is Parks's version of the Europeans' arrival in Africa: "QUEEN-THEN-PHARAOH HATSHEPUT: I
saw Columbus comin. / I saw Columbus comin goin over tuh visit
you. 'To borrow a cup of sugar,' so he said. I waved my hands in
warning. You waved back. I ain't seen you since."[110] Of great interest about the choruses is the way that Parks uses them to build
her main theme. The message about history subtly changes from
"write it down on a slip of paper and hide it under a rock" in the
Overture to "Carve it out of a rock" in the rousing Final Chorus.
This chorus has everybody "*stomping the ground with their foot,*"
singing the refrain, and "shouting" (i.e., the ancient foot-stomping
dance). The importance of Parks's play is that it charts the new jet
streams among plays utilizing history. Gone now are "the Victims"

in *Ti Yette* (1930) of the DuBois Era (1913–32), in *Our Lan'* (1947) of the second period (1932–51), in *Dutchman* (1964) of the third period (1951–65) and in *The Last Shine* (1969) of the fourth period (1965–72). Parks shows "the Victors" who, in the end, celebrate because they are their histories – histories learned from carved rock-books. Judging from the views as well as the vision in *The Death of the Last Black Man*, it is not surprising that Parks received an Obie award, for her earlier play, *Imperceptible Mutabilities in the Third Kingdom* (1989). *The Death of the Last Black Man in the Whole Entire World* is not only a significant watershed in African American theatre, it is also one of the most sophisticated plays in contemporary American theatre.

A comparison of the aims and methods of Parks's *The Death of the Last Black Man* and DuBois's *Star of Ethiopia* indicates the importance of both the Black Arts and the Black Experience schools of drama. DuBois wished simply to stop white racism and to stop African Americans from being raceless. He steered African Americans toward letting their "glorious" history guide their "eternal struggle" against racism. Parks, seventy-seven years later, had so internalized DuBois's objectives that they became the means by which she tapped into something even more important than either racism or racelessness. That something was the recognition that the source of these problems was lack of "ancestral knowledge and vision." The eternal struggle thus was broadened to encompass restoring this knowledge and vision to Americans. The renewal was critical because vision, after all, can determine what life is and what life ought to be. Racism and racelessness are but symptoms exhibited by people who have become spiritually blind. The search for "ancestral knowledge and vision," then, has come to define both schools of African American drama. It was cause for celebration that the schools had been at last united in their quests.

The celebration, unfortunately, had to be short-lived. Although there were now more quality plays than ever before, there were also too few places in which they could be produced. Beginning in the middle seventies, African American theatre organizations closed in unprecedented numbers. Of the forty-six most influential theatre companies founded during the late sixties and early seventies, for example, only six (or 13 percent) still performed a season of at least four plays in 1992. Although there existed in name more than two hundred forty theatre companies in 1992, no more than ten of these were economically healthy. The recession in the national economy was much to blame, but the principal cause was poor theatre management. The results of the closings were tragic. Fewer African Americans received training in the theatre arts early enough for them to be competitive. Consequently, there were fewer African Americans to participate in community and regional theatres. The question, then, becomes how can the few African Americans in theatre be encouraged to remain? More importantly, how can theatre organizations improve their governance and their development? Thoughtful and practical answers to these questions might begin with finding ways to stop African American theatre people from throwing up their hands.

3

Theatre People: Some Splendid Examples

> Let young Anglo-Africans, when they feel the weight and the manifest nature of the barrier in their way to eminence, remember . . . Ira Aldridge. We say this is a splendid example for the reason that the severe criticism of the London paper, in 1834, falling upon him when he had reckoned himself fit for the London stage, so far from discouraging [him] only acted as a stimulant to Mr. Aldridge, and drove him to a more severe course of dramatic study, which, after twenty years of persevering assiduity, placed him on that pinnacle of fame, to attain which he started out. What greater difficulties can there be in the way of any of our young?
>
> Dr. James McCune Smith

IT does not take much to make theatre people swear off theatre. Dr. Thurman W. Stanback (a former theatre chair at Bethune-Cookman College; later, professor of theatre at Florida Atlantic University) almost quit after the opening night at one college production. His lead actor, a full-time student and mother of teens, fell asleep on stage. Her leading man gave her cue after cue, waiting for her to rise from the sofa as if she had been asleep. He finally shook her. Half awake, she shouted out: "What y'all doing with all these lights on?"[1] Although Dr. Stanback found this incident slightly unfunny that night, he continued with the theatre, which he has been a part of for almost fifty years. Stanback's having had to smother several urges to leave over the years raises some questions: Would the young still flee theatre in droves if they knew that Trouble was Theatre's last name? Would the young give up as easily as they do if they understood how their role models in the theatre had been able to overcome racism, exploitation, rejection, family pressure, poor social environment, and career slumps? The performer Ruby Dee thinks they would not. She believes that although some fledgling artists might know the achievements of a particular star, they seldom know just what that individual had aspired to or had had to settle for as a young performer. They are unaware of the actor's "active search for opportunities, the sporadic success, the long periods of nothing to look forward to, the deliberate pretense of indifference, the deep self-doubt."[2] Dee recommends giving young performers more "knowledge of the history of entertainment, of the great contribution that our people have made to the theatre."[3] A feeling of "continuity of experience or sense of belonging to a tradition" can be gained, Dee believes, only through "complete descriptions" of lives.

What might be useful, then, would be to point out to the young some theatre people for further study. They should be individuals whose stories can provide just the examples of courage needed to help the young – and the tired – clarify and objectify their own grievances, thereby finding an alternative to despair in some sort of proactive program.[4] Such a proactive program could make a person's exposure to racism, for example, less damaging. The most helpful examples could be the way racism, the first Trouble of theatre, was handled by such masters as the actors James Hewlett and Ira Aldridge, as well as the dramatic reader–abolitionist William Wells Brown, the minstrelsy manager Charles Hicks, and the writer Alice Childress. They all dealt with racism by perfecting their craft, by externalizing their anger, and by publicizing discrimination. The sharpening of acting skills, strangely enough, increased the racism. Thus Hewlett was ridiculed in 1821 by the critic Manuel Noah and the English actor Charles Mathews only because Hewlett was the most talented member of Mr. Brown's

African Company. Noah himself revealed this in a backhanded way. In his review of the African Company's *Richard III*, Noah said that Hewlett's "conception of Richard III" was "not amiss," the only positive comment in an otherwise insulting notice.[5] In light of Noah's political agenda, his "not amiss" was high praise for this nineteenth-century multifaceted entertainer, who sang both popular songs and "operas," who performed as comedic characters and in dramatic roles, and pantomimes, and who danced ballets and jubas. It is significant that Noah's approval came at the beginning of Hewlett's acting career. After performing the role for five years, Hewlett had the *New York Star*'s critic singing hymns: Hewlett's "style, taste, voice, and action" were so "excellent" that he was a "credit [to] any stage." This was fairly strong stuff for a waiter at the City Hotel. The African American's talent led Charles Mathews to study Hewlett's style and language and thus fashion, and to popularize in Europe, the prototype for the first Negro minstrel character in 1825.[6] Hewlett was hurt when he heard that Mathews had "burlesqued" Hewlett's talent and "complexion." He had been extraordinarily nice to Mathews, having honored the English actor's request for a personal performance of *Richard III*. Hewlett dashed off to the *National Advocate* an open letter for Mathews: "When you were ridiculing the 'chief black tragedian' and burlesquing the 'real Negro melody,' was it my 'mind' or my 'visage' which should have made an impression on you?"[7]

This sophisticated question points to Hewlett's complete understanding of Mathews's and Noah's complex problem: They were jealous not only of Hewlett's acting ability, but also of his skin color. Hewlett apparently understood, then, as the psychiatrist Frances Cress Welsing theorized 145 years later, that fear and jealousy of African American skin color dominated the attitudes and beliefs about African Americans by some white people. The whites were obsessed because they feared obliteration.[8] In other words, Hewlett represented for the white actor Mathews the possibility of his being wiped off the stage by a rival talent and off the earth by recessive genes. It was only by understanding and then publicizing

Mathews's dysfunctional fears that Hewlett could direct his anger. Hewlett's example demonstrated that rebuke through the mass media of his time was an effective way to deal with racism in the theatre. Another effective antidote to racism was making a public spectacle out of the racists, a remedy used by the actor Ira Aldridge. Again, the bigots chose the most talented person of color they could find. Reviews of Aldridge's appearances throughout Europe between 1825 and 1867 were a golden tribute to him as the all-time most important American actor of Shakespeare.[9] European critics called him everything from "the greatest of all actors" to "the greatest thing in nature."[10] Nevertheless, one critic organized a conspiracy to run Aldridge out of London when Convent Garden booked him to perform *Othello* in 1833. In response, Aldridge, along with some white friends, passed out printed flyers: "Talent, let it come from what Country it may is deserving patronage. Therefore, fellow countrymen, do not permit a worthy and talented man to be CRUSHED by the slanders and libels of the low and contemptible."[11] Their demonstration worked, and, "by popular demand," Aldridge had to extend his appearance.[12] This example is important because it shows that racism has to be confronted, whether it is of an expected or a surprising origin.

An unexpected source characterized the dramatic reader and abolitionist William Wells Brown's brush with oblique bigotry when an agent of the Abolition Movement told Brown to stop reading his antislavery melodrama *The Escape; or, A Leap for Freedom* (1858). Some listeners allegedly had complained that Brown's powerful readings were scaring them. Indeed, Brown probably had, what with his booming voice and the romantic style he had learned by watching Ira Aldridge in London.[13] The abolitionist critics had often bragged that Brown could rivet "the attention of a large audience for almost three hours."[14] This is not surprising: The poor audience was probably too frightened to move. They would cry instead, no doubt watching Brown recall his time as a "slave custodian":

Before the slaves were exhibited for sale, they were dressed and driven out into the yard. Some were set to dancing, some to jumping, some to singing, and some to playing cards. This was done to make them appear cheerful and happy. My business was to see that they were placed in those situations before the arrival of the purchasers, and I have often set them to dancing when their cheeks were wet with tears.[15]

Brown was in no mood to have his abolitionist agent command him to stop his readings. He told the agent – from the platform and by private letter – that the readings were raising more money for the movement than anything done by the agent or anybody else. The agent shut his mouth.

Minstrelsy manager Charles Hicks was not so civil as Brown. Hicks acted out the bigots' worst fears. He knew just how to do this because by 1872 he had spent six years as co-founder, co-owner, and manager of Brooker and Clayton's Georgia Minstrels, the first successful African American minstrel troupe. He was such an "uppity nigger" that white managers were in "dread" of even seeing him.[16] Hicks was as rough as he was on them because he knew that the whites were exploiting African American actors by paying them incredibly low wages. He never missed a chance to tell the performers to demand higher wages. His advice was often ignored, however, because performers like Old Ida Jane and Sweet Mouth Willie were so glad to be out from behind a plow. Thus Hicks went around them – to the white managers, demanding that they either raise salaries or lose performers to him. He even joined white-owned companies in order to steal their actors. It took him just two months in the summer of 1876, for example, to persuade every African American performer in the J. H. Harverly and Tom Maguire Minstrel Company to work for him at a higher wage than they were getting from the white-owned company.[17] Hicks bragged about his successes in advertisements throughout the world, which were also warnings to white managers to be on the lookout.[18] When minstrel magnate Charles Frohman told Hicks that he had better stay away from Frohman's performers, Hicks took out full-page newspaper advertisements welcoming African Americans to work in his company for much higher salaries. So many of the best actors joined Hicks that Frohman quickly matched Hicks's wages. Whenever Frohman later heard that Hicks was even near the same town that his company was in, Frohman left.

Hicks's daring can be matched only by the likes of an Alice Childress. This diminutive writer was willing to take on all comers, including the Savannah, Georgia, school board. This school board, in 1974, tired of northerners' "Communist and integrationist trash" and banned Childress's *A Hero Ain't Nothin' But a Sandwich* (1973) from the Island Trees School Library. The poor board did not know who it was dealing with. Childress sued but lost. She appealed. Childress pursued this to the U.S. Supreme Court because of principle. Under no circumstances would she be deflected from her life's goal of writing material that will inspire people to become "winners" regardless of the "cruel odds." She had resolved early in her career as an actor, playwright, novelist, and screenwriter never to be tempted away from the serious topics occasioned by her goal. She cared nothing about building images by which others might measure African Americans' capabilities, or acceptability, or human worth.[19] Childress's concern about individual worth applies to all people. It is not at all surprising, therefore, that her prize-winning output has been heralded throughout the world for developing positive white and African American self-images. The novelist John O. Killens, himself a legend, has marveled at how Childress inspires all people to rise up "against oppression" without forcing them to wallow in "despair and pessimism."[20] The significance of the Childress example is – like the cases of Hicks, Brown, Aldridge, and Hewlett – that Childress was able to make clear that every person who experiences any kind of racism whatsoever is obligated to act. As Langston Hughes suggested, the offended must make so much loud and public noise that heads will spin.

Roaring verbal assaults, however, might not be the best way to handle the second Trouble of the theatre – financial exploitation.

As the experiences of Bob Cole, George Walker, and Charles Hicks show, quiet challenges equalized manager–artist relationships, upgraded African American companies' circuits, stimulated artists-controlled organizations, and raised artists's self-esteem. Cole's response to fiscal abuse transformed the company manager's ability to dominate artists. While he was the leading attraction with the Black Patti Troubadours during the 1895–6 season, Cole asked the company manager Rudolph Voelckel for a hefty raise. When Voelckel refused, Cole quit. Then he sued Voelckel over the rights to the songs and skits that Cole had written. Cole argued in court that because he had received low wages for the time that he was literally carrying the large company, he could refuse to obey the law requiring employees to relinquish rights to employers. It was because of this dispute that Cole founded in 1896 the first African American acting school. This quarrel also motivated him to write, in 1898, *A Trip to Coontown,* thereby beginning the first period of the Black Experience School of drama. The significance of the Cole–Voelckel feud, despite the judges' ruling against Cole, was that it "initiated a series of other controversies between white managers and black performers."[21] Cole had reversed manager domination of the performer.

George Walker, the "commander" of the Bert Williams–George Walker duo, defeated employer control of touring routes. Prior to Walker's altercation with minstrelsy czar Abraham Erlanger, most African American theatre companies got assigned to the "chitlin circuit," the string of theatre houses in the south and the midwest. Although Walker understood the need for beginning artists to perfect their skills outside of highly competitive markets, he believed that it was time for the Williams and Walker Company to play Broadway. He and Williams had behind them, after all, such hits as *The Policy Players* (1899), *The Sons of Ham* (1900), *In Dahomey* (1902), and *Abyssinia* (1906). Walker asked Erlanger, who controlled the minstrelsy syndicate, to book the duo on Broadway.[22] Erlanger told Walker to wait until the time was right, and Walker responded by creating a "stormy scene."[23] He and Williams vowed to show Erlanger. The William and Walker success story resulted. Their self-esteem, for understandable reasons, must have risen as they saw Erlanger slide into a box at the Majestic Theatre on Broadway during the long run of their hit, *Bandanna Land* (1908).[24] Walker's success, as well as that of Hicks and Cole, was, however, personally costly. Hicks had several of his companies stolen from him, a consequence not only of white managers' pooling their resources and offering higher salaries, but also, possibly, of their threatening the performers with black lists.[25] Hicks died in Suraboya, Java, in 1902; he had gone abroad because he could not get bookings in the major U.S. markets. Cole, suffering from mental illness, apparently drowned himself in 1911. Finally, much of Walker's ill health before his death in 1911 was worsened not only by his overworking to prove Erlanger wrong but also by Cole's inability to reconcile himself to seeing African American performers be rejected by their profession and their country.[26]

Rejection, the third Trouble, is the most pervasive problem facing African American theatre people. These professionals are brushed off not only because of racial prejudice but also because of artistic preferences, unjust accusations, poor judgments, jealousies, and politics. The most important thing about the rejections, historically, has been the variety of reactions to them. When racist authority figures put down the playwrights Charles Fuller and Ed Bullins, for example, these writers used their anger as a persistent stimulus to achieve. The actresses Ida Anderson and Laura Bowman, on the other hand, withdrew when they were rebuffed for their artistic preferences and developed other, successful, outlets for their talents. Not so fortunate was the actor-manager Billy Johnson, who left the business because his partner, Bob Cole, had accused him – probably unjustly – of stealing money. Johnson failed at his many efforts to earn a living. His anger was matched by those of the actors David Downing and L. Scott Caldwell, the writer Arna Bontemps, and the designer Felix Cochran, all of whom internalized their hostility and almost quit the business following poor judgments about their abilities. Instead of directing her fury inward, the international star Josephine Baker planned secret strategies to avoid open confrontations with the jealous colleagues who had tried to subvert her talents. There was nothing clandestine, however, about the attacks launched against the performers Paul Robeson, Lena Horne, Eartha Kitt, Richard B. Harrison, Marvin X, and Amiri Baraka. All of them had to overcome criticism for their political involvement.

The circumstantial details of these individuals' stories frame complex views about how to deal with rejection in the theatre. Thus Fuller and Bullins showed that anger resulting from abuse could drive people to achieve. Fuller's professor of creative writing at Villanova University had told him that his "people didn't need writers . . . [but] guys who could operate lathes."[27] The professor probably knew that he had abused his opportunity to assist his student in developing, shaping, and controlling his self-image.[28] Fuller, however, rebounded. Instead of anticipating, assuming, and accepting the professor's view of and attitude toward him, Fuller disproved the judgment by writing twenty-six plays, including works for which he received an Obie Award (1982) and the 1982 Pulitzer Prize for drama. In just the way Fuller invalidated his professor's biased judgments, Ed Bullins overcame a similar dismissal by his Los Angeles City College creative-writing teacher. This professor told Bullins to forget about playwriting and criticized Bullins's use of street language in his plays, as well as his refusal to obey sacrosanct prescriptions governing play structure. It did not matter to the teacher that Bullins wrote from his experience of North Philadelphia codes: Flunk and quit high school; join and leave the Navy; get high school General Education Diploma; marry and divorce childhood sweetheart; leave Philadelphia for an equally desperate California situation. Such rules too perhaps kept Bullins from either internalizing his anger or obeying the teacher's advice. The North Philly street mores, in fact, probably were responsible for Bullins's success in changing how people thought about drama and the theatre through his thirty-eight full-length plays, forty-three short plays, and nine musicals. Ironically, the professor's insult was partly responsible also for Bullins's receiving the New York Drama Critics Award and the Drama Desk–Vernon Rice Award along with three Obie awards, two Guggenheim fellowships, four Rockefeller Foundation Playwriting grants, and two National Endowment for the Arts Playwriting grants. Bullins contributed further to the development of Black Experience drama by conducting workshops and classes in his technique of playwriting (what the playwright Richard Wesley called his "graduate school"), and by publishing and performing his and his students' plays.[29] Whereas Fuller's and Bullins's professors had probably desired to frustrate these young writers, the professors might as well have aimed to motivate the two by *pretending* to thwart their ambitions. The encounters of Fuller and Bullins with racist professors were important because, as the psychiatrist Alvin Poussaint has explained, having to cope in an integrated educational environment, which is manipulated in part by a few racist whites, increases a student's "sense of control and achievement." The sense of control would come "not because of being in the presence of whites, but because of being in a proximate real world."[30] It was not surprising, therefore, that Bullins and Fuller together by 1992 had written more than one hundred fifty plays.

This same drive resulting from white racism applied as well to nonracial obstructions such as those experienced by Ida Anderson and Laura Bowman. Both women bucked trends, formed organizations, lost money, and found alternative funds. Anderson and Bowman disliked doing vaudeville and musical comedy. Although both women were musical-comedy stars (Anderson with the Lafayette Theatre, and Bowman with several companies), they preferred serious drama to mindless comedies. The women, therefore, separately formed their own dramatic companies, each of which initially did moderately well. Anderson played the major cities in the East, and Bowman's Dark Town Entertainers performed throughout the country. The irony of their choices was that although they offered the best chances of success, they also hastened failure. The urban, lettered elite of the east was where Anderson in 1916 would most likely find the market for her serious plays, but the small pool of potential audience members was rapidly depleted because of competition and cost. Although Bowman selected a larger circuit, her earnings and traveling/marketing costs were not offsetting. It was not surprising, then, that both women were soon looking for alternative financing. Anderson rejoined the Lafayette Players, and Bowman worked in vaudeville. Periodically, whenever they had raised enough money, they would return to serious drama: Bowman played in *Salome;* Anderson gave recitals and plays at socials and churches. Anderson's and Bowman's boldness in organizing their own companies at a time when men controlled the theatre business matched their daring in performing serious drama at a time when African American audiences wanted only to laugh. Thus these women dispelled the notion that women actors were fickle or were followers.

More of a surprise was that some men active in the theatre during this period did not fare as well as did Bowman and Anderson. The actor-manager Billy Johnson, for example, almost never recovered from his 1899 renunciation by his partner, Bob Cole. Cole, after one of his frequent illnesses, had returned to his and Johnson's hit show, *A Trip to Coontown* (1898), and he accused Johnson of stealing money. Johnson's thirteen-year absence from the theatre is traceable to this rejection and to Johnson's own lack of focus. Cole's accusation, interestingly enough, not only drove Johnson out of theatre, but it also compelled him to reenter it. It was the effort to prove his trustworthiness that caused Johnson, during the interim, to involve himself in one unsuccessful venture after another. The distraction of trying to erase the suspicions – which were, in fact, probably only the imaginings of Cole's slowly deteriorating mind – caused Johnson to fail in a vaudeville show, at songwriting, at playwriting, and in Chicago politics. The importance of Johnson's misadventures, however, is that they point to the need for theatre people to develop patience, persistence, and toughness. Johnson did not give up; his nineteen-year rise from song-and-dance man to specialty artist had taught him to expect things to be rugged.

Finally, his having gone through this stress made more meaningful for him his comeback with *Twenty Miles from Home* (1914), a quite successful musical comedy that he wrote with Tom Brown.[31]

Such recoveries seemed to be typical among African American artists, whether or not the initial trouble began with rejection by a teacher, director, producer, or artistic director. The discouragement by teachers – especially of young people – was particularly devastating. The actor David Downing, for example, withdrew from the New York High School of the Performing Arts after his tenth-grade acting teacher, for racist reasons, told Downing that he did not have what it took to be an actor. Although similarly insensitive remarks by Bullins's and Fuller's professors were destructive, these two college-age students were mature enough to see the racism. Downing, however, was crushed. Had his mother not been capable of cheering him up and his father of restoring his confidence, Downing would not have made his Broadway debut within a year. Nor would he have subsequently distinguished himself in roles as varied as Iago in *Othello* and Mitch in *I'm Not Rappaport*.[32] The importance of Downing's experience for young artists is that it lets them know they need not pay much attention to anybody's praise or condemnation. The ordeals of L. Scott Caldwell and Felix Cochran verified that the need to ignore judgments could be applied to professional artists. Their abilities were misjudged by directors. Caldwell, for example, might have thought that her years studying acting at Loyola University in Chicago had been wasted. Asante Scott, assistant director of the Negro Ensemble Company (NEC), rejected her application for membership in the company. Scott's rejection made Caldwell work even harder on the four pieces that she later used to audition for the company's artistic director, Douglas Turner Ward. Because she heard nothing from him, she returned home to Chicago, only to have Ward call to hire her as his last contract actor.[33] Caldwell later received rave reviews for her Broadway performance in Samm-Art Williams's *Home* (1979). She won the Tony Award for Best Supporting Actress in August Wilson's *Joe Turner's Come and Gone* (1986). Felix Cochran, too, must have wondered about his time spent studying design at Carnegie-Mellon University in Pittsburgh. For seven months he heard nothing from his hundreds of interviews with artistic directors in New York City. As he packed to return home to Syracuse, New York, he, too, got "that call." Marjorie Moon, artistic director of the Billie Holiday Theater (1972–), retained Cochran to design the set for *Inacent Black* (1981) by A. Marcus Hemphill, Jr. Cochran later designed Williams's *Home* and Charles Fuller's *A Soldier's Play* (1981).

Even more vulnerable than actors and designers were playwrights. Whereas Caldwell and Cochran could reverse poor judgments about them relatively quickly, it took Arna Bontemps fourteen years to prove to producers that his *St. Louis Woman* (1946) was stageworthy. Surprisingly, Bontemps's delay was caused by duplicitous African Americans. Some Harlem producers began the deceit soon after Bontemps and the poet Countee Cullen completed the play in 1932. Instead of the producers relinquishing their options because of a lack of financing, they continually asked for and got extensions. They never secured the money they needed, however, which did not stop them from bad-mouthing the project when it finally did reach Broadway. Even some well-known actors and civil rights leaders got involved. They stated that the African American image suffered still from the damage done by the musicals of the first period of the Black Experience School. The performers boycotted the show during its out-of-town runs. The actors allegedly wanted Bontemps to modify his "Back Street" characters. Certain stars used the strike, however, to demand that Bontemps enlarge their roles. Bontemps complied. He even modified some of the other outdated characterizations in order to suit midforties political realities. That some actors used this occasion for selfish reasons pointed to their contempt for both the images and the politics. Among the most disappointing people in the Bontemps affair were the African American leaders, specifically Walter White of the NAACP. He appears to have unashamedly mixed personal good and public policy when it came to his actor-children.

The troubling thing about the whole *St. Louis Woman* to-do was the loss of Bontemps to theatre. The years of lies and postures led Bontemps to swear off theatre. He wrote to Langston Hughes that serious people should invest no more "time, money, or affection" in theatre than they could afford to lose.[34] The performer Josephine Baker refused, however, in 1921 to let such things bother her. She simply ignored her fellow chorus-line dancers when, out of jealousy, they rejected her. The dancers in the *Shuffle Along* (1921) company were angry at Baker for "stealing the show right from under their noses." In retaliation, they dumped all of her makeup in the hallway.[35] Baker devised secret strategies to avoid open confrontations as she went right on stealing the show. She was so good, in fact, that she established the convention of having chorus girls comment humorously on the main action. Baker used her few moments and her considerable talents so well that she soon became not only a headliner but also the archetype of the international exotic "black flapper."[36]

The most common reason for rejection of African American theatre people was their involvement in the politics of desegregation, of war, or of the Black Liberation Movement. Typical were the cases of Paul Robeson, Lena Horne, Eartha Kitt, Richard B. Harrison, Marvin X, and Amiri Baraka. Robeson's "Trouble" seemed almost predestined. He recognized early in his acting career that the "content and form of a play" mattered considerably more than having "a *starring* role."[37] He believed that the "[African American] artist could not view this matter simply in terms of his individual interests."[38] He thought, in other words, that the artist "had a responsibility to his people."[39] Robeson decided, therefore, that if he were not offered a "worthy" role, he would play none.[40] He applied these principles as well to his songs, films, and politics, and it is no wonder that he was censured. Neither should it be a surprise that the government canceled his passport and questioned his patriotism. No person living by such high ethical standards in the United States could expect to be anything but a John the Baptist, especially at a time when racism matched oxygen. Equally un-

shocking were the efforts to demean, destroy, and quarantine
Robeson by forcing his "friends" to disassociate themselves from
him. Those who refused, like Lena Horne, too were denounced.
The entertainment industry blacklisted Horne during the fifties
because of her refusal to speak against Robeson, who was a family
friend. Horne, like Eartha Kitt – whom producers blackballed
during the sixties because of her opposition to the Vietnam War –
lost jobs because of her concerns about racial and international
problems. Horne and Kitt fought back, however. After an extended
period in seclusion, Horne returned to the stage as Savannah in
Jamaica (1957). Kitt's resurgence began with the Broadway production of *Timbuktu!* (1978). Upon entering the stage, she stared
directly into the audience and announced haughtily, "I am here!"[41]
Both women stood by their principles. The same morality and
intellect that did not allow Horne to desert or disparage her friend
Robeson prompted her, in 1991, to implore young artists to em-
power their art enterprises by creating and controlling the distribution networks.[42] As had Robeson, both women understood
that the theatre, along with the other arts, was a political and economic tool.

Apparently not understanding this about theatre resulted in the
actor Richard B. Harrison's being forsaken by some important African Americans in 1933. Harrison refused to turn theatre into a
cultural weapon to gain equal access. A committee of Washington,
D.C., ministers and NAACP representatives petitioned Harrison
during his Baltimore appearance in *The Green Pastures* (1930) to
refuse to play the National Theatre in Washington. They wanted
Harrison to help them change the theatre's policy of barring African Americans. A dumbfounded Harrison let the group know
that he felt obliged to honor his contract. This so angered these
people that they resolved to teach "de Lawd" a civics lesson. If
Harrison could not possibly break his contract, then they would
break it for him by kidnaping him. As they plotted, some members
of the group, who had initially gone along for the humorous ride,
finally understood that these intellectuals were quite serious.

Someone snitched to the police, who announced the plot over the radio. The daily newspapers so fueled the story that when Harrison arrived at the theatre, detectives surrounded him. Police jammed the theatre lobby. Guards even covered the stage entrance.[43] Harrison performed. Nevertheless, to soothe the furious African Americans, the theatre arranged a special performance for them. Their boycott of that performance highlighted the year for a lot of people. Although this might appear to have been a limited victory, the incident was significant: Many well-meaning white people realized for the first time the absurdity of barring African Americans from seeing any play, especially one about their own folk. The episode was important, therefore, for something other than its humor. Just imagine gentlemen from Washington's high society tying up Richard B. Harrison in some posh parlor.

This would have provided the kind of comic relief not seen in the bruising affairs surrounding the isolation of Marvin X and Amiri Baraka. Thirty-four years after Harrison was denounced for not desegregating theatre, the Black Panther Party rejected Marvin X for segregating theatre. Marvin X opposed the Panther policy of permitting white leftists and workers to join the Black Liberation Movement. Panther minister Eldridge Cleaver persuaded the party that whites were reliable allies, because the struggle was really against capitalism, which was the cause of racism. Marvin X, one of several Cultural Nationalists (including Sonia Sanchez, Amiri Baraka, Ed Bullins, and other Bay Area artists), told Cleaver that "Black Art and white people did not go together." Cleaver nevertheless enforced his position with a "goon squad" that had "brother fighting brother."[44] Marvin X's banishment in 1967 marked the first issue-oriented split in the Black Liberation Movement. The conflicts between the Marxists, who supported the left-wing whites, and the Cultural Nationalists, who opposed *all* left-wingers, were so ingrained and protracted that some leaders switched sides. Amiri Baraka, for example, joined the Marxists seven years after having supported Nationalist Marvin X against Marxist Cleaver. Baraka later indicated that he felt that Cultural

Nationalism was too narrow, limited, and reactionary to solve the combined problems of race and economics.[45] Baraka's public embrace of Marxism in 1974 not only caused his isolation in African American theatre, but it also fired debates in such national organizations as the African Liberation Support Committee and the Congress of Afrikan People.[46] Baraka was shunned in theatre. Most African American theatre people accepted the poet Haki Madhubuti's argument that African American interests and the interests of white workers were antithetical: "*White racism* preceded and advanced itself thousands of years before European capitalism and imperialism were even systematically conceived."[47] Baraka's theatre colleagues, therefore, did not support his 1979 revival of Hughes's *Scottsboro, Limited.* They also did not attend productions of Baraka's Marxist play *What Was the Relationship of the Lone Ranger to the Means of Production* (1979), which, admittedly, was mediocre. Baraka, however, rebounded, and he wrote *Song* (1989), one of the best plays in American theatre.

Although rejection has been the most prevalent problem faced by African American theatre people, the most debilitating is the fourth Trouble, the family pressure to stay out of the theatrical profession. Religion, along with community standards, usually has prompted such coercion. More prevalent from the late-nineteenth to the mid-twentieth centuries, these constraints were experienced in common by such performers as James Earl Jones, Billy Ewing, Rosalind Cash, Ira Aldridge, C. Luckeyth Roberts, Zakes Mokae, the Berry Brothers, and the Whitman Sisters. The root of the tension was the adolescent's typical need for parental approval and the parent's desire for spiritual and societal conformity. Nothing thwarted more a young actor's ambitions than did a parent's devoutness. Ministers' wishes also would often become divine commands. The magician Billy Ewing's minister father, for example, hated the sight of young Billy doing tricks with "devil" cards. When Reverend Ewing announced, therefore, that theatre would be Billy's "ruination," the father was voicing both his own and God's judgments. Billy had no choice but to put down the cards –

for a while. He later used these tricks, however, to develop his partnerships with the famous magician Thurston and with the vaudevillian Joe Byrd.[48] The tensions induced by religion in Billy Ewing's case were identical to those caused by community expectations. Neither the family of Rosalind Cash nor that of Zakes Mokae supported its child's interest in acting. Cash's mother, in fact, seemed stunned when Rosalind told her about winning a scholarship to study at the American Theater Wing. No "decent" girl from a "respectable family would be caught dead in theatre."[49] Mrs. Cash, of course, was voicing the attitude of her Atlantic City, New Jersey community, which considered theatre a good recreation but an evil business. The community doubted that theatre could ever make little-choir-member Rosalind into the star of such cinema and stage hits as *Uptown Saturday Night* (1974) and *Ceremonies in Dark Old Men* (1969). The same was true in Zakes Mokae's community. The very concept of theatre confused Mokae's father, because it translated as "playing" in his South African language of Sotho. What father could be proud that his grown son "played" for a living? Before Mr. Mokae died, however, he saw his own name in an article about his son, which caused the father to tell his son: "Anyway, it's a good thing, this thing you are doing." Mokae found out later that his father had shown the article continually to his friends, making himself "very famous."[50]

Despite such comforting outcomes, all of the actors cited earlier braved soul-wrenching obstacles in order to get into theatre. Usually, they handled such barriers either by outright defiance or by apparent compliance. Being disobedient had no embarrassing consequences provided the individual, like the actor-producer Billy King, ran away from home. King disregarded that he was needed on his family's large Alabama farm in 1885. He later made up to his family for this absence by rising from drifter to prominent producer and from being a bit actor to "one of the Big Four comedians."[51] It was he, in fact, who discovered and capitalized on Josephine Baker's clowning ability. King introduced the major innovation in musical comedy of using chorus dancers as comedic foils and commentators. This, alone, compensated for his having hopped the first vehicle leaving Alabama. Those would-be actors who stayed at home, however, suffered more than did King. Their parents often snatched them off the stage. Ira Aldridge and C. Luckeyth Roberts were unlucky in this way. The Roberts episode in 1898, in fact, was so dramatic that it stopped the show. Young Roberts, "dressed only in a raffia shirt," was rocking the theatre with his singing and dancing when Mr. Roberts entered. He saw his son on stage for the first time, grabbed the poor fellow by the shirt, and pulled him off the stage. The packed house roared because the audience thought that Mr. Roberts was part of the act. They called them back. The enraged father dragged the young boy home. Luckeyth poured on the charm, however, and he eventually changed his father's mind. He would become one of Palm Beach, Florida's leading society songwriters and performers.[52] The Ira Aldridge affair was, unfortunately, not so funny as Roberts's and probably caused Aldridge life-long remorse. Soon after his pious father removed Ira and his brother from Brown's African Grove Theatre in 1823, Ira sailed for Liverpool, never to return to the United States. There is no evidence that he and his father ever patched up their differences. Ira probably eased the pain of this rift somewhat by sending substantial sums of money to American abolitionist movements.[53] How unfortunate, however, that he never shared with either his father or his country the talent and international fame that made him "one of the finest Shakespearean interpreters of all time."[54]

Unlike Aldridge, the Berry brothers asserted their independence without rupturing their ties with their religious father. Ananias and James Berry overcame their father's objections when Mr. Berry discovered the earning potential of his talented sons. When in 1922 Ananias so captivated a Denver audience that the manager offered him a week's contract at the then unheard of salary of seventy-five dollars, Mr. Berry demanded that James, too, be hired.[55] Such relenting by parents was not too rare, provided that the children did little overt rebelling. James Earl Jones and the

Whitman sisters were typical of those young artists who delayed gratifying their ambitions out of respect for their parents' wishes. Jones succeeded because of the secret support of his grandmother, Mrs. Maggie Connolly. His grandfather John had admonished Jones during the forties not even to mention becoming an actor in his presence. So it was Mrs. Connolly, then, who was responsible for nurturing the hopes of the "big and awkward" Michigan farm boy and for turning him into one of America's most distinguished actors. Without her, there might not have been such critically acclaimed Jones performances as Deodatus Village in *The Blacks* (1959) in 1961, the title role in *Othello* in 1964, Jack Jefferson in *The Great White Hope* (1968), and Troy Maxson in *Fences* (1987). Like Mrs. Connolly, the Reverend Albany A. Whitman shaped the values and hopes of his children. The father of the Whitman Sisters (Mabel, Essie, and Alberta), Reverend Whitman insisted that his talented daughters place their education above the beckoning of show business. He denied George Walker's request, around 1894, that these Lawrence, Kansas, sisters be permitted to accompany Walker to New York. Reverend Whitman, however, did permit a professional manager a few years later to arrange the sisters' professional debut in Kansas City. This did not interfere either with their schooling or with their singing on Reverend Whitman's evangelical tours. Their father's beliefs about education stayed with the young women. Even as they became one of the most popular and respected companies in the country during the twenties and thirties, the sisters studied at Morris Brown College in Atlanta and at the New England Conservatory of Music. Thanks to their father, the Whitman Sisters not only entertained audiences, but they also educated theatre owners as their manager, Mabel Whitman, demanded and got for them salaries equal to those of the white performers.

Some people think that overcoming family pressure to stay out of theatre is nothing compared to overcoming the fifth Trouble – an impoverished environment. Proof of this might be seen in the actors Charles S. Dutton, Stephen McKinley Henderson, Margaret Avery, and Ron Dortch. All were members of poor families living in the very toughest sections of their towns. They each discovered theatre, which was their ticket to higher income and esteem, and they eventually made highly praised contributions to American theatre. Dutton, for example, grew up in the roughest projects in Baltimore. His rites of passage, like those of the French playwright Jean Genet, included street fighting, petty crime, reform school, murder, and the penitentiary. He found theatre while he was in prison, where he studied acting. While entertaining his fellow inmates by directing himself in Douglas Turner Ward's *Day of Absence* (1965), he experienced his moment of epiphany:

I remember that in the middle of a speech, I paused for a second and looked out in the audience at the sea of men, and I said to myself, "I've got these guys." It was a real sense of power that hit me. These guys were transfixed, suspended, staring at me on a stage. It was something about the recognition of me that night that made me think that I had what it took to be an actor. I didn't know the craft. . . . But in looking at their eyes I said, "Something's going on here. I think I might have found what I was born to do."[56]

His discovery led to studies at Maryland's Towson State University and at Yale University. He received two well-deserved Tony nominations, one for his performance as Levee in *Ma Rainey's Black Bottom* (1984) and the other for Boy Willie in *The Piano Lesson* (1987).

Stephen McKinley Henderson, Margaret Avery, and Ron Dortch found theatre while they were still in high school. Initially, instead of liberating them from poverty, theatre called their attention to poverty and racism. As one of the most talented young actors in Kansas City, Kansas, Henderson was the toast of high- and middle-income audiences. His own low-income roots, however, caused him to hate accepting rides home from his many admiring friends, and he often pretended that one of the better houses on his street was his home. He even disliked accepting dinner invitations because he did not know which piece of silverware to use. He won scholarships to the North Carolina School of the Arts and to the Juilliard School in New York. Chief among his acting credits was his highly praised performance – with John Cothran – in Athol Fugard's *The Island* (1973) at the 1981 Dublin Theatre Festival. He directed the well-received *Ali* (1992) by Geoffrey C. Ewing, the story of boxing champion Muhammad Ali's struggles outside of the ring. Henderson welcomed every opportunity to give free performances before low-income audiences, as well as to hold workshops for the many aspiring actors from low-income areas.[57] Margaret Avery underwent a change comparable to Henderson's. She grew up poor, the daughter of an alcoholic mother, and Avery has recalled coming home to find her mother passed out on the floor. Avery attended a school with wealthy children, and it was there that theatre taught her her first lessons about racism: As a member of the high school drama club, she played only maids. Avery said that this experience "was one of the worst things that could have happened. It breaks your spirit."[58] She later studied acting in college, which contributed to her winning roles in several musicals and films, the most notable being the motion picture *The Color Purple*. Avery received an Academy Award nomination for Best Supporting Actress for her work in that picture. Theatre also called attention to Ron Dortch's coming from "the poorest Goldsboro, N.C. people, who wore clothes given to them," but theatre also saved Dortch. His four-year scholarship to the North Carolina School of the Arts prepared him for his performances in London and throughout the United States. Among Dortch's most memorable roles was that of Rodney NYC Richards in Maya Angelou's *On a Southern Journey* (1983) at the Spirit Square Theatre in Charlotte, North Carolina.[59] Of his growing list of credits his 1990 "powerful portrayal of Othello" was the highlight of the Santa Cruz Shakespeare Festival.[60]

The significance of these stories is that high school and college theatre programs, and even those in correctional institutions, save people's lives. These low-cost programs offer the double-barreled benefits of helping young people – and prisoners – learn to accept who they are, to give themselves credit, and to develop their own values. Equally important is that students and inmates from poor neighborhoods are better-prepared acting students. They have better "*opening* connections into the character's experience" than many experienced actors. The reasons vary: The street smarts (or "emotional arsenal") of beginning inner-city actors serve them well on stage, and the stage, in turn, provides them with the sense of power and of self-esteem often missing in their other officially approved activities. Furthermore, these youths are better on stage because of the environment itself, which offers them contact with a varied, frequent, and concentrated mix of people, sights, sounds, smells, tastes, touches, movements, and physical states.[61] Inner-city people, therefore, have a better-than-average "file" of mastered emotions and vivid images. These beginners can select and use just the right imagery and feeling to make recalled emotions appear to be happening for the first time. Characters' experiences, therefore, come alive for audiences.[62] The important question is how low-income students and others can be taught to use their talents to develop characters, as well as to develop within themselves a sense of power and self-esteem. The first step is to persuade school and prison authorities that theatre programs are among the most productive and inexpensive tools available to help troubled youths and inmates become "self-confident, assertive, optimistic, and relatively free of anxiety." These traits are critical for raising student-retention rates and lowering inmate-recidivism percentages. This is because, as the Stanford University psychologists Ernest R. Hilgard, Richard C. Atkinson, and Rita L. Atkinson point out, a person becomes disruptive and defiant when his or her

self-esteem is lowered or threatened – when he is rejected by others because of color or status, when he cannot find a job, when he is conscripted into a war of which he disapproves. His self-esteem is enhanced when he has a sense of alternatives, a confidence that he can cope on his own terms with the problems that he faces.[63]

Theatre programs in prisons, as Dutton's experience proves, can help people take control over their lives. With only minuscule budgets, theatre programs can still entertain, enlighten, and provide release for people who are physically and economically imprisoned. This is done with plays, skits, revues, readings, and showcases about these individuals, their families, social relationships, job possibilities, and coping mechanisms. The implications of having thousands of men and women experience Dutton and Avery types of recognition and Henderson and Dortch types of salvation are significant. These actors' discoveries of theatre are themselves representative justifications for opening many more government-sponsored theatre programs in prisons, schools, and low-income community centers.

The sixth and final Trouble facing theatre people occurs during extended career slumps. This is when artists *really* must be able to "protect their self-esteem and to defend themselves against excessive anxiety."[64] The setbacks are caused by artistic and natural disasters, as well as by the performers' physical and mental disabilities or involvement in politics. Another cause is producers' predilection for hiring light-skin actors. Of all the causes for professional lapses, the most tragic have been artistic and natural disasters and physical and mental disabilities. The situations were akin to Greek tragedy, involving good, hardworking, and committed individuals who rose to lofty heights and fell from grace, although in some cases, they ascended to even greater eminence. The victims were usually from the African American theatre nobility. They endured some of the most pitiable human conditions, however, because of their flaw of trusting too much in another person's calculations. Their downfalls were of proportions large enough to challenge even the demigods who had infinite capacities for suffering. Whereas some sufferers, like Bob Cole and James Hewlett, never recovered, which made their stories true tragedies, other artists recouped.[65] If this pattern had not been a part of the lives of the songwriting team of Flournoy E. Miller and Aubrey Lyles, of the director Barbara Ann Teer, the composer J. Rosamond Johnson, the actors Bert Williams and L. Scott Caldwell, and the producer J. Leubrie Hill, other inspiring stories would be needed for the many theatre people mired in acute self-doubt.

The lives of the Miller-Lyles duo and the others do, however, offer inspiration. By briefly examining the initial stature, downfall, and climb back up of members of this group, one might develop useful paradigms for enduring misery. The initial heights included such achievements as making musical comedy a Broadway commodity, developing a major American arts institution, creating the formulas for popular songwriting and for producing, and setting the standard for acting. The team of Miller and Lyles, for example, not only restored musical comedy as a viable Broadway commodity with their long-running Broadway hit *Shuffle Along* (1921), but they also made theatrical history by introducing the Charleston dance to Broadway with their *Runnin' Wild* (1924). Continuing in this tradition of quality, Barbara Ann Teer molded a beg-and-borrow theatre organization with the somewhat apocryphal name of the National Black Theatre (1968–) into one of the sixty-three most important arts institutions in the United States. She did this within five years. J. Rosamond Johnson and Bob Cole established the constituents of popular songwriting with the several hit tunes that they wrote for their *A Shoofly Regiment* (1906) and *The Red Moon* (1909). Bert Williams and George Walker did likewise for musical-comedy writing between 1900 and 1910, whereas J. Leubrie Hill wrote the book on successful producing, with such shows as his *Darktown Follies* (1909).[66] L. Scott Caldwell showed young actors the kind of determination they would need when she moved from being a high school teacher to working as a professional actor. Then she demonstrated what the craft was all about in her leading roles in Samm-Art Williams's *Home* on Broadway in 1979 and in Wole Soyinka's *Play of Giants* at the Yale Repertory in 1984. These ground-breaking achievements typified those made by hundreds of other African-American theatre people, but the accomplishments of this group stand out because these individuals became "playthings of fate," whose careers were cut down at their peaks. Caldwell, for example, was hurled twenty feet by the impact of a taxi cab. The accident came while she was basking in the praise for her fine performance in *Play of Giants*. Hill was taking kudos for his

Darktown Follies of 1914 when a "mysterious illness" struck him. On the other hand, both Bert Williams and J. Rosamond Johnson enjoyed hits when their partners became ill. These calamities were not only devastating to those they struck but were also long term: Caldwell underwent painful physical therapy for two years, and Hill suffered for three years. Everything that Miller and Lyles wrote after *Runnin' Wild* flopped. Williams's depression following Walker's death in 1911 probably prevented him from performing again with another partner; he soloed instead between 1910 and 1922. Johnson tried to get over Bob Cole's mental breakdown in 1910 and Cole's death in 1911 by teaming first with Charlie Hart and later with Tom Brown, but neither pairing was successful. Those failures followed similar ones as a single act and as an opera director in London. Johnson's five years of suffering, however, did not top Teer's seven years of "running from pillar to post" to keep her theatre going.

The lesson of these sorrow years was that one should not expect "quick fixes," but should follow Bert Williams's advice to acquire the philosophy and independence necessary to protect oneself against humiliation and grief. Such independence would come not from being defensive, but from having a positive outlook, Williams asserted.[67] Thus Miller and Lyle refused to rationalize their inability to produce a hit by saying that public taste had deteriorated. Instead, they concentrated on writing continually, until they finally succeeded with *Sugar Hill* (1931). Rather than let the fire that destroyed her theatre also ruin her, Barbara Ann Teer separated her feelings of remorse from her belief that her company needed an even better building. Her vigorous campaign to raise funds netted $6 million in loans from the New York State Urban Development Corporation and the Columbia Broadcasting System Foundation. She constructed the new National Black Institute of Communication Through Theatre Arts, a modern steel-and-glass structure occupying a full city block.[68] J. Rosamond Johnson eventually found a substitute for his creative urges. He channeled his energy into developing young musicians by directing in 1914 the Music

School for Colored People in New York City. He turned the place into a highly respected school by quadrupling the enrollment, professionalizing the curriculum, and supplying employment. He later performed in *Porgy and Bess* (1935), *Mamba's Daughters* (1938), and *Cabin in the Sky* (1940). J. Leubrie Hill, throughout his illness, utilized feelings and ideas from his past in order to relieve his suffering and plan the future. It was the nourishment he got from reliving his success with *Darktown Follies*, in other words, that enabled him to revise the play in 1913 for a highly successful two-year run. Finally, not even the task of rehabilitating crushed vertebrae kept the bedridden L. Scott Caldwell from putting herself into other people's places and feelings. She worked, and it paid off. On her very first audition following her recovery, she won the role of Bertha in August Wilson's *Joe Turner's Come and Gone* (1986), for which she received a Tony Award.

The hurdles resulting from political involvement and bias against light skin required people to react in some unusual ways. Douglas Turner Ward, for example, studied alone when his career was put on hold because of his political activities. Ward headed the left-wing Labor Youth League in New York City as he began his career by writing *The Star of Liberty* (1950), a well-received cantata based on the life of Nat Turner. A court convicted him of draft evasion in 1951. The official charge was that he had refused to register for the Korean War draft. The real concern was that he was leading the league's effective campaigns against racism and war. While his case was on appeal, Ward returned home to New Orleans, where he kept writing. The U.S. Supreme Court overturned his conviction in 1953, permitting him to resume his career. The Ward case presents an opportunity to understand not only how individuals dealt with enforced isolation but also the reasons for most African Americans' historical involvement with left-wing causes. The Left attracted the youthful Ward, among other writers and artists, because he viewed it as the only "constructive alternative to entrenched American racism." This precocious young man found this racism so painful because he knew, very early in his life, the differences between the *real* and the *imagined* African American histories. He learned about these discrepancies in courses designed by the eminent historian Charles H. Wesley in 1946–7, when Ward was just a sixteen-year-old freshman at Wilberforce University in Wilberforce, Ohio. It was predictable, then, that while he was at the University of Michigan in 1947–8, Ward would join any group that dedicated itself to "eradicating racism." The only campus organization with such a mission happened to be composed of left-wing radicals. That these students, like other Communists, simply used the race issue as a tool to replace the capitalist system was unimportant to Ward, as long as racism was not a part of the New Order that they proposed. Ward's fight against the Korean War, like African Americans' later struggles against the Vietnam War, was, therefore, a manifestation of his genuine concern about racism. Although his willingness to forgo his career tested his commitment to oust discrimination against "those people outside of the margins of society," the stand also fortified his abilities.[69] He helped so many: In addition to sparking Charles Dutton's career, Ward founded in 1967 – with Robert Hooks and Gerald S. Krone – the Negro Ensemble Company. This organization developed the talents of thousands of theatre people – a list of their names reads like a "Who's Who" in world theatre, television, and film.

Ward's devotion in the forties to destroying racism made even more tragic the career-breaking racism, as well as the predilection for light skin, of the eighties and nineties. Valuable insights come from a comparison of the Nigerian actor Cyril Nir's problem in London and the dancer and singer Ida Forsyne's dilemma in the United States. Nir's problem derived from traditional racism. He endured his "Heigh-Ho" spear-carrying roles to become a leading actor with the Royal National Theatre of Great Britain. His road to there had started with his being a refugee of the Nigerian-Biafran War in 1968 and continued with his becoming an acting student in the Bristol (England) Old Vic School. During half of his program at the Old Vic, he received "disciplined training in the classics" by playing an assortment of leading roles. With the arrival of a new principal, who did not believe in nontraditional casting, Nir was given only minor roles. Unlike Aldridge and James Hewlett, he elected not to expose the racism publicly. He simply left the school.[70] Ida Forsyne, too, chose not to resist loudly when she was forced out of Harlem during the 1920s because of a preference for light-skinned dancers. Forsyne, a midnight-blue Chicago beauty, was a leading international star during the years between 1903 and 1921. She received rave reviews for her appearances with such organizations as the Black Patti Troubadours and Abbie Mitchell and her Coloured Students. Her credits included show-stopping performances in Will Marion Cook's *The Southerners* (1904), Gus Hill's *The Smart Set* (1904), and Will Mastin's *Holiday in Dixie* (1916), which featured her and Sammy Davis, Sr. Forsyne had "triumphant" engagements throughout Europe between 1905 and 1914, where she so mastered Soviet dances that she was known as "the Russian dancer" after she returned to the United States. When the Harlem Renaissance ushered in the craze for mulatto dancers, however, nobody hired her in Harlem. After working as a maid for the singer Sophie Tucker (1920–1), Forsyne, the international star, went on the chitlin circuit.

Nir's and Forsyne's abilities to suppress and set aside their pain and to concentrate on other tasks were responsible for their comebacks. By 1932 Forsyne was appearing as Mrs. Noah in Marc Connelly's *The Green Pastures* (1930) and in a revival of Eugene O'Neill's *The Emperor Jones* (1920). And Nir, before joining the Royal National Company, founded his own company. He also wrote the play *Small Beginnings* and entered it in the National Student Drama Festival, winning seven of the festival's thirteen awards, including Best New Writer and Best Director. The issue, however, was neither Nir's and Forsyne's troubles nor their comebacks. It was larger: Although African Americans loudly condemned the racism encountered by Cyril Nir, they only sighed about Forsyne's victimization. Were the Forsyne type of experience a "thing of the past," it could be dismissed as but another unfortunate chapter in the growing up of Americans. The Forsyne type of ordeal, however, still plagues African Americans, notwithstanding the careful explanations given by psychiatrists Frantz Fanon and Frances Cress Welsing for the causes and manifestations of both racism *and* color predilection. The years during which the talented actor Cicely Tyson had to struggle to get anywhere erase any doubts about the currency of the latter abnormality. Add to this that the "black and beautiful" actor Charlene Brown (*Sarafina!* [1989] and the television series "A Different World") felt obliged *in 1990* to thank Bill Cosby for employing dark-skinned performers.[71] Just as white Americans must work daily to rid themselves of racism, African Americans, too, must strive to eliminate their insidious prejudices against dark skin.

The importance of the preceding assortment of stories is that they educate. The lessons are so old that they border on being clichés: (1) African American theatre people must know and love who and what they are; (2) African American theatre people must have specific plans and purposes; and (3) African American theatre people must be patient, persistent, and tough. What makes these Three Sayings less hackneyed, however, is their governance of the mind and behavior of people, especially theatre people. Knowing and loving self, for example, is critical to people in the theatre, because many of them often are not only strangers to themselves but also runaways from themselves. Theatre substitutes for self, in other words, because some people avoid the steps that lead to real self-knowledge: learning from the example and from advice of one's nuclear family, reading widely, and understanding the differences between who and what one is. His obeying the first of these success determinants made Ed Bullins among the most important American playwrights. Without self-awareness, he could not have ignored his professor's ego bashing. Firmly rooted in his own sense of self, Bullins judged that the professor's reality, as well how he expressed it, disregarded, indeed, scorned, Bullins's North Philadelphia way of life. Bullins understood that the professor's command that he take the profanity out of his plays violated him and his whole life experience. Bullins refused, therefore, in 1965, to drop from his *Clara's Ole Man* a single one of the fourteen "mathafukkers" or twenty "shits." In terms of self-knowledge, this was among the most important artistic and personal decisions Bullins ever made. The second rung of the steps to self, the taking of advice from the nuclear family, is best reflected in the David Downing story. Imagine the predicament of tenth-grader Downing if he had not had his mother's and father's encouragement: The acting teacher's comment that Downing did not have what it took to become an actor could have robbed theatre audiences of intelligent interpretations of a wide range of characters. Thanks to the Downings's challenging of their David, he – as well as others – learned *not* to forget to forget judgments skewed to particular personal, political, and social preferences. Such advice from their African American families traditionally shaped the talents and principles of young theatre people. Alice Childress became a writer because she listened to her grandmother's early advice to write down all her thoughts. Because his father inculcated in him principles of hard study and selfless service, Paul Robeson made codas out of his father's teachings. Similar family-generated standards delineated nontransgressible borders for Rosalind Cash and Zakes Mokae. Cash's knowledge of "lines" and Mokae's full understanding of "play" confirmed for both that the extent to which the performer lived by early family beliefs often determined the degree to which the artist succeeded.

There are, of course, notable exceptions. Parents sometimes unintentionally confirm for young theatre people that they want no part of the parents' examples. Actor-producer Billy King, for example, discovered that he himself hated farm life from watching his hardworking farmer-father. King's running away from the plow mirrors the escapes of Ira Aldridge, Billy Ewing, and C. Luckyeth Roberts from the righteousness of their fathers. The important thing here is not judgment, but the family-generated discovery of who one is – whether by positive example, negative example, or words. Written words become the third – and probably the most reliable – way to find self. It is through reading, the Bert Williams story shows, that theatre people best understand self, gain perspective, and prepare characters. By reading, Williams stretched his range from a middle-class Caribbean who spoke impeccable English to the slow-witted southern Negro character who made do with English. Williams so mastered the character and the acting craft that W. C. Fields led the fight to make him the first African American member of Actors' Equity.[72] Reading led Williams not only to characters but also to himself. He mined histories of Africa and of African America. He devoured his well-worn copy of John Ogilby's *Africa* (1670), the "voluminous work" that traced the histories of African peoples. He even lent it to schools and friends, insisting that they, too, must learn about their history, as well as their politics, science, literature, and philosophy. Williams, in fact, so loved philosophy that, according to his wife, he often studied it until daybreak: "When I would call him in the morning, he would frequently say, 'Let me sleep, mother. . . . I was *wrestling* with the philosophers all night.' "[73] It was Thomas Paine, Confucius, Darwin, Voltaire, Kant, and Goethe who protected Williams from the grief and humiliation of racism. The philosophers taught him that racism existed because racists were not sure of themselves or of their places. It was philosophy, then, that helped Williams separate who he was (an intellectual) from what he did (minstrelsy). He realized this final way to self with burnt cork and with cotton gloves. He attached so much importance to his makeup and apparel that by 1915 neither his wife nor any producer could persuade him to remove either. The blackened face and gloved hand symbolized for Williams the differences between what James Hewlett, in 1824, had called "visage" and "mind." The lesson to beginning theatre people, then, is to develop their capacity to separate the perceived from the real self when dealing with such issues as racism (in Williams's case), poverty (Dortch's), or color prejudice (Forsyne's). Like Forsyne, the international star who transcended Harlem's predilection for light-skinned dancers during the twenties, the young and the tired should be *on*, but not necessarily *of*, the "chitlin circuit."

The Second Saying – that theatre people develop plans and purposes that are larger than themselves – is no less trite than the first, yet the most fascinating thing about the saying is its truth. History proves that the people who have made seminal contributions toward the development of African American theatre have done so because they consistently broadened the uses of their talents beyond self. Charles S. Dutton is such a powerful presence in American theatre because he yearns to improve life in the Projects, as well as to reduce prison recidivism. His acting, therefore, subtends his trips back to the street corner and to the penitentiary. Common were such activities as his delivering the 1991 commencement address to the twenty-nine college graduates who were inmates at the maximum security Maryland State Penitentiary. He told them that he had learned that the value of an education was the opportunity education offered to discover one's own humanity.[74] Stephen McKinley Henderson, by passing up paying acting jobs in order to coach or to perform for free, seconded his passions, which were to introduce low-income students to theatre and to equip them to escape poverty.

Often this drive to make a difference made the theatre person "a first," although the honor was by no means a part of the individual's plan or purpose. Alice Childress's motivation to clear the American stage of African American stereotypes forced her to clear new paths in American drama with *Florence* (1950), the first play to portray realistically the African American mother. Bob Cole, George Walker, and Charles Hicks similarly had to be firsts because what they wanted had not been wanted hard enough before them. The point is that the performers succeeded because their primary objective was to serve others, be it when they equalized manager–artist relationships, upgraded African American companies' circuits, stimulated artist-controlled organizations, or raised artists self-esteem. Thus Hicks's determination to raise wages for African Americans made him the feared and respected premium manager that he was. Furthermore, because artistic director Barbara Ann Teer wanted to raise the consciousness of all peoples, she was not content merely to rebuild the burned theatre space of her National Black Theatre, but she worked to expand the theatre, turning it into the National Black Institute of Communication through Theatre Arts.

Teer's task took the patience, persistence, and toughness recommended in the Third Saying. This saying, however, is the most complex of the three, notwithstanding its frequent use. How exactly is one "patient"? What did Reverend Albany A. Whitman really mean when he told his young daughters, Mabel, Essie, and Alberta, that they had to be patient about starting their professional theatre careers? He meant that they had to bear the pain of not going immediately to New York City with George Walker to begin their vocation. What Reverend Whitman did not tell them was how best to endure the anguish of accepting their father's refusal to let them go. It is significant for young theatre people to realize that neither Reverend Whitman nor anyone else can teach patience because these individuals cannot themselves experience another's pain. Patience, then, comes from the personal experience of having endured pain. All Reverend Whitman could have done was prepare his daughters for the hurt by telling them simply to expect it from his decision. Then he could have reminded them of the pleasure of having outlasted the last bout of aching. The sisters, subsequently, would have discovered the increasing correlations between pain and dividend. They would later have found that obeying their parents not only gave them the higher education that their father wanted them to have, but it also better prepared them for negotiating with racist theatre owners to get contracts equal to those of the white performers.

The experience of magician Billy Ewing, however, showed that young theatre people should not always be patient (or bear fully the pain). Had he totally obeyed his father's admonition to get rid of those "devil" playing cards, Ewing would not have been able to become partners with the world-celebrated magician Thurston and with the vaudevillian Joe Byrd. Patience, then, might not be so virtuous as impatience implies. Nevertheless, patience pays well, especially when selectively coupled with persistence. Advising young people in the theatre to be persistent is another way of telling the artists to believe in themselves. What, however, does that mean? Caldwell serves well as an answer. Her belief in herself as an actor translated into her affirming her ability to work for Ward's Negro Ensemble Company – notwithstanding assistant director Scott's initial judgment. Caldwell's inflexibility on the issue attested to her confidence that her preparation in college, on stage, and in workshops made her better qualified than all of the other candidates for the last NEC slot. Had Ward disagreed – luckily for him and for her, he did not – either Caldwell would have continued to believe she was indeed the best person auditioning, or she would have returned to studying. The designer Felix Cochran's case indicates that the former course is at times preferable. Cochran's eight months of rejections in no way daunted his belief in his abilities, which was borne out by his later Broadway designs. Persistence, then, toughened Caldwell and Cochran.

Toughness, however, is the most complicated aspect of the Third Saying. "Tough" denotes high insusceptibility to sense impressions and is the very opposite of the sensitivity every good theatre person desires. One cannot imagine an insensitive Bert Williams, Arna Bontemps, or Ida Forsyne. It should be no surprise to learn that Williams supported for three years at full salary his ill partner George Walker, or that for hours Williams told funny, charming, and true stories about animals to neighborhood children.[75] Such tenderness among most performers is perhaps the reason that they have such tough agents. The question, then, is how one can expect young performers to be both tender and tough when even seasoned artists are not. One answer is to help young theatre people develop the self-separations needed for being and for doing. Like Williams, young artists can best demand respect for their divides by knowing and respecting them themselves. James Hewlett, for example, roughed up Charles Mathews because Hewlett knew that Mathews had confused Hewlett's clowning Richard III with the actor's hardworking self. Mathews had publicly ridiculed Hewlett and the African Company. In response,

Hewlett publicly charged Mathews with not having enough intelligence to know the differences or enough sensitivity to respect them. What was important about Hewlett's action was his fearlessness regarding retribution. Toughness, then, also means that one corrects a wrong regardless of personal cost. Ira Aldridge certainly had every reason to fear the powerful critics who planned to bar his *Othello* from Covent Garden, and William Wells Brown must have known that the abolition aficionado had the power to take him off the lecture circuit. But both these performers risked the worst, because it was better than violating themselves and their histories. Furthermore, Mabel Whitman showed that confronting racist violators was the best way to set them straight. Toughness to this manager of the Whitman Sisters was the willingness to suffer financial losses in order to gain respect. In 1926 Whitman taught this lesson to the racist owner of a "high-class" theatre. On the night of their contracted performance, the Sisters heard from the theatre owner that the full house was not enough to pay them their agreed-upon price, because the price matched that paid to his white acts. Mabel, who knew that the Sisters' act was better than most white acts, demanded full payment – up front. The owner told her to take his offer or he would announce to the full house that the Whitman Sisters refused to perform. Mabel told him to make the announcement. His bluff called, the owner offered a compromise, but an angry Whitman told him that the Sisters would not work for him – for any amount of money. The important lesson Mabel Whitman's example teaches young theatre people is that they should expect to pay high costs for principles. Nevertheless, the costs might be a bargain compared to Charles Hicks's being shut out of major U.S. markets and dying alone in Suraboya, Java. Measured against the historic importance of his equalizing performers' wages, however, Hicks's painfully high personal costs seem worthwhile. Hicks's splendid example, then, as well as the experiences of all of the other theatre people discussed in this chapter, is a monument to prices paid and prices to be paid.

4

The Governance
of Theatre
Organizations

> If ever the history of the Negro drama is written without the
> scene of a committee wrangle, with its rhetorical climaxes af-
> ter midnight – the conservatives with their wraps on protest-
> ing the hour; the radicals, more hoarse with emotion than
> effort, alternately wheedling and threatening – it will not be
> well-written.
>
> Alain Locke

T HE funniest thing about the fussing that goes on in theatre boardrooms is that it is not funny at all. The fueding
is such a given within some "governing" bodies that many
talented people simply refuse to serve on the boards of African
American theatre organizations. These people say that it is a waste
of time, because the Lord God Himself must have spent the whole
Second Week trying to organize an African American theatre. The
questions that arise are Is theatre governance really as bad as all of
that? How accurate – and fair – is the charge that African American theatres open and close like morning glories? and If the average theatre life span is shorter than a pet canary's, what can be
done about it? These questions are vital because healthy African

American theatre organizations are a priori essentials of schools of plays and pools of talents. Finding thoughtful answers requires, first of all, that people stop considering African American theatres as a historical monolith. Like most other things, these theatres developed in stages. There are three developmental phases, but most theatre organizations do not survive past the first or second period. The first stage begins when a highly motivated individual decides to devote the thought, time, energy, money, and emotion needed "to put on some plays." Because of this huge personal investment, the organization becomes "My Theatre." The productions, for the most part, are initially crude. One should not, however, discount these first-stage organizations. The Hyers Sisters' Negro Operatic and Dramatic Company of San Francisco (1870s–?), and J. A. Arneaux's Astor Place Coloured Tragedy Company (1884–?) and Bob Cole's Worth's Museum All-Star Stock Company (1896–8), both in New York, drove the piles for modern African American theatre.

These early twentieth-century organizations offered not only affordable entertainment for urban communities but also essential training for fledgling actors. Dick Campbell and Muriel Rahn's Rose McClendon Players (1938–42), for example, gave their starts to a group of actors that included the now-eminent Ossie Davis. Located in Harlem, Frederick O'Neal and Abram Hill's American Negro Theatre (1940–50) sent to Broadway and Hollywood the likes of singer-actor Harry Belafonte; actor-director Sidney Poitier; and actors Hilda Simms, Ruby Dee, Isabel Sanford, Earle Hyman, Clarice Taylor, Helen Martin, Maxwell Glanville, and Gertrude Jeannette. Both these organizations let theatre people learn and perfect their crafts – under, what Davis has called, "the best instruction."[1] In this way, beginning playwrights could see their plays performed, and actors, stage managers, set designers, and assorted technicians could grow proficient through unpressured and error-laced trials. The importance of these primary organizations, especially to the Harlem community, was in the really "high-grade" entertainment that they provided.[2] The community overwhelmingly supported these organizations: The American Negro Theatre, according to the theatre historian Ethel Pitts Walker, played to over fifty thousand patrons, who saw 324 performances over nine years.[3] In addition, Broadway producers flocked uptown to performances of this theatre in order to cast their plays. Thus the American Negro Theatre – first-stage or not – was critical to the very notion of African American theatre, whereas Ed Bullins's Black Theatre Workshop (1968–71) is an example of the importance of the later theatre organizations. Still, some ninety percent of these infant theatre companies failed to make it through their fourth season, which translated into only sixteen consecutive productions.

The reasons for this failure rate varied, from men going off to war to, in one case, a woman's taking off with the entire company. The Anita Bush All-Colored Dramatic Stock Company (1915–16) personalized these tragedies when a wealthy woman literally stole the company from the trusting Bush. According to historian Francesca Thompson, Marie Downs offered to assist the financially troubled Bush company, provided that Bush changed its name to the Marie Downs Company. Bush consented. Without Bush's authorization, Downs moved the company from the Lincoln Theatre to the rival Lafayette Theatre. Downs, furthermore, sold *her* company to entrepreneur Robert Levy, who added it to his Lafayette Players.[4] Bush, however, was too tired to take this dowager on alone, and she let go of the organization that she had founded. In much the same way, the talented but overworked Theodore Ward gave up the primary company of professional writers, the Negro Playwrights Company (1940–2). If either Bush or Ward had had even a rubberstamp board, they might not have suffered this fate, the same fate that struck such other newborn organizations as Ed Cambridge's Drama Group at the "Y" (1952–5), the Elks Community Theatre (c. 1948–?), the Harlem Showcase Theatre (c. 1946–c. 1950) and the Committee for the Negro in the Arts (1950–c. 1954).

These first-stage organizations functioned like social clubs. They were basically run by their founders, along with boards consisting of casts, relatives, and close friends who would generally confirm a founder's decisions. The boards had distinct advantages and drawbacks. Their principal benefit was that members were highly motivated, hard working, and trustworthy. These traits spelled short-term success. The social-club board of Langston Hughes's Harlem Suitcase Theatre (1938–9), for example, was responsible for his designing New York City's first avant-garde theatre space; for his producing the play *Don't You Want to Be Free?* (1938); and for his running the play for a then unheard of thirty-eight performances during the theatre's four-month first season. These accomplishments resulted from the board's keying its interest and know-how to its commitment to the founder. Such devotion carried with it the major weakness of this board, however: Not much got done during the founder's absence. Whenever Hughes took on other assignments, the board simply squabbled, as it attempted to function without its coach and referee. Even the person assigned that position by Hughes was second-guessed as board members asserted their special relationships with Hughes. The board, predictably, killed the organization. In fact, this was the pattern for each of the three theatres founded by Hughes: The Suitcase Theatre collapsed after Hughes moved to California; Hughes's New Negro Theatre in Los Angeles (1939) closed when he relocated to Chicago; and Hughes's Skyloft Theatre in Chicago (1942) died when he left for Europe.[5] One must conclude then, that if primary theatre organizations do not become secondary, they usually die when the founder departs.

Theatre organizations enter the second developmental phase when they add community leaders and professionals to their boards. It is important to note, however, that the power of decision-making still rests with the founder–artistic director. Sometimes the artistic director asks for a vote, the outcome of which the founder can accept or reject. The advantage of these boards, which function like societies or associations where there is presidential veto power, is that they can smell out and hunt down trouble. Such a board would have prevented a hostile takeover such as the one suffered by Bush. There are also, however, some pronounced disadvantages. Some influential board members successfully pressure founders and directors to accept policies that are not in the long-term interests of the group. Gough D. McDaniels's Baltimore Krigwa Group (1929–33), for example, first flourished because of the political clout of Edward Lewis, president of the Urban League, and the theatre expertise of the legendary S. Randolph Edmonds, who at the time directed dramatics at Morgan State University in Baltimore. Edmonds helped the Group garner national attention with its stunning performances of such representative works as John H. Pollard's pageant *Golden Racial Hours* (1929); McDaniels's *A Long, Long Trail* (1932), a one-act play based on his experiences in World War I; Georgia Douglass Johnson's *Blue Blood* (1927); Willis Richardson's *The Flight of the Natives* (1927); and May Miller's *Ridin' the Goat* (1929). These plays helped set the national agenda for African American community theatre by boosting W. E. B. DuBois's national little theatre movement, to which the Baltimore Krigwa Group belonged. The group demonstrated that audiences wanted to see serious plays about African American life and history. Little theatres throughout the country flooded DuBois with requests for more plays, making it imperative that he publish in his *Crisis* magazine more of the winners from his national competitions.

Ironically, Edmonds's expertise and the Baltimore Krigwa Group's success pointed out the weakness of the local society board: The same influential board members who had brought money and people to the organization later used their leverage to dictate theatre policy. Urban League president Lewis told Edmonds and McDaniels to broaden their play selections beyond the African American experience. Lewis wanted not only to integrate the Krigwa Group but also to satiate interracial tastes for Broadway hits. Although Edmonds objected, Lewis forced the issue because of his prominence. Constantia W. Jackson, assistant director of the Krigwa Group, reported on the showdown:

Mr. Lewis brought to one of our meetings a Mr. Bernard S. Davis, white, who was working with the Baltimore Emergency Relief Commission. Mr.

Davis had been a member of the [Johns Hopkins University] Homewood Playshop. Mr. Lewis and Mr. Davis felt that a Little Theatre Group should be a community project in which any persons with interest and dramatic ability could become members. There were some who disagreed with this idea and a very fiery meeting resulted.[6]

When Edmonds's opposition to the policy did not dissuade the majority on the board from adopting it, he, along with several other members, resigned. Bernard Davis became artistic director of the newly integrated organization, which, ironically, changed its name to the Negro Little Theatre (periodically, between 1933 and 1946). After directing George Kelly's Broadway hit *Craig's Wife* in 1934, Davis left the group in 1935 because of his job reassignment to another city. The Edmonds faction, in the meantime, founded the Monumental Theatre Group (1933–5). Because the African American community in Baltimore could not support two competing organizations, both died. If the Krigwa Group had had a board insulated from the pressure of the power-hawker Lewis, perhaps Baltimore would not have been without an African American theatre company between 1946 and 1953.[7]

Similar problems plagued organizations governed by association boards, which consisted principally of nationally known figures. Founders understandably chose these "names," who generally rubber-stamped decisions, for such task-specific goals as opening avenues, extending the "right" invitations, and influencing outside negotiations. How DuBois himself used this kind of board illustrated both its boons and shortcomings. DuBois used his boards to cut through red tape for his Horizon Company (periodically, between 1913 and 1924) and his Krigwa Players little theatre network (1926–46). A partial list of DuBois's board members for the performance of his *Star of Ethiopia* in Washington, D.C., shows how the design worked: Secretary of the Interior Lane and his wife helped DuBois got free use of the American League Ballpark for the pageant; the president of the board of education provided DuBois with access to school buildings for rehearsal spaces for the pageant's twelve hundred actors; the superintendent of schools encouraged teachers and students to be actors; and prominent local ministers not only developed audiences from among their congregations but also extended DuBois invitations to their conventions. DuBois used these same people in other negotiations, such as those he had with the New York City Public Library. By dropping his board members' names, DuBois persuaded hesitant library authorities to donate space for a theatre, which would become the home of several major Harlem theatre groups.[8] The flaw in DuBois's management through an association-type board emerged after he quit producing theatre in 1938 when his organization, like those of Hughes and McDaniels, folded.

This was typical as well of the influential second-stage organizations of the sixties: Robert Macbeth's New Lafayette Theatre (1966–72) went first; Delano Stewart's Bed-Stuy Theatre (1965–73) was representative of those that soon followed. The lodestar organization, the Negro Ensemble Company (1967–90), also lost its space. Woodie King, Jr's, New Federal Theatre (1970–88) became principally a production company in 1992, sponsoring touring circuits. Even Barbara Ann Teer's National Black Theatre (1968–), now in its newly built space, teetered. Nor could legatees sustain theatres, because funders generally supported the founder rather than the organization. The death of Hazel Bryant, for example, forced her successor, Shirley J. Radcliffe, to add Bryant's name before the name of the theatre in an effort to maintain fiscal support. The Hazel Bryant's Richard Allen Center for Culture and Art (1965–88), nevertheless, folded – in the sense that it no longer presents seasons of at least four plays. The same thing happened to the Roger Furman's New Heritage Repertory Theatre Company (1964–) after Furman's death. The conclusion here is that unless secondary theatre organizations become tertiary, they too, like the primary organizations, will die.

Second-stage organizations enter the third phase only by empowering their boards. This means that the founder–artistic director gives to the board *complete control* over determining the organization's mission, establishing fiscal policy, providing adequate resources, hiring the artistic directors, developing and maintaining community resources, and executing the by-laws. Statistics show that boards with these powers help organizations survive longer. Of the forty-six most influential theatre companies founded during the late sixties and early seventies – all of which were second stage – none still performed in 1992 a season of at least four plays. But of the five most influential and board-controlled organizations founded during the late seventies and the early eighties, only one has floundered. Doing quite well are the Jomandi Productions in Atlanta (1976–), the Penumbra Theatre Company in St. Paul (1978–), Crossroads Theatre Company in New Brunswick, New Jersey, (1978–), and the Lorraine Hansberry Theatre in San Francisco (1982–). Only the Oakland Ensemble Theatre (OET) (1976–) in 1990 produced less than a four-play season. Even OET has been recovering, the producing director Sharon Walton has said, thanks to its strong board and the "wonderful support from our funders, the public, and the theatre community."[9]

The evidence overwhelmingly supports the need for founders and puissant artistic directors to surrender their power to boards that are in no way obligated to the founders. This is about as easy as getting a devoted parent to give up custody of a beloved baby. The task, therefore, is to persuade founders that relinquishing control not only ensures their "child" a long and happy life, but it also guarantees the founder a place of honor in theatre history. The founder, additionally, will be delighted to find out just how smoothly an empowered board operates. This was the case for Samuel Wilson, Jr., who struggled for ten years with a social-club board to run his Baltimore Arena Players. His toil began in 1953, when he founded the Players from among the former members of the Krigwa Group/Negro Little Theatre and the Monumental Theatre. The Players inherited its predecessors' props, limited funds, and practices: "A few of us," according to Wilson, "did everything: made and sold the tickets, built the costumes, did the lighting, built and painted the sets, everything. When it came time to act, we were so tired that we could hardly see."[10] They developed, however, quite a loyal following – literally, that was, because they performed in church basements and school auditoriums "from one end of Baltimore to the next." While playing cards one night, the board of directors heard that a funeral supply company had recently vacated its warehouse. The board leased this space, with the option to buy. Wilson soon realized that if the Players were ever to rehabilitate the site, the group needed the help of some people with clout. He invited Camilla Sherrard, a retired school administrator, to found an empowered board in 1962. Sherrard did not want to be "bothered with all this because I didn't know a thing about theatre. But they kept after me and kept after me."[11] She finally took on the task, but only because Wilson had assured her that the board would have total control. Switching to a powerful board was one of Wilson's smartest moves: Not only was the Players in 1992 the oldest continuously operating African American community theatre, but it also played to houses filled to 80 percent of capacity in its $2 million refurbished complex.

A detailed look at the operations of the empowered board of the Players might remove for other founders any doubts about handing over full governance to their own boards. In other words, relief might come to owners when they find out how an empowered board actually chooses it members, regulates monetary matters, provides adequate resources, develops community resources, and limits its participation in the day-to-day operation of the theatre. Choosing board members is such an example because the Baltimore community so respected the Players that people vied for the opportunity to serve on the board. In selecting its new members, the board paid strict attention to its own composition, as well as to the competence, recruitment, processing, and orientation of prospective members. Composition was important because all sections of the city needed to have a say. The board also had to satisfy specific needs, however, such as those presently covered by the individuals on the 1992 board: a downtown theatre executive, a certified public accountant, a banker, a business executive, an entrepreneur, a corporate attorney, an arts attorney, a judge, a newspaper publisher, a public relations executive, a minister, and a deacon.[12] Guarding against elitism, the board added actors, educators, club and church women, and students. The all-important process of choosing new members began, of course, with the nominating committee, which solicited widely for names and conducted in-depth interviews. The committee, typically, sent letters requesting nominations to all influential community leaders, as well as to the mass media and trade publications. This process ensured widespread community input, as well as fresh ideas from all economic classes. The nominations, in other words, came not only from current board members and theatre personnel but also from civic groups, school associations, neighborhood groups, merchants associations, audiences, churches, and ministerial alliances. The amazing result was that the Arena Players solved the persistent problem of getting religious people and representatives of religious organizations to join a theatre board.

One important reason for getting church leaders to serve on boards, as DuBois showed, was that these leaders influenced large potential audiences. Perhaps if, for example, Deacon Hampton Glover had chaired the board of directors of the Footlighters Theatre in West Palm Beach, Florida (c. 1945–55), instead of only the board of the Mt. Carmel Missionary Baptist Church in West Jupiter, the theatre group's fate might have been different. The Footlighters, in 1992, would not be simply a pleasant memory, unlike the ninety-year-old church, which remains a valuable community organization. The Footlighters might be enjoying a long existence if it too had had on its board the shrewdest old heads in the area: Chairman Glover, Thomas Hay, Sr., Allie Hunter, and Thomas Hay, Jr. These self-educated farmers, dairy farmers, and gardeners might have made the Footlighters successful, because they would have known how to charm people into investing more time and money into the organization. Indeed, these Bible-quoting deacons would have known that the Footlighters would die without these investments. And so it did.

Getting deacons intimately involved in the governance of theatres has been difficult because of the antipodal natures of the theatre and the church, the historical problems existing between the two institutions, and the complicated steps needed to resolve the conflicts. The problems exist as part of Nature's checks and balances: Religion trims excesses, theatre explores them. Church people – and business people – correctly demand that theatre subscribe to codes of public morality. Theatre people rightly expect complete artistic freedom. These divergent views predate by almost two thousand years the clashes between the church and the theatre during the Era of Black Revolutionary Drama (1965–72). First-century Roman mimes were, in fact, the ones to cast the first stone in what turned out to be a fierce competition not over people's souls, but over their allegiances. The early Christians proselytized against the theatre's mimes and good times, which caused the era's theatre people to ridicule and antagonize further the Christians. In the first of several maneuvers designed to do away with the huge crowds that flocked to theatrical festivals, Christians shifted the celebration of Jesus' birth from May to December 25th, the date of the theatre's biggest festival. Theatre supporters retaliated by performing live sexual acts on stage, then Christianity's deadliest "sin." The Christians ultimately played their trump card: In the sixth-century they damned all theatre people to hell. The Trullan Synod not only banned all mime and theatre, but the synod also denied citizenship and church membership to all professional entertainers and their consort. Theatre people did not care. The effects, however, were long-range: The church rescinded the doctrine only recently, that is, in the eighteenth century.

It is not surprising, then, that early-nineteenth-century African American church leaders, following the Europeans, eschewed theatre. These ministers were not aware of the traditional African belief that religion and theatrical celebration were inextricably bound. One understands, therefore, why the early pastors of the Abyssinian Baptist Church in Harlem, for example, would have disagreed with the Reverend Calvin O. Butts III, the pastor in 1992. According to Reverend Butts, the church should not only tolerate theatre but also produce it: "Life is supposed to have celebrations, too. That's godly."[3] The evidence that Reverend Butt's notion was anathema to his predecessors was that the founders of Abyssinian in 1816 had not helped Mr. Brown resist in 1823 the closing of his African Grove Theatre. Brown, of course, had not helped himself. He had packed his theatre throughout the week, including *Sundays*, with ale-swigging and women-seeking men, not to mention handkerchief-waving women who shamelessly flirted with the handsome James Hewlett. Such behavior prevented even the liberal Father Peter Williams of the Protestant Episcopal Church from speaking out for Brown's theatre. The clergy evidently persuaded all parishioners to turn their backs on Brown. A search of the writings of the New York City businessman Philip A. Bell, publisher of the *Colored American*, finds not even one mention of Mr. Brown. This is perplexing, because Bell loved theatre. After he moved to California in 1862, he even became a theatre critic.[4] Perhaps the pressure from his minister friends forced Bell to forsake Brown. Brown's African Grove Theatre (1821–3), therefore, became the first American theatre officially closed because of collusion between bigoted whites and religious African Americans.

One possible way to win over religious leaders is for theatre organizations to raise three questions concerning the historical differences between African American theatre and the church: (1) To what extent are church–theatre problems historically improving or deteriorating? (2) How can the theatre help the church understand that the spectacle in drama, like that in the Scriptures, does not state, but vivifies the theme? and (3) How can the church and the theatre better serve their mutual needs and interests? Viewed within the context of the fourth-period *Imani* plays of the Black Arts School, which proposed to overthrow the church, the 1991 situation was not so bad. Some churches themselves, in fact, originally housed theatre companies, like New York's H.A.D.L.E.Y. (Harlem Arts Development League Especially for You) Players

(1985–) and the Quest Theatre of West Palm Beach, Florida (1989–). The best symbol of the easing of tensions was in the person of the Reverend Spencer Jackson. Reverend Jackson directed the Black Heritage Theatrical Players of Chicago (1974–c. 1982), which performed at churches and events throughout the area. He used theatre to develop "youth and adults artistically, socially and religiously."[5] Notwithstanding these advances, a great majority of church people as well as business people still felt that theatre was sacrilege, or a thief of that which belonged to God. These people would attend such plays about religion as Langston Hughes's ever-popular *Tambourines to Glory* (1963), Vinnette Carroll and Micki Grant's *Don't Bother Me, I Can't Cope* (1972), and Vy Higginsen's *Mama, I Want to Sing* (1983). But devout parishioners would not brook most secular plays, even if the works aimed, as the playwright OyamO put it, "to please Black folks with 'positive images' and to please white folks with 'safe images.'"[6]

Not even the positive images, however, pulled in enough church people. The principal reason was that theatre neglected to assist the church to understand that in drama as in the Bible spectacle functions only to enliven the theme by showing faults. In other words, playwrights, like the prophets, revealed positive messages through negative examples. The story of Job, for instance, taught that one must fear God and avoid evil. Job painted grotesque pictures of burning sheep, slain servants, drunken and dead children, and pus-dripping boils. This spectacle so seared the mind that the lesson could never be forgotten. So, too, did the sensuous spectacle in Song of Solomon make the lesson unforgettable. Its wise man did not violate God by sharing with readers the invitation from his "black" and "comely" lover "to lie all night betwixt my breasts."[7] He used this sexual imagery to make clear that "if a man would give all the substance of his house for love, it would utterly be condemned." If church people and business people can appreciate these biblical uses of spectacle, then they can understand as well the cursing, drinking, and fornicating in, for example, Ed Bullins's *The Duplex* (1970). Irrespective of Bullins's not being a moralist, the themes in his *Duplex* and in the Song of Solomon are indistinguishable. One could not expect church officials, of course, to rally soon to this view. Given time and discussion, however, church people and theatre people might narrow their differences. Their disagreements might disappear if pastors and artistic directors were to appoint joint committees charged with finding answers to the following questions: (*a*) How can the theatre help the church to enhance the theatricality of its services and professionalize the performances of its seasonal pageants? (*b*) How can the church help dramatists and performers "witness" God's love and mercy in every performance? (*c*) How can the church assist the theatre in understanding the importance of stimulating the audience's imagination by letting some negative images and words occur offstage? (*d*) How might the theatre aid the church in appreciating the necessity of giving artists complete artistic freedom to create? (*e*) How can the church help the theatre to appreciate the abuse suffered by religious people through the representation of decadence – even when it is used to encourage morality? (*f*) How can the theatre help the church in its fund drives? (*g*) How can the church help the theatre in its audience-development activities? (*h*) How might the church and theatre cooperate to make sure that never again will a racial bigot or a speculator be permitted to manipulate them out of satisfying mutual interests?

Because the Arena Players did address these issues, religious organizations became not only the group's partners, but also its board members. Their presence demanded that the board's member selection committee avoid even the appearance of favoritism. The Players solved this problem by coding names on applications. Nominees made the shortlist by scoring highly on evaluation sheets. The nominating committee painstakingly interviewed each finalist. These were by no means run-of-the-mill interviews because candidates came well-informed: They each had received a packet containing an overview of the theatre's programs and policies, meeting and time requirements, term lengths, and job expectations.[18] The questions at the interview uncovered the candidate's genuine interest, competence, and availability. Following the full board's approval of the nominating committee's recommendations, the board would process and orient the new members. Thus new members could learn about their individual responsibilities, as well as about the Player's history and governance. Each new member was given the biographies of the organization's artistic and administrative leaders; current financial reports; board minutes; board members' names, addresses, and phone numbers; a list of committees; information on programs and activities; and meeting dates. The importance of all of this information was that it bound and obligated the member to the organization. Any failure to meet responsibilities lay squarely on the member. Orientation was usually fun for a new board member: The parliamentarian gave advice about legal and fiscal responsibilities; the artistic staff explained its duties; and the member's chosen committee chair discussed assignment(s). This careful process ensured the organization a well-composed board of qualified people who had been widely recruited and were thoroughly oriented.

The Players' empowered board relied on its finance and fund-raising committees for preparing, monitoring, revising, and raising the budget. The finance committee received a budget draft from the artistic and managing directors. The draft itemized projected earned income, along with operating costs for personnel, plays, activities, and programs. After validating the cash flow projections, the finance committee approved the projected budget and presented it to the full board. The board approved the budget and assigned it to the fund-raising committee. This committee decided on the amount to be raised and the plan for raising the money. The committee, assisted by the board, implemented the plan, which had to acquire all of the contributed income necessary to make up the difference between projected income and expenses. Through its finance committee, the board accounted for every penny raised: It did this by monitoring quarterly reports of expenditures and incomes, thereby avoiding fiscal crises by seeing early any deviations from the projected expenses and earnings. The board revised the budget as needs dictated. The close coordination of the planning, finance, and fund-raising committees resulted in a successful program and substantial income for the Arena Players. The board raised in 1985, for example, $3 million from seventeen national and local corporations, charities, and foundations. The Players received grants from the National Endowment for the Arts, the Maryland State Arts Council, and the Mayor's Advisory Committee on Art and Culture. As of late, the Players has relied less on grants, having found that funders are often mixed blessings. It was well-meaning foundations and agencies, ironically, that both gave birth to and accidentally murdered several second-stage theatres of the sixties. These agencies had restricted their grants principally to operational expenses. Their prohibiting the use of their money for endowments resulted in, of course, boom-and-bust theatre organizations. Agencies, in fact, controlled the future of sixties theatres by tightening and loosening choke hold leashes that too often were tied to politics.[19]

It was important, therefore, that Arena's board decided to rely less on grants and more on community-based co-sponsorships and campaigns. In the co-sponsorship program, for example, the Players permitted clubs, churches, and other groups to sponsor performances. These groups would receive one-third of the profits generated from ticket sales. The club, by the way, could set its own ticket prices as far above the standard admission price as the co-sponsor wished. The Players, however, still collected only two-thirds of the standard price. This popular program, along with the development of community resources, accounted for the Players' 80-percent-full houses. The board, in fact, shone best in its community projects: It assisted community groups by offering expertise, by donating free advertising space, by providing meeting space, and by contributing evenhandedly to political campaigns. The know-how it offered to community groups included helping churches and schools produce and direct plays, pageants, and events. Civic and fraternal organizations often called on the theatre, not only for staging their affairs but also for coaching speeches. The board authorized free program advertisements, along with meeting space, to nonprofit organizations. Groups used the facility free – or for a minimal charge – for their fashion shows, talents contests, forensic events, rallies, and so on. The Players made sure that all politicians had equal access to its facilities, because the Players believed in nonpartisan participation in the political life of the community. Politicians, consequently, were quite generous to the group. While Maryland's governor William Donald Schaefer was the mayor of Baltimore, he often supplied funds and assisted the board in securing matching grants and in acquiring real estate. State senator Clarence Blount got several $100,000 matching grants from the state.[20]

The high-level and well-covered contacts by the board made the board appear to be running everything. The truth was that the board did not meddle in the day-to-day operation of the theatre. The board's *only* operational obligation was to appoint the artistic director. This was not the case until the celebrated watershed for the board – between artistic director Samuel Wilson and staunch board member Clifton Sherrard. Sherrard, who was the husband of the board's founding president, decided that the artistic staff needed to upgrade "the quality of its plays and its production." He submitted to Wilson a "professional script from a friend." The Players' play-reading committee summarily rejected the script, principally because Sherrard had violated the unwritten rule "to keep his whatever out of artistic business." Sherrard so resented the committee's "insult" that he decided to produce and direct the play himself. The opening skirmish began, appropriately enough, with auditions: "Those people," claimed Sherrard, "led by you-know-who [referring to Wilson], sat right out there in that lobby and told every actor coming to audition not to have anything to do with this production." Sherrard finally got a cast by tapping several outside sources – including some university actors from Morgan State. Then he decided to let somebody else direct, which belled

Round Two: "Everybody I asked originally agreed – until you-know-who got to them. And I was paying good money, far more than those old two-bit hens down at Arena. After having person after person pull out because of *his* threats, I finally got a dear friend to direct." The technical troubles making up Round Three persuaded Sherrard to move the production from the Arena play-house to a plush downtown theatre, "staffed by union people":

We played to a full house every night. And you should have seen me. When I stepped out there on that stage – dressed all up in white – I want you to know that I was some kind of sharp. When I stepped out there to introduce the play, you don't know how good I felt. Just to be able to show those ole biddies that you don't control me. The nerve of them. And after all I've done for them. After all the money my wife and I have raised. Well, I showed them.[21]

"You should have seen that mess," said Wilson. "You have never seen so much overacting and under-direction in all your life."

Thanks to this brouhaha-ha-ha, the Players' board prohibited members not on the artistic staff from producing, directing, or act-ing in shows anywhere in the greater Baltimore metropolitan area. The board, in fact, limited itself in the performance area to owning only the obligation of hiring, evaluating, and firing the artistic di-rector. Had the board not restricted itself, it would probably have suffered a turnover similar to that of the McCree Theatre of Flint, Michigan (1970–). This board manages the daily operations of the organization, giving the artistic and the managing directors de-tailed instructions. The workload makes it difficult to find and keep members. By the board's own admission, this results in:

No core group of actors and directors; not enough board members to form effective committees; weak management (part-time staff); unclear view of future; lack of space; lack of organized fund raising; inadequate promotional resources; negative image because of recent past; and loss of funding sources.[22]

The president of the McCree board was optimistic in 1992 that "fresh faces" would give the theatre "new life."[23] It would be surprising, however, if the overwork did not soon diminish the new members' enthusiasm.

The encouraging news is that all African American theatre organizations do not die after only a few years. Only those with unempowered boards do. The question is How can founders/artistic directors give *complete control* to boards without suffering too much from withdrawal symptoms? One understands the founders' dilemma, especially for such family-owned enterprises as Marla Gibbs's Crossroads Theatre in Los Angeles (1981–) and Nora Vaughn's Black Repertory Group in Berkeley, California (1964–). Yet even these owners must know that the chances of their organization surviving them for at least eight years are 67 percent better with an empowered board. The second-stage board simply is unable to find substantial amounts of money, because funders, major contributors, even audiences, identify with the founder, not with the organization. If this were not the case, Shirley Radcliffe of the Richard Allen Center for Culture and Art in New York and Voza Rivers of the New Heritage Repertory Theatre would not have seen such Draconian cuts in their funding following the deaths of the companies respective founders, Hazel Bryant and Roger Furman. If founders want their theatres to be living monuments in their honor, then the founders must yield power – *now*. The first step might be to have funding agencies deal with the officers of the board, along with the owner. Funders welcome the chance to interact with a board, as long as they are confident that they are dealing with the people who are accountable. Another major step toward turning over the reins would be to change in the public's mind its sole identification of the organization with the owner. The founder might see to it that every public information release about the organization features the officers of the board, not the founder. The founder, for at least two seasons, might attend only final dress rehearsals, giving the job of ambassador at other performances to officers of the board. This symbolic public pulling away might be matched with real internal disappearances. Thus the founder might attend board meetings less frequently, checking from a distance the health and well-being of the "baby." All critical decisions would be shifted gradually to the board. As the board made errors, its members could learn to straighten up things themselves. This whole business would be no less difficult for the founder than slowly dying. This sacrifice, however, would ensure life.

5

Development

From all the moaning and groaning about the death of Black theatre, and from seeing theatre after theatre close because of money and space, it is quite plain that we have to find some better ways of developing audiences, marketing plays, developing our talent, finding money and sharing our resources.

Hazel Bryant

HAZEL BRYANT'S "better ways" might be the oldest ways. There has got to be a means of raising money for theatre. For example, theatre could adapt the Missionary Baptist Church's ancient form of collection, called a "love offering." The offering lets a visiting preacher know just how much the congregation liked his sermon. There is always the risk, however, that some – like the old sister known for sipping her gin – will use it to show how much they hated the preaching: The sister could have done without the visitor's going on about "backsliders rattling them cups." As she walks around the table where the visitor's donation is being collected, she looks straight into his eyes, making sure that he sees what she does – she puts a dollar in his basket and takes twenty dollars out. The importance of such an incident is in the question that it raises: How can theatre organizations so develop their audiences, market their shows, cultivate talents, form coalitions, and raise funds that the companies will be able to sense the direct link between product and well-being? More importantly, how does theatre reflect its awareness that the organization will

191

pay for performances – as well as for anything else – that offends
the audience? Applied to the issue of increasing audiences, these
questions encourage serious study of how past organizations addressed such needs as finding better sites, diversifying seasons, or
supporting communities.

These needs are interconnected. The critic Peter Bailey's studies of the relationship of theatre location to audience development
showed for example, that African Americans often refused to attend theatres in poorer areas.[1] Nevertheless, history has proved
that some people will still seek out good entertainment, even
though it is offered in cramped quarters in shady neighborhoods.
Brown's African Company had audiences fighting to see *Richard
III*, despite the wooden seats that splintered people's behinds.
Ricardo Kahn's Crossroads Theatre Company (1978–), before
moving into its multi-million-dollar facility, performed in a New
Brunswick sewing factory. Ed Bullins's BMT Theatre (1988–91)
brought well-dressed audiences to a tiny Oakland storefront in an
area where just walking alone required prayer. The people came
because the plays were the best fun in town. The people kept coming because the producers had sense enough to diversify their seasons with plays of escapism and heritage. Brown's *The Drama of
King Shotaway* (1823) certainly answered producer-director Larry
Leon Hamlin's call to put audiences "in touch with their history
and culture."[2] One can bet, however, that Brown's audiences did
not have the same complaint that was voiced by the audiences sur-
veyed by Bailey, that is, that the history plays had "too much moaning and groaning and not enough hope."[3] Brown undoubtedly
spiked *Shotaway*, like he did his *Richard III*, with so many popular
songs and dances that people could not get enough history, even
though the plot was about an uprising. Although site must be
considered, audiences will apparently come when a performance
commands them to come. The best way to get audiences was by
showing them how much the theatre cared about the community. In
their efforts to do this, organizations offered projects ranging from
forays to forums. Some theatres, for example, assisted civic orga-

nizations with events, provided groups with meeting space, participated in a particular group's meeting, and, in some cases made token donations. Other theatres found it quite beneficial to offer free family events, to travel to "new" audiences, and to adapt plays to familiar locales and events.

In Chicago, Val Gray Ward's Kuumba Workshop (1968–) developed its audience by consistently taking part in public seminars. In 1971 Ward mobilized public opinion against the film *Sweet Sweetback's Badasss Song* (1971). She felt that the film debased women as sex objects. Kuumba sponsored a symposium featuring seven well-known speakers (three for the film and four against). The film's opponents, of course, won. This motivated Kuumba along with its supporters to boycott *Sweetback*. In a further commitment against sexual abuse, Kuumba assisted William Gaddis in producing segments of an antiabuse film. Gaddis's film, which he based on his experiences as a Chicago pimp, depicted the destructive elements of prostitution. The importance of the Kuumba example was its demonstration to potential audiences that the theatre would actively work to solve issues deemed critical by the community. Because of such off-theatre-site contact, more people came to the theatre to see what else Kuumba did.

Similar benefits resulted when a theatre helped community organizations professionalize their events or shared its space with other groups. Phillip and Ethel Pitts Walker's African American Drama Company of California (1978–) assisted churches, schools, and hospitals in writing and producing many of their theatrical and special events. By doing so the Drama Company won new audiences. Similarly, Amiri Baraka's Spirit House Theatre in New Jersey (1966–c. 1986) increased its audiences through community outreach. Baraka, additionally, offered not only regular classes in the creative and martial arts but also tutorials in history, mathematics, science, and English. This connection between education and theatre was carried even further by Gustave Johnson and James Spruill's New African Company of Boston (1968–), which held workshops in public schools and community centers. The company developed a teacher's curriculum manual, which included lesson plans, photos, drawings, and hints for teaching theatre arts. Baraka's and Johnson and Spruill's audiences doubled because of these activities. Equally useful was the attendance by a theatre representative at other groups' meetings, as well as extending invitations to other groups to meet at the theatre. Larry Hamlin, along with other members of his North Carolina Black Repertory Company in Winston-Salem (1979–), poked his head into "every social or organizational meeting they could, constantly talking about their theatre, doing scenes on the spot, and inviting the members to come and see their productions."[4] George Hawkins's Ensemble Theatre of Houston (1976–) offered special touring productions for children and seniors. These efforts paid off, probably because the theatres, like the Kuumba Workshop, also would make small, symbolic, financial donations. The workshop contributed 5 percent of its gross earnings to such organizations as the Institute of the Black World in Atlanta, and Provident Hospital, the Black Women's Committee for the Care and Protection of Our Children, and the DuSable Museum, all in Chicago. The significance of these contributions was that they let people know that the theatre's hand was not *always* out. The amount was unimportant, because everybody knew that the theatres themselves were exceedingly poor. Especially helpful, as well, were free, family-oriented events such as were held by Marian Maxwell's Yard Theatre in the nation of Jamaica (c. 1969–). Maxwell invited musicians, poets, neighbors, and Rastafarians to her big yard to interact and to perform. These events pulled in people, some of whom simply stood and listened, while others played and acted. Guests came and went as they wished. The National Black Theatre of New York (1968–) held similar events in 1974, called Sunday afternoon "Blackenings." These were almost community support groups: ordinary folks and well-known artists met, talked, and created. In 1976 Hazel Bryant's Afro-American Total Theatre (1966–9) (later, the Richard Allen Center for Culture and Art [1965–88]) held a lunchtime theater series, where Midtown Manhattan audiences could see one-act plays. This event proved quite successful. Vernell A. Lillie's Kunta Repertory Theatre (1974–), which is part of the Department of Africana Studies at the University of Pittsburgh, donates a percentage of tickets for each production to people with limited incomes and with social and health service organizations. Helpful, too, were tours that brought the theatres to special audiences, such as the Freedom Community College's performances in the Newark, New Jersey, public housing projects in 1968. Some theatres increased their audiences by adapting plays to familiar locales and events. The Dashiki Project Theatre of New Orleans (c. 1965–), for example, in a 1967 production, changed the locale of Errol John's *Moon on a Rainbow Shawl* (1962) from Trinidad to New Orleans. The successful production was critical of the New Orleans Public Service, Inc.

The success in building audiences can be attributed not only to community involvement but also to innovative and frugal models for the marketing of productions. The theatres traditionally relied on guest appearances, fashion shows, seminars, soap-box-theatre hours, art exhibits, dance recitals, parades, happenings, and mass-media parties to get the public's attention. Guest appearances became such staples in some theatres that they never had a "dark" weekend. If no plays were up, a theatre might give, as Larry Neal suggested, "concerts of soul or cosmic music. Other groups should be invited to perform on the off season."[5] Promotion by using guest artists was quite effective, as DuBois demonstrated with special appearances in the Washington, D.C., production of *Star of Ethiopia* (1913). DuBois inserted as actors in his pageant, among others, the highly respected historian Charles H. Wesley, seen as chief of the Kushites; civil rights activist Mary Church Terrell, as Harriet Beecher Stowe; and the director Montgomery Gregory, as an abolitionist.[6] Bobby Seale, co-founder of the Black Panther Party, appeared as a guest performer in the Panther acting company, the Black Guards (1965–6), which Marvin X directed. Such guests as Sun Ra and his Myth-Science Arkestra often appeared with Baraka's Black Arts Repertory Theatre/School (1964–6) and later at the Spirit House. Because popular actors were very busy, theatres invited them simply to do dramatic readings.[7] Many colleges and universities welcomed guest artists to work with their student-actors.[8] A great success for Bryant's Richard Allen Center in 1975 was the Countee Cullen Great Storytellers, in which well-known guest storytellers read to children. The guest artists did not, however, always have to be national figures. Baltimore's Arena Players (1953–), for example, lured a well-known community activist to perform. Although many local people had known this person for his community-development work, few knew that he could act. The community, which flocked to his performances, came not only to see the play but also to support its friend.

Audiences also responded well to fashion shows as special marketing tools. The Dashiki Theatre, for example, had overflow spectators for its African-inspired fashion show called "Watu Wazuri" (The Beautiful People) in 1970. Divided into "Authentic," "Roots and Slavery," "The New Breed," and "The Genteel Black," the enormously popular show featured original music and dance. The affordable prices of the fashions made the event even more appealing. Although expensive and time-consuming to mount, the show worked because the organizers spent so much time planning it and developing community support. A slightly different fashion show was used by the Black Butterfly Company of Philadelphia (c. 1968–), directed by Chaka Ta (clarence maloney) in 1972. Chaka Ta fused African fashions with poetry, music, drama, and dance into a show that was so popular that organizations throughout Pennsylvania booked it.

Although not so popular as fashion shows, pre- and/or post-production seminars so improved the audience's understanding of some productions that there were noticeable increases in attendance. Blackarts Midwest of Minnesota (c. 1968–), for example, ran pre-performance workshops in 1969 that explained not the particular play, but rather the principles of African American theatre. Directed by Colden X, the group distributed information, including booklists. Following the performance, the group held another seminar on the impact that the issues in the play had had on the community. Similar discussions today could make more accessible such period works as the fourth-period Black Revolutionary plays and the first-period musical comedies. An organization might even re-stage a typical evening of entertainment such as that seen at Brown's African Grove Theatre: some opening comic songs (called "Opera"), cut versions of Shakespeare and/or an African American classic, classical and modern dances, and pantomimes – all accompanied by much food, drink, and music. Such fare, set in its historical context, could be as much a box-office smash now as it was for Mr. Brown. Equally refreshing and informative could be re-creations of the Soap Box Theatre (1937–9). These Depression-era improvisational theatre productions encouraged audiences to discuss and role play personal, social, and political conflicts. This theatre not only altered and molded beliefs, attitudes, and practices, but it also developed audiences from among people who had not previously viewed theatre as a communication tool.

Visual art exhibits, too, helped market shows, especially if the art works were by local artists. Flint's McCree Theater (1972–) – directed by Charles Winfrey – illustrates best how to use art exhibits as a marketing tool. Winfrey's exhibits, which ran concurrently with each major production, showed scenes, people, and conditions similar to those in the plays. The viewers, artists, and actors engaged in lively discussions about the paintings, often within the context of the play. Paintings and theatre tickets sold briskly. This was akin to the African Company's using dance recitals to promote special occasions. For the opening of his new play, *The Drama of King Shotaway*, Brown presented James Hewlett in an original Native American ballet, *Balililon*. Brown, therefore, premiered not only the first African American play but also the first ballet. Such special times occasioned parades and happenings. Like Baraka's Black Arts Repertory Theatre/School in 1966, as well as like many minstrel shows, theatres promoted each new production with a downtown lunchtime parade, complete with actors, musicians, dancers, and majorettes. The importance of such events, of course, was that the media enjoyed covering them, as well as covering "happenings" like that used by playwright Charles Fuller to market a show he was directing at a Philadelphia housing project. Fuller's "happening" netted an unexpected full house for his theatre workshop production, which addressed the violence that plagued the African American and Hispanic communities. Fuller staged an outdoor shoot-out between rival gangs. He had the cast chase an actor through the projects. The neighbors, always ready for some excitement, joined the chase, which ended at the theatre. Fuller asked the "posse" to stay for the play, and the people did.

Whereas this sixties event might today occasion real trouble, other "happenings" appropriate to the play's theme might also fill theatres. Such events would prove especially helpful if the theatre informed the media about the "happening" beforehand. The broadcast media's love of graphic stories makes it important for theatre organizations to cultivate good, one-on-one relationships with directors of radio and television news, arts, and public affairs. Yet it has been with such marketing that African American theatre companies have had the most trouble. Not so successful now as in the past are such events as "media nights" and "media parties," featuring buffets, drinks, complimentary tickets, and performances, along with live music. It was, for example, at such a jointly sponsored party in 1974 that all of Chicago's theatre companies persuaded the African American media to publicize their plays. Popular media personalities like Earl Calloway (fine arts editor of the *Chicago Defender*) and Vernon Jarrett (columnist and television celebrity) gave much needed preproduction publicity to the companies. This advertising bonanza brought in considerably larger audiences. Some theatres sponsored public relations workshops, where companies learned how best to utilize such free advertising outlets as speakers' bureaus, talk shows, billboards, public service announcements, and community distribution sites.[9] It was important for the theatre to get placed not only in the free local listings but also in such national services as *Black Masks* magazine. After all of this work, however, most shows drew only 37 to 42 percent of capacity for the run, according to Gary Anderson, artistic director of Plowshares Theatre in Detroit (1989–).[10] Furthermore, Anderson reported that radio advertising was the best way in 1991 to market African American theatre: African Americans, according to a recent U.S. government survey, received just under fifty percent of their news from radio.[11] The marketing plans of the national tours of *Beauty Shop* (1990) and *Mama, I Want to Sing* (1983), according to Anderson, supported the survey findings: radio advertisements ran all day two weeks prior to the opening of the shows, and no print advertising occurred outside of African American newspapers. Both shows played to sold-out houses throughout the United States. Blanket radio marketing is, of course, expensive. Perhaps that expense, however, is as essential as the cost of scripts, costumes, and make-up. It simply makes no sense for companies to continue investing tens of thousands of people-hours into performances that only a few hundred see. Along with holding such marketing events as the DuBois ticket contests, "happenings," parades, dance recitals, art exhibits, soap-box hours, seminars, fashion shows, and guest appearances, theatres might also consider devoting one-quarter of the total production budget to radio advertisements.[12]

Among the greatest successes enjoyed by theatres in the past have been their development of raw talent in writing and performing. The methods for cultivating these gifts were not at all standard. The Free Southern Theatre (FST) (1964–82) limited writer training principally to writing, whereas Ed Bullins's Black Theatre Workshop (1968–72) incorporated writing into the whole experience of putting on plays. At the Free Southern Theatre the writing director, Tom Dent, had poets and playwrights work either for *Nkombo* (the workshop magazine) or for an acting workshop showcase. There were no assigned themes, subjects, or styles: The only goal was to express oneself honestly about the history and culture of African peoples. Writer training at the Black Theatre Workshop, on the other hand, encouraged writers to assist in scenery construction, house management, and audience development. The writers created works for poetry shows, one-act showcases, calendars, and newsletters.[13] Both workshops produced important works and writers. Some theatres even reserved slots for workshop plays, which significantly improved the writers' attitudes and output. The Black Arts/West of Seattle (1967–82), for example, annually gave well-received performances of several one-act workshop plays.[14] In order to encourage writers further, some organizations and publications, following the examples of *Crisis* and *Opportunity* magazines of the twenties and thirties, held playwriting contests. Among the richest prizes was the James Arthur Baldwin Award, established in 1989 by the New World Theatre at the University of Massachusetts at Amherst and the Amaryllis Arts Foundation. This $3,000 prize competition also offered a production at Smith College. Professional productions were also features of the Penumbra Theatre Company's prize and of the Theodore Ward Prize for Playwriting, a $2,000 award sponsored by Chicago's Columbia College Theatre/Music Center. The Baltimore Arena Players held one of the most unusual contests: It coproduced a performance on a local television station of the play by the winner of the $1,000 first prize.[15] The only contest currently being sponsored by a periodical is *The Massachusetts Review*'s Doris Abramson Playwriting Award of five hundred dollars.

The significant improvement in playwriting more than justifies the need for each theatre company to consider sponsoring not only playwriting workshops and contests but also criticism workshops. In addition, the number of complaints about white reviewers calls for the review-writing workshops that are directed toward African American newspaper reviewers. These journalists have received their on-the-job play-review training from editors who have no particular expertise.[16] This training, unfortunately, does not reflect the changing role of the African American critic. During the sixties and seventies the critic's function was to help theatre organizations build audiences. This audience development entailed fighting influential – and generally negative – critics like Walter Kerr of the *New York Times*. Because Kerr, along with several other whites and a few African Americans, was either unaware of – or unsympathetic to – African American experiments with Western structure, characterization, and theme, he often wrote scathing reviews. African American theatre people called the reviews racist, prompting most African American critics to become only promoters. The contemporary reviewer, however, need not feel obligated to aid either "in keeping a Black production alive" or in letting the audience be "the supreme critic," as Ed Bullins predictably advocates.[17] The audience, as the critic Clayton Riley asserts, needs honest criticism to help it better appreciate the complexities of theatre. Theatre companies, similarly, should welcome outside opinions of their work, if for no other reason than to assess others' understanding of the writer's and the director's objectives.[18] Within this context, many organizations might build a cadre of first-rate critics with specialties in African American theatre. Although workshops might vary considerably, they should all satisfy the objectives outlined in Appendix A. If each theater were to offer workshops, then reviewer training might catch up with such other development programs as the schooling of actors.

Whereas formal actor training mushroomed after midcentury, its early development was quite slow. It began in 1819 with James Hewlett's closely studying from the gallery of the Park Theatre such great English stars as Edmund Kean. Hewlett, in 1821, passed on his skills to the other members of Brown's African Company. This on-the-job education changed to formal instruction seventy-five years later, when in 1896 Bob Cole opened his acting school with the Worth's Museum All-Star Stock Company. The formal training, however, did not predominate. Although some early-twentieth-century actors like Charles Burroughs studied at such conservatories as the Boston School of Expression, most other actors learned their craft in workshops and apprenticeships at community and educational theatres. These were plentiful because in the twenties DuBois had founded his Negro little theatre movement and Locke his college theatre program. Locke's 1921 college theatre proposal had blossomed by 1992 into actor-training programs in almost all of the ninety-two Historically Black Colleges and Universities (HBCU). Three of these programs have been accredited by the National Association of Schools of Theatre: Howard University, chaired by Al Freeman, Jr., who succeeded longtime chair Carole Singleton; North Carolina A. & T., chaired by Mary Tuggle and formerly directed by H. D. Flowers; and Grambling University, chaired by Allen Williams, who in 1992 was president of the National Association of Dramatic and Speech Arts (NADSA). The success of these college programs must be attributed to NADSA (1936–), which was nourished by its founder S. Randolph Edmonds and by presidents Thomas E. Poag of Tennessee A. & I., Thomas D. Pawley of Lincoln in Missouri, Floyd L. Sandle of Grambling, Lois P. Turner and Edward Fisher of Fayetteville State, Lillian W. Voorhees of Fisk University, Granville Sawyer of Texas Southern, Singer Buchanan of Kentucky State, John M. Stevenson of Savannah State, Juanita Oubre of Winston-Salem State, Joan Lewis of Clark College, and 1992 executive secretary Sandrell Martin of Miami. These people, among many others, have helped actor training for students and adults reach maturity.

Although the study of acting began for children much later than it did for adults, children's programs have taken much less time to mature, thanks to the efforts of Professor Irene C. Edmonds while she was at Florida A. and M. in Tallahassee, where she developed a youth theatre. Many college theatre programs developed similar youth theatres. Among the best was the Howard University Children's Theatre, directed until 1992 by Kelsey Collie.[19] Evidence of Howard's early commitment to children's theatre was the prominence that the university gave to the popular children's play *Mushy Mouth* (1960), by Henriette Edmonds, daughter of Professors Randolph and Irene Edmonds. The Howard University Children's Theatre deserved being featured at the 1990 National Black Arts Festival in Atlanta. This event saluted youth programs, which, following the sixties, have become intense and abundant. Typical of children's programs connected to community theatres was Baltimore Arena Players' Youtheatre (1965–), offering training for five-to-eighteen-year-olds in acting, dance, tap dance, music, speech, mime, movement, beginning ballet, and stagecraft. Youtheatre proffered paid apprenticeships in stage and house managements, as well as in technical theatre. Children's theatre, in fact, became popular additions to the repertories of several professional theatres in New York City and Chicago in 1974. Aduke Aremu's Harlem Children's Theater was among the best known for its *Liberation of Mother Goose* (1976), which gave the traditional nursery rhymes an African American perspective. More than sixty-five children performed each Saturday morning in 1975 at the Apollo Theatre in such Aremu plays as *Babylon II* (1975), *JuJu Man* (1975), and *Land of the Egyptians* (1975). Young audiences converged on Ernest Hayes's New Faith Children's Theater, which did *The Young Magician* (1976); the Richard Allen Center for Culture and Art's Countee Cullen Storyteller Series; the Theater for Little Folks at the Billie Holiday Theater (1972–); the AMAS Musical Theatre's (1968–) Eubie Blake Children's Theatre; and the Alonzo Players (1967–). Puppet shows also became quite popular, as seen from Brad Brewer's show *The Jackson Five Meets Malcolm X* (1975) and the Harlem Studio Museum's *Rosa Parks and the Bus Boycott* (1976) by Shroeder Cherry. One noteworthy youth theatre was the Chicago Black Ensemble's (1976–) children's theatre school in the Cabrini Green Homes, where it performed *The Other Cinderella* (1976) by Jackie Taylor.

This development of acting talent far outpaced the instruction in technical theatre. So desperate, in fact, was the need for African American technicians in 1983 that Hazel Bryant called on Historically Black Colleges and Universities to institute technical theatre curricula and to persuade more theatre students to enroll. She recommended that in addition to instituting the usual technical courses (set and lighting design, drafting, model making, scene painting, script analysis, and electrical works), the HBCU theatre

program introduce courses in theatre career development, technical theatre practicum, union relationships and certification programs, and professional theatre culture. Such specialized courses,
Bryant stated, would ensure the survival of HBCU theatre programs as they worked "to fill gaping holes in the Black presence in
professional theatre, and to improve technical performances in the
non-professional theatres." In order to motivate students to become technical theatre majors, Bryant said that the students had to
be made to understand that "technical theatre required the same
creative and embellishing energy, discipline, dedication, and rigor
as the performance theatre." Students must be informed, she argued, that "theatre technicians make more money than the average
theatre performer, and that outstanding designers and technicians
are accorded every bit as much respect as actors and singers."[20]
Charles McClennahan, among the busiest of New York City set
designers, developed in 1986 parts of the Bryant program. He created a network of African American professional designers called
the Black Design League, which trained and placed design students. McClennahan, working with Lyl Burn Downing of Jobs For
Youth, set up student summer internships with New York City theatres. McClennahan's program modeled for community and regional theatres the way they could satisfy the still-growing need for
adequately trained technicians.

The significance of this training program, as well as of programs
in writing and performance, is that they had such gratifying outcomes. Alumni of the writing and acting workshops, for example,
founded and ran several highly regarded national publications and
theatre organizations: BLKARTSOUTH's *NKOMBO* and *Plain
Truth*, the Miami Theater of Afro-Arts' *Deep Down in My Soul*, and
the New Lafayette Theatre's *Black Theatre* magazine. Typical of the
achievements of those trained in the performance workshops were
contributions by the former students of Ed Bullins's Black Theatre
Workshop, as well as of the workshops of BLKARTSOUTH and
Oscar Brown, Jr. Following the closing of the Black Theatre Workshop, the students began independent work: OyamO started a

Harlem theatre called the Black Tempo (1972–?); Neil Harris and Milburn Davis assisted in the development of the Black Magicians (1972–?); and Richard Wesley and Martie Charles founded the Black Playwright's Workshop (1970–?), out of which came Wesley's *The Black Terror* (1971) and Charles's *Where We At* (1971). BLKARTSOUTH's students founded a senior citizens group in the Guste Homes Housing Project. Directed by Iona Reese, the group toured community centers and churches. Oscar Brown, Jr., directed members of the Chicago gang Black P Stone Rangers in the musical *Opportunity, Please Knock* (1973). Not only did the play enjoy local success, but, after traveling to the West Coast, the group gained national attention.

The formation of theatre coalitions has been, since 1967, along with national organizations and festivals, among the newer and more successful methods used to develop African American theatre organizations. The varying purposes, objectives, goals, and activities of these coalitions and organizations reflected the historical changes in the philosophies and practices of African American theatre.[21] One of the most revealing changes occurred in coalition philosophy. Thus the Organization of Black American Culture in Chicago (OBAC) (1967), the first coalition of visual artists, writers, and theatre people, consisted of such at-odds groups that it was first necessary to analyze each separate group's philosophy for servicing "the cultural needs of the Black community."[22] Synthesizing the groups' agreements and modifying their differences, in other words, were necessary first steps to developing "a collective definition of their functions."[23] By the time of the founding of the second of these coalitions, the Black Theatre Alliance of New York (1971), the purpose had changed to such practical issues as funds, press notices, and audiences.[24] Markets, not philosophies, dictated trends and shaped the coalitions. Because a national consensus on the function of African American art had emerged within five years, in other words, the groups were influenced by forces in the market. The highly competitive New York City market, for example, compelled the various companies to combine their efforts

quickly. So desperate was the need for assistance that the Black
Theatre Alliance expanded within seven years from seven to forty-
eight companies, including nineteen dance companies. The
laissez-faire Chicago arts market, on the other hand, allowed internal conflicts to develop within the OBAC. The friction caused
the visual artists to leave the OBAC in 1972 and to found the
Coalition of Black Revolutionary Artists (COBRA). This trend
toward speciality grouping grew rapidly between 1972 and 1976
for almost paradoxical reasons. The continual bickering in Chicago led to the formation of the Black Theater Alliance (1974) to
serve as an information clearinghouse for the city's competitive and
cantankerous theatres. This quarreling eased with the creation of
the Midwest Afrikan American Theatre Alliance (1976), which
had as its healing purpose the establishment of "a cultural para-
digm for analyzing and re-claiming the rich legacy of Afrikan
Americans."[25] The need to specialize services to members, however, caused the New York Black Theatre Alliance to divide. The
Audience Development Committee in New York (AUDELCO),
for example, originated in 1973 to boost attendance.[26] The only
coalition to buck these genre and specialty groupings was the
Southern Black Cultural Alliance (1972).[27] This coalition accommodated all philosophies and types in a comprehensive effort to
strengthen each organization.

The coalitions and organizations founded in the eighties focused more on such specific areas as arts fiscal policy. The coalitions highlighted historical studies, women's issues, performance
skills, and showcases. The attempts to influence fiscal policy
of the arts linked the needs of the theatres with those of their
neighborhoods. Whereas the Black Arts Council of Dallas (1984)
lobbied for its share of the city's $3 million cultural arts bud-
get, the Black Theatre Collective of New York (1986) initiated
a multi-billion-dollar revitalization of the member theatres' communities.[28] This intense lobbying by African American companies
paid off not only for the companies and their neighborhoods but
also for other ethnic theatres. The San Francisco Area Multi-

Cultural Production Fund (1988), for example, provided benefits to the Asian American Theater Company and El Teatro Campesino, as well as to the Oakland Ensemble Theatre (1974–) and SEW Productions/Lorraine Hansberry Theatre. The California Arts Council, through the fund, helped these organizations produce outstanding new works by leading multicultural artists. The African Continuum Theatre Coalition (ACT Co) (1989) of Washington, D.C. similarly emphasized the financial development of its members.[29] ACT Co offered its Management Assistance Project to selected organizations in order to develop their administrative infrastructures. A selected organization would be provided for six months with a resident financial consultant to advise on management, audience development, and fund-raising.

These purposes of advising were consistent with those of the national organizations of individuals, which added the purpose of personal development of skills in research, writing, performing, and producing. The National Conference on African American Theatre (1983), for example, annually invites eminent scholars, artists, and lay people to share their recent research on a theme in African American theatre history or criticism.[30] African American feminism and international feminism were concerns of Black Women Theatre (BWIT) (1983) and the International Women's Playwrights Conference (1988). The importance of BWIT was that it added gender to its organizing principle, which was otherwise the same as had been behind OBAC, the first coalition of artists. The differences between them was that the BWIT actors, singers, dancers, writers, directors, producers, and technicians were professionals. BWIT's similarity to OBAC, however, was striking, because BWIT too addressed issues of roles and philosophies.[31] The International Women's Playwrights Conference both telescoped internationally and narrowed generically BWIT's purposes.[32] Another coalition, the Black Theatre Network (BTN) (1986), along with two national arts festivals, assembled scholars and artists to engage in dialogue and give performances. BTN offered professional workshops and seminars,[33] whereas two festivals showcased talent. Atlanta's National Black Arts Festival (1986) was important for its inclusion of theatre, dance, literature, folk art, film, music, and performance art.[34] The North Carolina Black Theatre Festival (1987) in Winston-Salem presented twenty nationally respected theatre organizations. The festival aimed to "sensitize the nation to the importance and the plight of Black theatre in America; and to make people aware that Black theatre may very well become non-existent in the next ten years if steps are not taken now on a national level to ensure its longevity."[35] In addition to being clarion calls for African American theatre, both festivals measured current preferences for schools, periods, and classes of plays. Analysis of the twenty-five plays performed at the 1989 and 1990 festivals, for example, showed that only two were plays from the Black Arts School. Of the twenty-three Black Experience plays, all came from the latest period (since 1975). Eighteen of the twenty-three Black Experience plays were in the Unified Binding Relationships and the Unified Flow classes. The significance of these data was that they made credible OyamO's complaint that organizations neglected historical and Black Arts plays. More theatres needed to adopt the Roger Furman policy of mixing in his New Heritage Players' repertory classic and contemporary plays from both schools. This would have ensured that theater-goers saw plays featuring the wide range of African American life and history.

Analysis of the coalitions' activities showed that, for the most part, the groups were successful in satisfying their aims: improving public relations; developing audiences, talents, and archives; pooling resources; creating communications arms; and raising funds. The coalitions enhanced their public relations through awards ceremonies and regional festivals. Indicative of the importance assigned awards ceremonies were the reactions to the cancellation notice of AUDELCO's sixteenth-annual Recognition Awards. As soon as the word spread in 1988 that funding cuts had caused the termination, the African American community rallied to help director Vivian Robinson save the awards. Heading up special fund-raising drives were Lloyd Williams, president of Uptown Chamber of Commerce; Woodie King, Jr., director of the New Federal Theatre; and Percy E. Sutton, then chair of Inner City Broadcasting. MacDonald's and Paragon Cable made hefty contributions.[36] Every coalition prized such ceremonies, because they honored theatre people both current and past, as indicated by the names on the awards: typical were the Hazel J. Bryant Award of the Midwest Afrikan American Theatre Alliance and the Mr. Brown Award of the National Conference on African American Theatre.[37] The awards publicized the organizations as well as the achievements of the honorees.

An equally important means of promoting coalitions were local and regional festivals, which predated national festivals by seventeen years. The Black Theatre Alliance in New York (BTA) inaugurated the festivals in 1971, when several companies presented plays over five weeks. This initial series of plays, which the Negro Ensemble Company hosted the first year, climaxed in 1974 with twenty-nine companies participating at a downtown theatre. Because of finances, BTA ceased its festivals, as did AUDELCO, which presented its October Festival from 1983 to 1988. The African Continuum Theatre Coalition, however, still presents an annual November Festival. Among the most innovative of the festivals was the one sponsored by the Southern Black Cultural Alliance. The alliance would discuss a new theatre form one year, and most of the organizations would present examples of that form at the next festival. The 1976 festival, for example, focused on multimedia plays.[38] The Black Theatre Alliance in Chicago held the most unusual festival. Each evening a different organization gave a reception and a performance. The festival ended with all organizations participating in "Black Reflections," which accommodated all tastes. The coalitions, unfortunately, were somewhat less successful at meeting their goals of cooperatively developing audiences, training students, and building archives. Among the most successful audience-development activities were surveys and vouchers. The New York BTA conducted surveys, from which it concluded that audiences might increase if performances were more varied, entertaining, and polished. Organizations com-plied, and attendance rose – thanks also to the vouchers used by AUDELCO. At theatre parties, AUDELCO disseminated information about Theatre Development Fund vouchers, which admitted the holder to any participating BTA performance for only eighty cents. Another such plan was "A Taste of Chelsea," which, for a forty-five-dollar "Passcard," allowed a person to attend up to twenty-nine theatre performances. As a bonus, the person was given a discount at fourteen restaurants and shops.

The coalitions' training mission focused on teaching creative writing and essay writing, as well as technical theatre skills. Typical of coalition writing programs were those sponsored by the Frank Silvera Writers' Workshop, the Organization for Black American Culture, and the Black Theatre Network. The Writers' Workshop, founded and directed by the highly regarded playwright Garland Lee Thompson in 1973, sponsored professional readings and critiques of plays. OBAC's weekly meetings paired beginning and professional writers, making the sessions more personal than the Silvera Workshop sessions. BTN's much-needed Young Scholars Competition encouraged undergraduate and graduate theatre scholarship. This program partly satisfied the need for better training in African American theatre reviewing and criticism. Professionals like Shirley Prendergast and Joe Gandy answered Hazel Bryant's call for improved technical theatre training. Prendergast and Gandy held workshops designed to enlarge the supply of stage managers, lighting and sound technicians, and set and costume designers. The late Duane Jones's New York BTA-CETA Artist Project added practical experience to the Prendergast and Gandy workshops.[39] Jones's project placed over sixty student-artists with BTA companies for paid, on-the-job training as lighting and stage technicians. Jones offered similar training to set and costume designers, choreographers, graphic artists, writers, actors, and administrators. This was among the most significant training programs offered by any coalition. Funding cuts, again, stopped these much-needed practicums. The coalitions' attempts to develop theatre collections did not match Jones's success in achieving their training objective. The only significant archives projects directly connected to a coalition were the Armstead-Johnson Foundation for Theatre Research, directed by Helen Armstead-Johnson, and the Theodore Ward Collection.[40] What saddens about the coalitions' failure to develop collections is the alpine amount of historical materials lying in various organizations' drawers, closets, and garages – awaiting an accidental burning and trashing. Only greater and more successful joint-collecting efforts can prevent such needless waste.

Even less successful than the building of collections were the coalitions' efforts to pool their resources, create communications arms, and raise funds. Although there were several proposals for resource pooling, there is no evidence of a single successful program. Communication ventures were only slightly better. The failure in communication occurred not within a coalition, but among and between coalitions. Intracoalition communication organs ranged from newsletters to monthly calenders listing plays, workshops, and other activities. Some coalitions even produced information and service directories, such as those published by the African Continuum Theatre Coalition, the New York Black Theatre Alliance, and the Black Theatre Network. Particularly noteworthy is the second edition of *The BTN Black Theatre Directory* (1991), edited by Addell Austin Anderson.[41] This directory advanced considerably the possibilities of sharing information among the 579 individuals, 46 college and university programs, 22 black theatre organizations, 6 regional arts organizations, 18 other theatre-related organizations, and 106 theatre companies that it listed.[42] Hamlin's North Carolina Black Repertory Company listed 205 theatre organizations in 1992. The publication of theatre news depended principally on such short-lived magazines as *Black Theatre* and *Black Creation.* Occasional news was in *The Black Scholar, Impressions, First World, Black Books Bulletin,* and *The Western Journal of Black Studies.* Among the most thorough and reliable news sources were

the April issues of the magazine *Black World* between 1966 and
1976, edited by Hoyt W. Fuller. The most valuable 1993 source
was *Black Masks*, published and edited by Beth Turner.

News, however, was not the most disappointing area of mission
failure by the coalitions. Fund-raising was. Most of the individual
companies were initially successful in getting grants. The grants
inevitably decreased in size, however, sometimes by as much as 80
percent. Duane Jones's efforts on behalf of the New York BTA
made his one of the few successes in coalition fund-raising. Jones
initially received sizable grants from the New York State Council
on the Arts and the National Endowment for the Arts. He got
smaller sums from such private foundations as the Louise Ottinger
Charitable Trust, the Shubert Foundation, the Urban Coalition,
and the Rockefeller Brothers Fund. The Rockefeller grant helped
the BTA house in a five-story building on New York's Theatre
Row the coalition's studios, rehearsal spaces, and administrative
offices.[43] When the grants dried up, however, so did everything
they had paid for.

Although the coalitions could take pride in their training programs, festivals, audiences-development initiatives, and improved
public relations, they could not come up with a plan to improve the
difficult financial conditions that plagued most African American
theatre organizations. Such a plan is still desperately needed today.
The plan must modify the nature of both theatre and theatre financing. To appreciate the fundamental changes required, one
might ask whether theatre should adopt the same policies on membership, organization, service, and financing that a church would
have. The answer is "Yes," especially in light of a revealing comparison that can be made between Mr. Brown's African Company
and the African Methodist Episcopal Zion Church. The comparison works, notwithstanding that church and theatre serve antipodal needs. The AME Zion Church, which was only a few blocks
from the theatre, was organized on June 21, 1821, exactly four
months before Mr. Brown opened *Richard III*. The differences between the church's open membership and the theatre's talent-

restricted membership manifested themselves financially and politically. The church required its many members to pay affordable weekly dues and tithes, whether or not the members attended a particular worship services. Mr. Brown paid his members for services, whether or not he made a profit. His tickets, therefore, were the highest priced in all of New York City. These ticket prices alienated the theatre from most of the city's ten thousand free African Americans. Thus the theatre had to face alone its many political enemies and economic crises. No poor people – who would be the most likely to join protests – identified enough with the theatre to take to the streets in its support. "Mother Zion," however, was home not only to such celebrated members as Frederick Douglass and Sojourner Truth but also to some of the very poorest New Yorkers. The church, consequently, did not worry about racist politicians and editors like Noah. Mother Zion's services to poor people made the church a viable community institution. What could Brown have changed for his theatre to have survived? Mr. Brown might have reorganized the African Grove Theatre so that its organizational structure more closely resembled that of Mother Zion. Such a possible reorganization is outlined in Appendix B.

Notwithstanding internal changes in local theatres, a vast national assistance program is necessary to help theatres finance their programs. Because powerful interests compete for the few federal and private dollars, the "New African American Theatre" itself must supply the funds. From where can the money come? One possibility is from the development of an endowed fund, to be called the National Endowment for African American Theatre, Inc. (NEAAT). To summarize the proposal, the details of which are in Appendix C, the purpose of NEAAT would be to raise and invest $25 million over the next twenty-five years. Theatre organizations would receive grants from the interest. In order to raise the money, an organizing committee would call four African American theatre summits: Planning; Economic; Politics and Education; and Religion, Entertainment, and Sports. The Planning Summit would have leading African American-theatre artistic directors, managing directors, and board chairs draft and approve the "NEAAT Prospectus," which would state goals, membership criteria, fund-raising methods, grant-distribution formulas, and plans of action. The Economic Summit would have prominent investment bankers, brokers, corporate chief executive officers, and theatre executives develop detailed plans for raising and investing money. The Politics and Education Summit would have members of the Congressional Black Caucus, as well as officials of various national, state, and local governments, education systems, and organizations develop action plans for lobbying their agencies for funds. The final summit (Religion, Entertainment, and Sports) would have national and local ministers, personalities, and entrepreneurs develop plans for fund-raising events using their institutions and fans.

The key to persuading so many national and community groups and leaders to become actively involved in NEAAT is to point to theatre's track record in improving a person's self-image, strengthening families, and developing communities. With the splendid examples of, among others, the actors Charles Dutton, Stephen McKinley Henderson, Margaret Avery, and Ron Dortch, African American theatre has proven its ability to turn individuals away from crime, from self-hatred, and from poverty-induced self-pity. These and other pent-up frustrations can be relieved, theatre has shown by such community-support group activities as the Sunday afternoon "Blackenings" of Barbara Ann Teer's National Black Theatre. Theatre has established that it can make people feel worthwhile – people as young as the children of the Cabrini Green Homes, who performed in the Chicago Black Ensemble's children's theatre, and people as old as the senior citizens from the Guste Homes Housing Project, who acted with BLKARTSOUTH Youth Theatre in New Orleans. Not only have the very young and old benefited from theatre, but also the angry. With his performance of the musical *Opportunity, Please Knock* (1973), done by the Black P Stone Rangers of Chicago, Oscar Brown, Jr., showed that theatre can disarm even tough street gangs. Theatre's history is one of turning alienated strangers into nuclear, extended, and assembled families, as exemplified by Marian Maxwell's family-oriented Yard Theatre in Jamaica and, in Baltimore, the Arena Players' family night. Theatre organizations have helped not only to fortify individuals and families but also to build a sense of community by assisting businesses, social-action activists, schools, and churches. Predominant examples are the Baltimore Arena Players' aid to community organizations trying to raise money and Val Gray Ward's Kuumba Workshop's donation of 5 percent of its gross earnings to other organizations. That the Black Theatre Collective of New York (1986) initiated a multi-billion-dollar revitalization of the theatres' communities demonstrated the theatre's recognition that its well-being and that of business were inextricably bound together.

The distrust between the African American business and theatre communities was a relatively recent development. That trend, in fact, violated the proof given by entrepreneur and owner Robert T. Motts that theatre was a sound investment and that such companies as his Pekin Theatre of Chicago could make a fortune. The record of the fruitful marriage between theatres and other businesses is, in fact, evidence enough that African American businesses need to make saving theatres a priority. The same applies to civic organizations concerned principally with social causes. Theatre organizations have stayed literally down in the trenches in the struggles to mobilize communities to help themselves curb crime, reduce violence, prevent racism, and stop sexual abuse. The theatre's record in schools has been no less exemplary. Theatre organizations have reenforced education through such academic efforts as the tutorials by Baraka's Spirit House Theatre and the seminars by the Blackarts Midwest of Minnesota. Of equal importance has been theatre's practical assistance, as typified by the help Phillip and Ethel Pitts Walker's African American Drama Company of California gives schools in improving their plays, fashion shows, talents contests, forensic events, rallies, and so on. Education systems serve themselves, therefore, by helping to save theatre organizations. So, too, do the churches, where such early examples of cooperation as the relationship between the AME Church and the DuBois Horizon Company cry out to be duplicated. That theatres organizations like the H.A.D.L.E.Y. Players of New York and the Quest Theatre of West Palm Beach found early homes in churches and that Reverend Spencer Jackson used his Black Heritage Theatrical Players of Chicago to save souls and minds are evidence that Reverend Calvin O. Butts's belief that churches must produce theatre has taken hold. Theatre organizations, then, have good cause to expect those being helped by them to return the favor.

Even with the community's full support, however, the goal of raising the $25 million for NEAAT will require persuading governmental agencies and private foundations to change their policies against contributing to endowments. A survey of the six major private foundations and corporate funders (the Rockefeller Foundation, the Pew Charitable Trusts, the Andrew W. Mellon Foundation, the Dayton Hudson Foundation, the AT&T Foundation, and Philip Morris Companies) showed that they did not contribute to endowments, nor did the national public endowments. The Rockefeller Foundation said that its priority was to help organizations get on their feet. Staying upright was principally the organizations' responsibility. These policies, however, were self-defeating: After theatre companies had spent their grant money, not only did they have no reserves, but they also did not have sufficient audiences and alternative incomes to supplant the grants. By not funding endowments, then, a funder could unwittingly cause the deaths of the very companies that it wanted to keep alive. Just as an organization came to rely on a certain level of funding, the allocation either was drastically reduced or was eliminated. The Frank Silvera Writers' Workshop, for example, had its 1983–4 National Endowment for the Arts grant of $20,000 cut to $3,500 the next year. During the 1985–6 funding cycle, the NEA cut the grant to Woodie King, Jr.'s New Federal Theater by $20,000; the Negro Ensemble Company by $50,000; and Roger Furman's New Heritage Players by 27 percent, along with a 50 percent cut by the New York State Council of the Arts.[44] No theatre, as the funding agents must have known, could have sustained these cuts without experiencing systemic disruptions and morale problems and thus compromising the quality of its productions. Whereas the desire of funding agencies to see immediate results from their investments is understandable, the foundations were defeating their own goal of building strong minority theatre organizations. Only fundamental policy changes, permitting theatres to invest at least a portion of the grant as a hedge against future difficulties, can solve this problem. Theatres – even quite well-managed ones – simply have been unable to build audiences, as well as corporate-underwriters, large enough and fast enough during the tenure of the grant to off-set the loss of the money. If foundations, therefore, wish to see long-term results from their investments, then the agencies either must fund endowments – with the provision that only the interest be expended – or they must require that for each dollar granted, a theatre raise at least thirty-three cents for an endowment. Without this change, theatre organizations will continue to be on intimate terms with hard times.

The financial straits of African American theatre apply as well to other Western theatres. In other words, all theatre companies experience cyclical cash flow crises, brought on principally by downturns in the national economy. Whereas, for example, eight African American theatres in New York City closed their doors during the 1990–1 season, fifteen other major New York City theatres also shut down that year, according to Alisa Solomon.[45] These theatres, Solomon said, suffocated under huge debts, heaped upon the companies by an ever-more stingy environment, an increasingly bureaucratic system, and an out-of-touch corporate community. Stinginess, of course, is nothing new to African American theatres. For the Frank Silvera Writers' Workshop to have had its grant from the NEA cut in 1984 by 83 percent for the one year and eliminated the next invokes wonder: Are the subsequent problems worth the NEA's making and the theatre's accepting grants in the first place? In other words, perhaps the New Federal Theatre, the Negro Ensemble Company, and the New Heritage Players would

have been better off if they had earlier relied solely on the re-
sourcefulness that they would later develop during the seven years
following the NEA's draconian cuts. The purpose here certainly is
not to trash funders. They make inestimable contributions to African American theatre, and one must admire their refusal to impose on or to dictate to theatre companies. The foundations are not
at all simply ribbons and balloons – as is evident by arts-program
director Rachel Newton Bellow's steering the Mellon Foundation
toward the more intellectual aspects of the performing arts.[46]

African American theatres gain even when corporate funders
serve their own self-interests in pursuit of increased sales along
with visibility. Thus the AT&T Foundation used both production
and marketing money to extend the Broadway run of Richard
Wesley's *The Talented Tenth* (1990).[47] Furthermore, the Ford
Foundation's deemphasizing, during the seventies, of institutional
operating grants in favor of establishing a cash reserve program –
later the National Arts Stabilization Fund – was a step in the direction of helping African American theatre organizations develop
fiscally sound management strategies. Not even this level of assistance, however, could keep African American theatre alive for
extended periods. Only endowments can replace the short-term
solutions for developing audiences, marketing shows, cultivating
talents, forming coalitions, and increasing finances. To build an
audience, for example, takes more than producing the most innovative entertainment in town. Even balancing a season with plays of
escapism and plays of heritage cannot possibly offset the 72 percent losses in 1986 from grant cuts. Such cuts mean theatres do
not have access to the extensive radio advertising they need to
reach the 50 percent of African Americans who use radio as their
principal source of information: Not many organizations can afford
the $140 fee for a sixty-second advertisement in 1993. Theatres
have continued to draw just 32 to 47 percent of capacity, as they
rely on everything from public service announcements to talk show
appearances – often aired only a day or two before the opening. No
wonder, then, that companies have little time to give the training

needed to increase the supply of African American technicians. The once significant gains in playwriting and acting have dropped as well as workshops have disappeared. The need for criticism workshops is greater now than it was during the sixties. Daily critics – this time, Frank Rich of the *New York Times* – still savage such plays as Leslie Lee's *Black Eagles*, the story of the Tuskegee Fighter Squadron:

The play has almost nothing to say about its fascinating subject beyond the documentary facts. The play unearths a neglected chapter in American history only to present it onstage as a talking mural suitable for study in a dogmatic high-school civics class.[48]

Informed African American critics might have informed Rich that *Black Eagles* (1991) followed the traditions of the Contribution class of the Black Arts School of drama during the DuBois Era. Like Frances Gunner's *The Light of Women* (1930), *Black Eagles* simply sings out the praises of African American people – airmen, this time, instead of women. There was to be no "dramatizing of the transforming journey both the men and their nation took," as Rich expected.[49] One, however, does not expect Rich to know what competent critics of African American theatre must know – gained, somehow, in workshops not yet organized.

One should not, however, write off African American theatre. Hope lives through its coalitions. A close look at these notions of sharing show that theatre companies have in place the skeleton for their own renewal. The present structures show that the coalitions are capable of making individual organizations stable and disciplined. The New York Black Theatre Alliance, for example, was responsible for many organizations surviving for years on grits and guts. AUDELCO assisted its organizations in building the track records necessary for funders to fund. The African Continuum Theatre Coalition's Management Assistance Project was critical in giving its members an administrative infrastructure professionally capable of management, audience development, and fund-raising. Coalitions took the lead in training young people in the theatre arts in order to resupply the losses of talented people to film, television, and professional theatre. Duane Jones's project at the New York Black Theatre Alliance became the model for placing hundreds of student-artists with companies for paid, on-the-job training. Coalitions helped companies save and economize. It was the Chicago Black Theatre Alliance that synchronized diverse company philosophies so that the groups could better invest their time, money, and energy into community projects. The salvation of African American theatre, then, rests in strengthening coalitions. This might best be done through a national coalition of coalitions. Because the theatre, like the church, requires substantial incomes that are not terribly sensitive to economic recession, the national coalition would need to offer fiscal independence to the nonprofit African American theatre organizations. The National Endowment for African American Theatre, Inc. (NEAAT) answers these needs. Its raising and investing of $25 million over the next twenty-five years, in other words, will best provide continual and substantial financial support to hundreds of local African American theatre organizations. Whether or not the national African American community adopts this particular plan, however, is not absolutely essential. What is of critical importance is that a think tank of scholars, artists, business people, and community leaders soon devises some sort of long-term financial rescue plan to save theatre companies. These companies are too important repositories of African American life and history to lose. Although the very idea of such a massive plan is daunting to many, history shows that realizing such a goal within a quarter century is too important for us not even to try.

Conclusion

THE future of African American theatre, its history shows, swings by an intricately woven hanging rope, on which sway the classes, periods, and schools of drama, along with the theatre people, organizations and coalitions. So robust and dancing is this theatre that it invites forgetting. Hidden is James Hewlett, "de son of New York," who made handkerchief-waving women and ale-swigging men forget "de vinter of our discontent": Manuel Noah plaited the murder and mayhem in and of Mr. Brown's *Richard III* and his African Grove Theatre. Noah knew that without strong cables to hold up the laughter loads, African American theatre organizations would so often be born and die that there would not be certificates enough to record them, nor graves enough to bury them. If only the publisher and editor Beth Turner had been there to warn Mr. Brown:

This extraordinary assemblage must not be allowed to disperse before it tackles the increasingly serious problem of Black theatre. . . . While we all gather to enjoy each other, renew friendships, catch up on the news, revel in each other's achievements and celebrate surviving, . . . let us also take time to hone serious plans, to forge the alliances imperative to the continuation of Black theatre, to make commitments for cooperative actions and to set into place means of continuing our dialogue.[1]

Suppose that Mr. Brown had listened. He would have knitted tougher ropes, opening lines to the African American leadership in New York City. He would have sent invitations to join his theatre's empowered board to such notables as clergymen Bishop Varrick and Peter S. Williams, editors Samuel E. Cornish and John B. Russwurm, entrepreneur Phillip A. Bell, and politician Peter A. Jay. Convincing would have been his argument that Noah had tried to make the African Company a cultural weapon in his battle to preserve slavery, that Noah had, in other words, made clowns and dupes out of the African Grove community in order to defeat suffrage. Mr. Brown would have revealed the reason that Noah had plucked the actor Edwin Forrest from obscurity in order to make Forrest a star, the idol of the masses.[2] So persuasive would Mr. Brown have been that most of those he approached would have agreed to serve on his board, especially because he had agreed to give the board *full* ownership of the theatre's governance. The board, in its turn, would have invited such wealthy African Americans as James Forten, the Philadelphia sail manufacturer, to serve on it. The board also would have requested that Mr. Brown write *The Drama of King Shotaway*. So important was Brown's message, that the board would have wanted it spread throughout the states. The board, therefore, would have asked David Ruggles to join. Ruggles had national connections gained through running the Underground Railroad in New York, and he undoubtedly would have suggested that the board set up African Grove theatres in every major seaport. The board would have sent Mr. Brown to start theatres in Boston, Philadelphia, Baltimore, Washington, Richmond, Norfolk, Charleston, and New Orleans. The New York board too would have set up a National Cash Reserve Fund, which would oversee all theatres. Founding the national board of this reserve fund would have been David Walker of Boston, Bishop Richard Allen and philanthropist Robert Purvis of Philadelphia, journalist William Lloyd Garrison, and Underground Railroad leader Levi Coffin.

The national African Grove theatres would have been ready for Manuel Noah. When in 1849 he published editorials aimed at embarrassing the abolitionists into abandoning their cause, the African Grove would have produced plays to accompany such abolitionist orators as William Wells Brown. Together they would have cut apart Noah's argument. Ira Aldridge would have performed at these rallies. He would have traveled to African Grove theatres from Boston to Fort Negro, Florida – battling Noah's minstrelsy and vaudeville. Charles Hicks's companies, too, would have traveled under the auspices of the African Grove, making fun of funmakers who tried to debase African Americans. The Hyers Sisters would have opened African Grove theatres in California, taking serious theatre throughout the west and the midwest. Jesse Shipp would have managed international tours of William Wells Brown's *Escape; or, A Leap for Freedom,* starring Bert Williams, George Walker, Ida Anderson, and Laura Bowman. Bob Cole would have headed the African Grove Theatre School and would have written musical hits celebrating such abolitionists as Charles Lenox Remond (the first African American professional antislavery lecturer), Henry Highland Garnet, Martin R. Delany, Sojourner Truth, Harriet Tubman, and Frederick Douglass. These shows would have traveled to most African American communities, keeping heritage alive. The New York African Grove Theatre would have produced in 1913 William E. B. DuBois's *Star of Ethiopia.* When in 1916 Alain Locke called for the staging of *real* African American lifestyles – regardless of what "our traditional enemies" might think – the Washington, D.C., African Grove would have regarded it as more than just philosophic discourse on the nature of Truth and Beauty. The African Grove by then would have been secure enough to accept Art-Theatre. Because there would have been less national paranoia about Noah's negative stereotypes, the theatres would have produced the Locke school playwrights. The characters in the musical comedies would have been welcomed by the public, as would those in Langston Hughes's *Little Ham* and Arna Bontemps's *St Louis Woman*. People would have received them for what they were – comical looks at a people, not looks at a comical people. The public would have accepted too each class of drama, in witnessing of the ever-changing needs and expectations of the people: from Randolph Edmonds's *Bad Man* and Willis Richardson's *Compromise* to the play fighting for breath in the head of the latest would-be playwright.

Thanks to Mr. Brown's acting on Beth Turner's warning, there would have been no forty-six-year silence in Art-Theatre (between the *Richard III* of Mr. Brown and the minstrelsy of Charles Hicks); no ninety-year absence of Protest theatre (from Brown's *Drama of King Shotaway* to DuBois's *Star of Ethiopia*); no 87 percent failure rate of 1960s organizations; and no dependence on disposable income. It would have been second nature for theatre organizations to shore up their internal structures, to tie themselves tightly to their communities, and to locate substantial subsidies consistently. Carefully composed, recruited, selected, and oriented boards would have been a given. Thanks to Mr. Brown's national financing plan, African American theatre history would have had no record of any hanging-rope theatre organizations to disgrace so noble a people. African American theatre would be flourishing.

APPENDIX A

❧

Goals for a Theatre Criticism Workshop

D EVELOPING a group of creditable critics in African American theatre requires workshops that aim to satisfy the following broad goals:

1. To develop an understanding of and respect for the schools, periods, and classes of African American drama;
2. To cultivate the ability to analyze a script;
3. To generate basic knowledge about the principles of directing, acting, scene design, costume design, lighting design, and sound design;
4. To improve the skills needed to research the performance and critical histories of a play, as well as the political, socioeconomic, and historical issues addressed; and
5. To enhance writing skills.

APPENDIX B

New Theatre
Organizational
Structure

I n order to benefit from a broader base of support that is integral to an African American theatre organization, the companies might reorganize themselves so that they were more like church organizations.

1. An empowered board of directors would be analogous to the church's board of trustees;
2. The artistic director would be similar to the minister;
3. The management and the artistic staffs would become the board of deacons; and
4. The subscribers would be the church's members.

FUNCTIONS AND ROLES

All theatre segments would function as they presently do, except for the audiences, which would subscribe to services, not only to plays. The theatre would be a referral center for one-stop social services. The theatre would connect neighborhoods to such services as day care, after-school care, and senior citizens' care. There could be tutoring, victim counseling, and family planning, as well as programs to prevent the abuse of women and children. Support groups could be organized for recovering substance abusers. The theatre would be the meeting house for any neighborhood clubs and groups that wished to meet there.

THE PERFORMANCE SERVICE

Membership would entitle subscribers not only to all social services, but also to a Performance Service (PS). The PS would be a secular ceremony patterned somewhat after the Kuumba Workshop's and the National Black Theatre's rituals. PS would consist of seven parts: Devotion, Invitation, Offertory, Silence, Performance, Discussion, and Closing.

DEVOTION

Members would lead and control the Devotion, which would last no longer than fifteen or twenty minutes. They would sing hymns, popular songs, and raps; play musical instruments; recite poems, sayings, testimonies, and prayers; and do popular dances and shouts.

THE INVITATION

During the Invitation, new members would be solicited. As new members came to the front to join, the artistic director would announce them, assign them to a ward, ask their committee assignment preferences, and introduce them to the ward trustee. This procedure would allow new members to make public commitments. The membership would be divided into wards. Each ward's name would correspond to the day of the week and time of day on which that particular PS would meet: Saturday-Three would meet on Saturdays as three o'clock. The ward leader would be an elected trustee, who collected and accounted for membership dues and contributions. The trustees would represent ward interests on the board of directors.

THE OFFERTORY

After the orientation of each new member during the Invitation, the artistic director or a designee would conduct the Offertory. Each ward trustee would publicly announce the contributors' names and the amounts or items he or she had collected. Members without money could donate food and clothing or volunteer time and expertise. Following trustee reports, the Public Offertory would permit members and guests to walk to the front of the theatre and announce additional offerings. This would instill pride in giving.

THE SILENCE

Following the Offertory, the artistic director would lead a one- or two-minute period of Silence. The Silence would prepare the membership for the Performance.

THE PERFORMANCE

The Performance would be a professionally mounted production.

THE DISCUSSION

The Discussion, a forty-five minute question-and-answer-and-debate session on the issues raised in the play, would follow the

Performance. Highly respected authorities on the issues would lead the Discussion.

THE BENEDICTION

After the Discussion, a minister would close the PS with the benison.

APPENDIX C

The National Endowment for African American Theatre, Inc.

PURPOSE

The purpose of the National Endowment for African American Theatre (NEAAT) is to support community, educational, regional, and touring theatres with matching grants. These organizations must be not-for-profit, and they must perform plays that deal principally with the African and the African American experiences.

JUSTIFICATION

All theatre organizations experience cyclical cash flow crises, brought on mainly by funding cuts resulting from national economic recessions. Most African American theatres, unfortunately, fold during these cycles. This historic pattern will stop only if the national African American theatre community itself – consisting of more than two hundred fifty organizations – structures assistance that is not totally dependent on national funders and disposable family incomes.

MEANS

NEAAT will raise and invest $25 million over the next quarter century. The interest from the investment will be used to match funding for endowments, planning grants, and production budgets.

PROCEDURES AND ACTIVITIES

Four American American theatre summits will be called.

1. The Planning Summit will consist of the artistic directors and chairs of the boards of directors of influential theatre organizations from throughout the United States.

   a. The purposes of the Planning Summit are to organize and incorporate NEAAT; to write the by-laws for NEAAT; to write guidelines for grant distribution; and to plan the Economic Summit, the Politics and Education Summit, and the Religion, Entertainment, and Sports Summit.

   b. Among the questions to be considered in organizing NEAAT are those concerning membership criteria:

   (1) Should the theatre organization be required to have a fully empowered board of directors (i.e., chooses it members, regulates all monetary matters, provides adequate resources, develops community resources, and hires the artistic director, as well as withdraws from day-to-day operations)?

   (2) Should the organization have produced at least four plays per season for the last three consecutive seasons preceding the application?

(3) Should the company be required to establish an endowment?

(4) Should the company be required to pay annual NEAAT dues of 1 percent of its annual gross earnings?

(5) Should the organization be required to invest at least 10 percent of any NEAAT grant into the theatre's endowment?

(6) Should the theatre be obligated to volunteer annually two hundred NEAAT-approved and agency-verified hours to the public school system, the interdenominational ministerial association, the minority business association, a senior citizens' agency, or a community group chosen by the local theatre?

(7) Should the theatre be required to donate 10 percent of the tickets for each show to low-income people?

(8) Should the organization be compelled to make its space available free to community organizations?

c. Questions concerning the distribution of grants might include the following:

(1) To what extent should the amount of the last payment the theatre made into its endowment determine the amount of the NEAAT grant?

(2) To what degree should the total number of paid admissions for the last season influence the NEAAT formula?

(3) How should the number of volunteer hours of community service govern the formula?

(4) What role should the evaluations of community service reports from the community agencies play in deciding the amount of grant?

(5) How should the evaluation of performances by professional critics and audience responses be included in the amount of the grant?

(6) To what extent should the geographical spread of grants determine recipients?

(7) How many consecutive grants should a theatre be allowed?

(8) What contingencies should temporarily suspend certain criteria?

d. Among the questions to be considered for planning the summits are

(1) What specific goals and issues are to be addressed?

    (2) Based on the goals and issues, which experts should be invited?

    (3) What should be the criteria for evaluating each summit?

2. The Economic Summit will consist of corporate executives, entertainment lawyers, investment bankers, brokers, chief executive officers, funders, and theatre executives.

  a. The purpose of the Economic Summit is to develop detailed plans, strategies, and timetables for raising, investing, and managing $25 million.

  b. Among the questions to be considered are

    (1) How can NEAAT theatres best help local corporations, merchants associations, and chambers of commerce?

    (2) How best can NEAAT theatres ensure that their audiences patronize all business contributors to NEAAT?

    (3) How can corporate and private funders be persuaded to change their policies against funding theatre endowments?

    (4) Which senators and representatives can be approached about changing public policy to permit the funding of theatre endowments by government agencies?

    (5) By which means should NEAAT get placed into the annual budgets of major corporations?

    (6) What specifically should be the criteria for developing an investment portfolio?

    (7) What safeguards should be instituted to guard against theft, fraud, and mismanagement?

    (8) What plan of action should be utilized to begin raising funds?

3. The Politics and Education Summit will consist of members of (or representatives from) the Congressional Black Caucus (CBC), as well as officials of national, state, and local governments, educational systems, and organizations.

  a. The purposes of this summit are to prioritize the needs to be served by the theatre organizations, and to develop plans for soliciting contributions for NEAAT from the groups represented.

  b. Among the questions to be considered are

    (1) How can local theatre organizations best assist local political and educational organizations?

    (2) How can prominent theatre companies help the Congressional Black Caucus (CBC), the National Association for Equal Op-

portunity in Higher Education (NAFEO), the National Education Association (NEA), and the American Federation of Teachers (AFT)?

(3) How can the CBC best assist NEAAT in getting public funds?

(4) How can other national, state, and local public officials best help NEAAT to lobby their agencies for funds?

(5) To what extent can local theatre organizations help public school systems with their theatre programs?

(6) How best can theatre companies help theatre arts departments in the Historically Black Colleges and Universities (HBCU)?

(7) What plan of action should be utilized by the CBC, NAFEO, NEA, and AFT to help NEAAT raise funds?

4. The Religion, Entertainment, and Sports Summit will consist of representatives from the national church organizations; from leading entertainers, producers, and promoters; and from sport figures and club owners.

a. The purposes of this summit are to prioritize the needs to be served by theatre organizations, and to develop plans for soliciting contributions for NEAAT from the groups represented.

b. Among the questions to be considered are

(1) How can the theatre help the church to enhance the theatricality of its services and to professionalize the performances of its seasonal pageants?

(2) How can the church help dramatists and performers "witness" God's love and mercy in every performance?

(3) How can the church assist the theatre in understanding the importance of stimulating the audience's imagination by letting some un-Christian representations occur offstage?

(4) How might the theatre aid the church to appreciate that artists must have complete artistic freedom in order to create?

(5) How can the church help the theatre to appreciate the abuse suffered by religious people through the representation of decadence, even when it is used to encourage morality?

(6) How can the theatre help the church in its fund drives?

(7) How can the church help NEAAT in its fund raising?

(8) In what ways can theatre assist in marketing for entertainers and sports figures?

(9) How can entertainers and owners be persuaded to hold benefits for NEAAT?

EVALUATION

Each summit will have to measure the extent to which it has set
realistic and specific goals, made viable plans for realizing the
goals, developed suitable action plans, and met planned deadlines.

Notes

INTRODUCTION

1. Marvin Carlson, *Theories of the Theatre: A Historical and Critical Survey, from the Greeks to the Present* (Ithaca. N.Y.: Cornell University Press, 1984), 9.
2. W. E. B. DuBois, "The Drama among Black Folk," *Crisis*, August 1916, 11.
3. Philip S. Foner, ed., *W. E. B. DuBois Speaks: Speeches and Addresses, 1890–1919* (New York: Pathfinder Press, 1970), 227.
4. Johnny Washington, *Alain Locke and Philosophy: A Quest for Cultural Pluralism* (New York: Greenwood Press, 1986), 169.
5. Alain Locke, "Steps toward the Negro Theatre," *Crisis,* December 1922, 66–8.
6. Alain Locke, "Enter the New Negro," *Survey,* 1 March 1925, 631–4.
7. W. E. B. DuBois, "Criteria of Negro Art," in *The Seventh Son: The Thought and Writings of W. E. B. DuBois*, vol. 2, ed. Julius Lester (New York: Vintage Books, 1971), 319.

237

8. There is no irrefutable evidence that confirms "William" as Mr. Brown's first name. Historians, in fact, have also suggested "James" and "Henry." Professor Fannin S. Belcher of West Virginia State College discovered "James" in the 1820 and 1821 directories of New York City. Omanii Abdullah used "Henry" in James V. Hatch and Omanii Abdullah's *Black Playwrights, 1823–1977. Annotated Bibliography of Plays* (1977). Abdullah did not cite his source. Jonathan Dewberry discovered "William" in the 1823 Record of Assessments for New York City's 8th Ward. Dewberry, "The African Grove Theatre and Company," *Black American Literature Forum* 16 (Winter 1982):129.

9. Dixon Ryan Fox, "The Negro Vote in Old New York," *Political Science Quarterly* 32 (1917):257.

10. Ibid., 255.

11. Dixon Ryan Fox, *The Decline of Aristocracy in the Politics of New York* (New York: Harper & Row, 1965), 269.

12. Manuel Noah, "Africans," *National Advocate*, 3 August 1821, 2.

13. Fox, "The Negro Vote," 259.

14. Noah, "Africans," 2.

15. Noah, review of *Richard III*, *National Advocate*, 21 September 1821, 1.

16. *National Advocate*, 25 September 1821, 2.

17. Noah to William Dunlap, dated 11 July 1832; in *A History of the American Theatre*, vol. 2, (New York, 1832; reprint, New York: Burt Franklin, 1963), 383.

18. *Memoir and Theatrical Career of Ira Aldridge, the African Roscious*, (1849), 11.

19. Stephen Price's motivation for sabotaging Mr. Brown's productions was economic. From his "capacious" segregated galleries for African Americans and prostitutes, Price netted approximately nine hundred dollars per week. (Price's gallery for African Americans held approximately seven hundred fifty people. If the gallery were only 80 percent filled – a quite conservative estimate – Price, at a ticket cost of twenty-five cents per person, would have made nine hundred dollars for each six-performance week.) The galleries met Price's costs, which were estimated from Dunlap's budget at the Park in 1798. (A. M. Nagler, *A Source Book in Theatrical History* [New York: Dover, 1959], 524). Price's profit came from the orchestra and the three tiers of fourteen boxes each. When Brown emptied the African American gallery, as well as some of the boxes, he cut tremendously Price's profits. Added to this was that trends in theatre changed in 1822 from Shakespeare to circus, which forced Price literally to steal

a rival circus by convincing its owner that Price himself planned to open an even larger circus on Broadway. Price, therefore, whom even Macready called a "despised cut-throat," had ample reason to seek to destroy Brown's African Grove Theatre.

20. *National Advocate,* 27 October 1821, 2.

21. Leo H. Hirsch, Jr., "The Negro in New York, 1783 to 1865," *Journal of Negro History* 16 (October 1931):420.

22. Mr. Brown advertised on a playbill that the play was "Founded on facts taken from the insurrection of the Caravs in the Island of St. Vincent / Written from experience by Mr. Brown." Whereas Carlton W. and Barbara J. Molette say that they do not believe Brown's claim, there is ample circumstantial evidence that Brown might have been a combatant in the 1795 uprising (Carlton W. and Barbara J. Molette, *Black Theater: Premise and Presentation* [Bristol, Ind.: Wyndham Hall Press, 1986], 29). (*a*) Brown was the right age. Dr. James McCune Smith has said that Mr. Brown was a tall black man who retired as a steward in 1816. According to the "Passenger Lists" at the National Archives, stewards retired when they are around age forty-seven. Brown, then, was probably born around 1769. This would have made him twenty-six years old when the uprising started. (*b*) For the title of his play, *The Drama of King Shotaway,* Brown anglicized the French "Chatoyer," which was the name of the Paramount Chief of the Garifuna on St. Vincent's. (*c*) Brown was so familiar with the participants in the uprising that he named his characters after them: According to I. E. Kirby and C. I. Martin's *The Rise and Fall of the Black Caribs,* (Caracas, 1985), Prince DuValle in the play was the name of Chatoyer's brother and field marshal; Queen Margaretta and Queen Caroline in the play were the names of two of Chatoyer's five wives (Kirby and Martin, 62–3). (*d*) Had Brown wished to base his play on any other Caribbean uprising, he could have chosen from among ten during the very same period. He evidently chose this particular uprising because, as he advertised, he had first-hand knowledge about it. Brown probably paid homage to the Paramount Chief Joseph Chatoyer, whom Brown called "King," because everybody called the Park Theater's owner Stephen Price "King Stephen." Thus *The Drama of King Shotaway* probably is telling how Chatoyer masterminded the March 14, 1795, capture of a British fort, and during which he replaced the British flag with a French flag. According to Kirby and Martin, the British recaptured the fort that night in a surprise attack, in which Chatoyer was killed (85–7). Because Stephen Price was such an Anglophile – he had managed Covent Garden

Theatre – Brown's having Chatoyer (i.e., Brown himself) slay the British was a way for him to avenge through drama the troubles that Price had caused Brown.

23. Although there are reports of Mr. Brown's starting a theatre company in Albany, New York, in December 1823, there is no proof. A thorough search of all contemporary newspapers in Albany unearthed only one mention of a Mr. Brown, in a parade. Because Brown was so good as publicizing his company in New York City, it would be difficult to imagine that he would not have been able to generate similar coverage in Albany. This raises serious doubts about a Brown theatre in Albany.

24. Dr. James McCune Smith, "Ira Aldridge," *Anglo-African Magazine*, January 1860, 27.

25. Ibid.

26. Bernard Hewitt, " 'King Stephen' of the Park and Drury Lane," in *The Theatrical Manager in England and America*, ed. Joseph W. Donohue, Jr. (Princeton, N.J.: Princeton University Press, 1971), 108–9.

1. THE BLACK EXPERIENCE SCHOOL OF DRAMA

1. Manuel Noah, "Africans," *National Advocate*, 3 August 1821, 2.

2. Review of *Richard III*, *American*, 10 January 1822, 2.

3. Ibid.

4. Ibid.

5. Noah, review of *Richard III*, *National Advocate*, 21 September 1821, 2.

6. Ibid.

7. Jonathan D. Sarna, *Jacksonian Jew; The Two Worlds of Mordecai Noah* (New York: Holmes & Meier Publishers, 1981), 50.

8. A measure of how well Edwin Forrest perfected the southern Negro character appeared in a newspaper review of his role as Ruban. After blackening himself and rigging his costume, Forrest could not find anyone to play his wife, a nonspeaking role designed for comic relief. Forrest persuaded his "African washerwoman," who lived nearby, to play the role: "I want you to go on the stage with me and play my wife," said Forrest. The astonished and incredulous washerwoman responded, "De debbil you does." "Yes, Dinah, but hurry along, or we shall be late," said Forrest. So they hastened arm-in-arm to the theatre and arrived just in time. "The appearance of the darkies was greeted with loud applause, and when Ruban began to let out the regular cuff, as he always could, in his most irresistible way, with wide and suddenly breaking inflection of voice, breathing guffaws, and

convulsive doubleshuffle, the enthusiasm of the audience reached the highest pitch" (William Rounseville Alger, *Edwin Forrest, the American Tragedian* [New York, 1877], 108–9).

9. Alain Locke, "The Negro and the American Stage," in *Anthology of the American Negro in the Theatre: A Critical Approach*, ed. Lindsay Patterson (New York: Publishers Company, 1968), 21–22.

10. Tom Fletcher, *100 Years of the Negro in Show Business* (New York: Burdge & Company, 1954), xvii.

11. Sterling Brown, *Negro Poetry and Drama* (Washington, D.C.: Associates in Negro Folk Education, 1937; New York: Atheneum, 1969), 140.

12. William E. B. DuBois, "The Colored Audience," in *The Seventh Son: The Thought and Writings of W. E. B. DuBois*, vol 2, ed. Julius Lester (New York: Vintage Books, 1971), 52.

13. Ibid.

14. DuBois asked Cole to write Protest musicals after seeing a performance of Cole and J. Rosamond Johnson's *The Red Moon* (1909). The play tells the story of the cooperation between Native Americans and African Americans to rescue a woman's bi-racial daughter, who is kidnapped by her irresponsible Native American father. DuBois undoubtedly saw the possibilities of further highlighting the important historical links between the two oppressed peoples.

15. H. D. Albright, William P. Halstead, and Lee Mitchell, *Principles of Theatre Art* (Atlanta: Houghton Mifflin, 1968), 58.

16. Robert C. Toll, *Blacking Up: The Minstrel Show in Nineteenth-Century America* (New York: Oxford University Press, 1974), 36.

17. Mabel Rowland, ed., *Bert Williams: Son of Laughter* (New York: English Crafters, 1923; reprint, New York: Negro Universities Press/Greenwood Publishing, 1969), 116–7.

18. Allen Woll, *Black Musical Theatre: From "Coontown" to "Dreamgirls"* (Baton Rouge: Louisiana State University Press, 1989), 12.

19. Alain Locke, "Max Rheinhardt Reads the Negro's Dramatic Horoscope," *Opportunity*, May 1924, 145.

20. Alain Locke, "The Negro in the American Theater," in *Theatre: Essays in the Arts of the Theatre*, ed. Edith J. R. Isaac (Boston: Little Brown, 1927), 290–303.

21. Alain Locke, *The Negro and His Music* (Washington, D.C.: Associates in Negro Folk Education, 1936; reprint, New York: Arno Press and The New York Times, 1969), 61.

22. James Weldon Johnson, *Black Manhattan* (New York: Knopf, 1930; reprint, New York: Atheneum, 1969), 98.

23. William E. B. DuBois, "The Negro and the American States," in *The Seventh Son*, 2:311.

24. Alain Locke, ed. *The New Negro* (New York: Albert & Charles Boni, 1925; reprint, New York: Atheneum, 1969), 10.

25. Ibid.

26. DuBois, "The Negro and the American Stage," 2:311.

27. Ibid.

28. Willis Richardson's *The Chip Woman's Fortune* was the first serious play by an African American to appear on Broadway. It was part of a May 15, 1923, premiere of a triple bill by the Ethiopian Art Players of Chicago. Locke so admired the play and the Players that he named his school "Art-Theatre," and he viewed the Players' style as the new wave of African American theatre.

29. Brown, *Negro Poetry and Drama*, 123.

30. Willis Richardson, *House of Sham*, in *Plays and Pageants from the Life of the Negro*, ed. Willis Richardson (Washington, D.C.: Associated Publishers, 1930), 286.

31. Albright, et al., *Principles of Theatre Art*, 52.

32. Locke, "Youth Speaks," *Survey*, March 1925, 660.

33. Evidence of the success of *Don't You Want to Be Free?* was its 135 performances in New York, along with its successful runs in Los Angeles and Chicago. New York audiences, according to Hughes biographer Arnold Rampersad, "wept, complained, fought back, sang mournfully and joyfully, endured, and prevailed together, all in one intense hour or so. On the opening night of April 21, an overflow crowd, at the end of the play, rose as one. Cries for the author brought a beaming Langston to the stage to renew his promise of a Harlem repertory theatre: 'We want to build a theater for you folks, a theater for which you may write, in which you may act. This is your theatre.' " (*The Life of Langston Hughes*, vol. 1 [New York: Oxford University Press, 1986], 359).

34. Langston Hughes, *I Wonder as I Wander: An Autobiographical Journey* (New York: Hill & Wang, 1956), 199–200.

35. Charles H. Nichols, ed., *Arna Bontemps–Langston Hughes Letters: 1925–1967* (New York: Dodd, Mead & Co., 1980), 70.

36. Rose McClendon, fearing her own inexperience as a director, recommended that Flanagan appoint John Houseman director. Although Houseman was himself not a racist, he nevertheless could not persuade the play-selecting National Service Bureau to produce expressionistic indictments of racism. That the FTP eventually produced Theodore Brown's *Natural Man* (1940) and J. Augustus Smith and

Peter Morell's *Turpentine* (1936) did not compensate for the many plays submitted but ignored. As a result, the FTP did not have the expected impact on the development of African American play writing.

37. Doris E. Abramson, *Negro Playwrights in the American Theatre, 1925–59* (New York: Columbia University Press, 1969), 198.
38. Rowland, *Bert Williams*, 217–18.
39. Ibid.
40. Jessie Fauset, "The Gift of Laughter," in *Anthology of the American Negro in the Theatre*, 34–5.
41. Brown, *Negro Poetry and Drama*, 140.
42. Fauset, "The Gift of Laughter," 34–5.
43. DuBois, "The Negro and the American Stage," 2:311.
44. Locke, "Negro Youth Speaks," in *The New Negro*, 47.
45. Margaret B. Wilkerson, "*A Raisin in the Sun* and the Afro-American Folk Tradition" (Paper delivered at the Third National Conference on African American Theatre, Baltimore, Md., 10 April 1986), 4.
46. Ibid.
47. As an example of the popularity of Binding Relationship plays, *A Raisin in the Sun* was still in 1986, according to Margaret Wilkerson, probably the most-produced play by an African American writer. This class of drama did not lose its popularity until the fifth period (1990), when the Flow class made up almost fifty percent of Black Experience drama.
48. A. Clifton Lamb, "Acceptance Speech for The Mr. Brown Award" (Second Annual National Conference on African American Theatre, Baltimore, Md., 18 April 1985), 1.
49. S. Randolph Edmonds, then a professor of English at Morgan College, founded the Intercollegiate Theatre Association (ITA) in 1930. The founding colleges, known as the "Negro Ivy League," were Howard, Morgan, Hampton, Virginia Union, and Virginia State.
50. Wilkerson, "*A Raisin in the Sun* and the Afro-American Folk Tradition," 4.
51. S. Randolph Edmonds founded in 1936 the Southern (later, the National) Association of Dramatic and Speech Arts (NADSA) at Southern University in Baton Rouge, La. NADSA, which still meets each April, is the oldest American theatre organization.
52. Locke, "The Negro and the American Stage," 21.
53. Locke, "Negro Youth Speaks," 51.
54. Ibid.
55. Sterling Brown singled out Ethel Waters' singing "Supper Time" in Irving Berlin's *As Thousands Cheer* (1933) as a "startling and effective

innovation" among musicals that attached protest in order to gain social relevance (*Negro Poetry and Drama*, 136–7).

56. DuBois to Dr. Jesse Edward Moorland and to Abram L. Harris, in
The Correspondence of W. E. B. DuBois, ed. Herbert Aptheker (Amherst: University of Massachusetts Free Press, 1973), 2:352, 470.

57. Herbert Aptheker, ed., *Against Racism: Unpublished Essays, Papers, Addresses, 1887–1961, by W. E. B. DuBois* (Amherst: University of Massachusetts Press, 1985), 103–4.

58. Ibid.

59. DuBois to Dr. Jesse Edward Moorland, in *Correspondence of DuBois*,
2:352.

60. Walter White, *A Man Called White* (New York: Viking Press, 1948),
338.

61. Ibid., 338–9.

62. "Negro Press' Gripe on New Colored Shows Cues Lena Horne 'St.
Loo' Nix," *Variety*, 19 September 1945, 1.

63. White, *A Man Called White*, 339.

64. Nichols, *Arna Bontemps–Langston Hughes Letters*, 192.

65. Ibid., 188.

66. Ibid.

67. Ibid., 180–1.

68. Ibid., 194.

69. Darwin T. Turner, "Langston Hughes as Playwright," in *Langston
Hughes/Black Genius: A Critical Evaluation*, ed. Therman B. O'Daniel
(New York: Morrow, 1971), 86.

70. Rampersad, *The Life of Langston Hughes*, vol. *1*, 326.

71. Locke, "Negro Youth Speaks," 48.

72. Brown, *Negro Poetry and Drama*, 121.

73. Oscar C. Brockett, *History of the Theatre* (Boston: Allyn & Bacon,
1987), 564.

74. Locke, "Negro Youth Speaks," 53.

75. Ibid.

76. Locke, *The New Negro*, 11.

77. Cited in Dick Brukenfeld, review of *House Party*, *Village Voice*, 1 November 1973, 60.

78. Ed Bullins, *The Theme Is Blackness* (New York: Morrow, 1973), 9.

79. Helen Armstead Johnson, "Playwrights, Audiences and Critics," *Negro Digest*, April 1970, 18.

80. William Branch's *A Wreath for Udomo* is based on Peter Abraham's
1956 novel of the same name. Abraham as recently as 1990 denied
Branch the rights to publish the play. The script can be found in both

the Howard University Library and the Schomburg Collection at the New York City Public Library.

81. Amiri Baraka, "The Descent of Charlie Fuller into Pulitzer Land and the Need for African-American Institutions," *Black American Literature Forum* 17, (Summer 1983):51.

82. Beth Turner, "Charles Fuller: Black Pride, Integrity, Success," *Black Masks*, September/October 1987, 11.

83. Ibid.

84. Barbara T. Christian, *Black Feminist Criticism: Perspectives on Black Women Writers* (New York: Pergamon Press, 1985), 221.

85. Audre Lorde, "My Words Will Be There," in *Black Women Writers (1950–1980): A Critical Evaluation*, ed. Mari Evans (New York: Anchor Press/Doubleday, 1984), 265.

86. Ibid.

87. Ibid.

88. Ibid., 263.

89. Ibid.

90. Jerome Brooks, "In the Name of the Father: The Poetry of Audre Lorde," in *Black Women Writers*, 270.

91. Ibid., 274–5.

92. Ibid.

93. Paula Giddings, "Nikki Giovanni: Taking a Chance on Feeling," in *Black Women Writers*, 215.

94. Christian, *Black Feminist Criticism*, 33.

95. Ibid., 52.

96. Ibid.

97. Ibid., 75.

98. Ibid., 77.

99. Lorde, "My Words Will Be There," 266.

100. Ibid.

101. Ibid.

102. Eugenia Collier, "The Closing of the Circle: Movement from Division to Wholeness in Paule Marshall's Fiction," in *Black Women Writers*, 313.

103. Locke, "The Negro and the American Stage," 21.

104. Allen Woll, *Black Musical Theatre: From "Coontown" to "Dreamgirls"* (Baton Rouge: Louisiana State University Press, 1989), 271.

105. Stephen Holden, review of *Yesterdays*, *New York Times*, 8 October 1990, B-3.

106. Frank Rich, review of *Once on This Island*, *New York Times*, 19 October 1990, B-3.

107. Laurence Holder, *Zora,* in *New Plays for the Black Theatre,* ed. Woodie King, Jr. (Chicago: Third World Press, 1989), 139.

108. Rosemary L. Bray, "An Unpredictable Playwright Reverses Himself," *New York Times,* 15 April 1990, H-7; John J. O'Connor, review of "Jammin': Jelly Roll Morton on Broadway," *New York Times,* 2 November 1992, B-2.

109. Cited in John C. Thorpe, "Behind the Wings of the *Colored Museum,"* *Black Masks,* January/February 1986, 3.

110. Cited in O'Connor, review of "Jammin'."

111. National Ad Hoc Committee to End Crimes against Paul Robeson, *A Statement of Conscience: The Dimensions of Paul Robeson and the Crimes against Him* (New York: Black Theology Project, 1978).

112. Statement released by Paul Robeson, Jr.

113. National Ad Hoc Committee, *Statement of Conscience.*

114. Ibid.

115. Roger P. Ross (public affairs officer), "USIE: Request for Special Story on Paul Robeson," American Consul, Accra, Ghana, 9 January, 1951.

116. C. Gerald Fraser, "33 Playwrights Protest 'Censure' of *Robeson,"* *New York Times,* 18 May 1978, C-20.

117. Ntozake Shange, *For Colored Girls Who Have Considered Suicide When the Rainbow Is Enuf* (New York: Macmillan, 1977), 59–63.

118. P. J. Gibson, "George Houston Bass: Artist, Scholar, Visionary," *Black Masks,* December/January 1991, 5.

119. *The Piano Lesson* (New York: Dutton, 1990), front flap.

120. August Wilson, *Two Trains Running, Theatre* 21 (Winter 1990–1):46.

121. August Wilson, *Joe Turner's Come and Gone* (New York: New American Library, 1988), 68–9.

122. August Wilson, *Fences* (New York: New American Library, 1986), 21.

123. Wilson, *Two Trains Running,* 68.

124. Wilson, *The Piano Lesson,* 101.

125. August Wilson, *Joe Turner's Come and Gone,* 52.

126. August Wilson, *Ma Rainey's Black Bottom* (New York: New American Library, 1981), 70.

127. Sandra G. Shannon, "Lloyd Richards: From Lorraine Hansberry to August Wilson: An Interview," *Callaloo* 14 (Winter 1991):132.

128. For information on jazz ensembles, I am indebted to saxophonist Antonio Zamora, jazz-group leader and director of the Purdue University Black Cultural Center, telephone interview, 28 March 1991.

129. Wilson, foreword to *Two Trains Running,* 42.

130. Nelson George, "Native Son," *Village Voice,* 4 September 1990, 22.
131. Patti Hartigan, "The Richards Mystique," *American Theatre,* July/August 1991, 15.
132. Wilson, *Two Trains Running,* 52.
133. King, *New Plays for the Black Theatre,* 1.
134. Ibid.
135. Albright et al., *Principles of Theatre Art,* 56.
136. Ed Bullins's *Salaam, Huey Newton, Salaam* is taken from Marvin X's work-in-progress, "Autobiography of a North American Afrikan."
137. Brockett, *History of the Theatre,* 568.
138. Ibid.
139. Brown, *Negro Poetry and Drama,* 123.

2. THE BLACK ARTS SCHOOL OF DRAMA

1. DuBois's budget for the New York production of *Star of Ethiopia* was six thousand dollars. DuBois contributed five hundred. Mrs. Amy Spingarn contributed the balance ("Budget," DuBois Collection, Library of Congress, Washington, D.C. [hereafter, DuBois Collection]).
2. DuBois surrounded himself with talented people. For his pageant and his Krigwa Players, he developed an artistic "cabinet," which included Charles Burroughs as director and Louise Latimer as coordinator, along with Frank L. Horne and Zora Neale Hurston as writers. DuBois chose Burroughs not only because he had been DuBois's student at Wilberforce, but because Burroughs, DuBois thought, was "one of the most gifted dramatic exponents and critics of any color" (DuBois to the sponsors of *Star of Ethiopia,* DuBois Collection). Burroughs did indeed "know what he was doing," as DuBois wrote to a colleague, because Burroughs had been well-trained. After graduating from the Boston School of Expression, Burroughs for years gave lectures and Shakespeare readings for the New York City Board of Education. He directed all of DuBois's shows. With Burroughs's assistance, DuBois by 1925 earned enough credit to warrant his own important place in the development of African American theatre.
3. DuBois, *"The Star of Ethiopia," Crisis,* August 1916, 339–41.
4. Ibid.
5. "Newsclippings," DuBois Collection.
6. Alain Locke, "Steps toward the Negro Theatre," *Crisis,* December 1922, 67.

7. Ibid.
8. Locke to Archibald Grimke, undated, Alain Locke Papers, the Moorland-Spingarn Research Center, Howard University, Washington, D.C.
9. Philip S. Foner, ed., *W. E. B. DuBois Speaks: Speeches and Addresses, 1890–1919* (New York: Pathfinder Press, 1970), 229.
10. "Star of Ethiopia," DuBois Collection.
11. DuBois, "The Drama among Black Folk," *Crisis*, August 1916, 171.
12. Ibid.
13. DuBois, "Criteria of Negro Art," in *The Seventh Son: The Thought and Writings of W. E. B. DuBois*, vol. 2, ed. Julius Lester (New York: Vantage Books, 1971), 319.
14. DuBois, "The African Roots of War," in *The Seventh Son*, 1:452.
15. Alain Locke, "The Legacy of the Ancestral Arts," in *The New Negro*, ed. Alain Locke (New York: Albert & Charles Boni, 1925; reprint, New York: Atheneum, 1969), 254.
16. Maud Cuney-Hare, *Antar of Araby*, in *Plays and Pageants from the Life of the Negro*, ed. Willis Richardson (Washington, D.C.: Associated Publishers, 1930), 38–9.
17. DuBois, "Criteria of Negro Art," 2:317.
18. Ibid.
19. "Crisis Magazine," DuBois collection.
20. Langston Hughes, "Southern Gentlemen, White Prostitutes, Mill-Owners, and Negroes," in *Good Morning Revolution: Uncollected Social Protest Writings by Langston Hughes*, ed. Faith Berry (New York: Lawrence Hill & Co. 1973), 49.
21. Ibid.
22. Ibid.
23. Ibid.
24. Ibid.
25. VeVe Clark, "Restaging Langston Hughes's *Scottsboro Limited:* An Interview with Amiri Baraka," *Black Scholar*, July–August 1979, 62–9. For one of several of Hughes's disavowals of being a Communist, see Langston Hughes, "My Adventures as a Social Poet," in *Good Morning Revolution*, 139.
26. Hughes to Arna Bontemps, dated V-J Day, in *Arna Bontemps–Langston Hughes Letters: 1925–1967* ed. Charles H. Nichols (New York: Dodd, Mead & Co., 1980), 183.
27. Many of Hughes's early beliefs that the Soviet Union was a raceless and classless society were refuted by Robert Robinson. His accounts, as well as the events in 1990, made Communism appear racist and

elitist. See Robert Robinson, *Black on Red: My 44 Years inside the Soviet Union* (Washington, D.C.: Acroplis Books, 1988).

28. Hughes to Bontemps, in *Arna Bontemps–Langston Hughes Letters*, 183.

29. In his review of a 1982 revival of *Mulatto*, John S. Patterson reported that the play still had the power to make audiences uneasy: "It works because it stages the barbarism which informed black/white relationships from slavery days until very, very recently. . . . No one laughs at the work, no one takes a condescendingly distant attitude toward it. Hughes's subject matter is still so explosive that it transcends despite the overwrought dramaturgy in which it is framed." See "Langston Hughes: Harlem Renaissance Man," *Other Stages*, 28 January 1982, 5.

30. William Branch, *A Medal for Willie*, in *Black Drama Anthology*, ed. Woodie King and Ron Milner (New York: Columbia University Press, 1972), 471.

31. In the final chorus of *Trouble in Mind*, Childress implies that Wiletta would be fired. This event clearly violated Childress's labeling the play a "comedy drama." Childress later added a third act, which was unpublished. According to Doris Abramson, Wiletta and the director resolve their differences in this new version: Because the director is threatened by Wiletta's intention to notify all the newspapers, he rehires her. See Doris Abramson, *Negro Playwrights in the American Theatre, 1925–59* (New York: Columbia University Press, 1969), 189.

32. Loften Mitchell, *Black Drama: The Story of the American Negro in the Theatre* (New York: Hawthorn Books, 1967), 170–1.

33. Loften Mitchell, *A Land Beyond the River*, in *The Black Teacher and the Dramatic Arts*, ed. William R. Reardon and Thomas D. Pawley (Westport, Conn.: Negro Universities Press, 1970), 353.

34. Mitchell, *Land Beyond the River*, 358.

35. Mitchell, *Black Drama*, 180.

36. Calvin C. Hernton, "A Fiery Baptism," in *James Baldwin: A Collection of Critical Essays*, ed. Kenneth Kinnamon (Englewood Cliffs, N.J.: Prentice-Hall, 1974), 112.

37. Baldwin, *Blues for Mr. Charlie* (New York: Dial Press, 1964), 90.

38. Amiri Baraka, *The Autobiography of LeRoi Jones/Amiri Baraka* (New York: Freundlich Books, 1984), 187.

39. LeRoi Jones, *Dutchman and The Slave* (New York: Morrow, 1964), 33.

40. Amiri Baraka, "Black Theatre Forum," *Black Theatre #5*, 1971, 27.

41. Ibid.

42. Ibid.

43. Ibid.

44. Baraka, *Autobiography*, 253.
45. Ibid., 275–6.
46. Ibid.
47. Ron Zuber, *Three X Love*, in *Black Drama Anthology*, 438.
48. Marvin X, "An Interview with LeRoi Jones," *Black Theatre #1*, 1968, 22.
49. *Slave Ship* is so powerful that it can have unexpected effects on audiences. After a Free Southern Theatre production of the play, for example, the Gilbert Moses–directed performance had some people in Greenville, Mississippi, ready to revolt. They "were only reluctantly persuaded to go home. And then there was the entire audience in West Point, Mississippi, which rose to its feet, waving fists and singing, 'When We Gonna Rise Up!' (the song which is included at the end of every performance)" (Val Ferdinand, "On Black Theater in America: A Report from New Orleans," *Black World*, April 1970, 28).
50. LeRoi Jones, "In Search of the Revolutionary Theatre: New Heroes Needed," *Black World*, April 1966, 21.
51. Ibid.
52. Amiri Baraka, *Slave Ship* (Newark, N.J.: Jihad Productions, 1969), 11–12.
53. Amiri Baraka, *The New Nationalism: Kawaida Studies* (Chicago: Third World Press, 1972), 12.
54. Alice Childress, *Wine in the Wilderness* (New York: Dramatists Play Service, 1969), 37.
55. Edward Palmer, "Black Police in America," *Black Scholar*, October 1973, 27.
56. Rodney King, who was from the Los Angeles suburb of Altadena, was stopped by police for allegedly driving 115 mph on an interstate highway. While a police sergeant, along with twelve other officers, watched, at least four officers hit King between fifty-three and fifty-six times with their sticks. They shocked him with a 50,000-volt stun gun. They kicked him six times, knocking out his teeth, burning and bruising his skin, and lacerating his mouth. The police claimed that King had lunged at them ("Video Taped LA Police Brutality Stirs Calls for Ouster of Chief," *Jet*, March 25, 1991, 12–13).
57. Dennis Martin admitted to widespread police brutality on the television program "Our Voices," Bev Smith, moderator, the Black Entertainment Television Network, March 1991.
58. Ibid.
59. Palmer, "Black Police in America," 23.

60. M. Ron Karenga, *Beyond Connections: Liberation in Love and Struggle* (New Orleans: Ahidiana, 1978), 13.
61. Joseph Scott, "The Black Bourgeoisie and Black Power," *Black Scholar,* January 1973, 12.
62. Ronald Walters, "Population Control and the Black Community," *Black Scholar,* May 1974, 46; June 1974, 30.
63. Tariq Ibn Hassiz, "On That Black Administrator Sitting in Darkness," *Liberator,* March 1971, 11.
64. Alvin Pouissaint, "The Black Administrator in the White University," *Black Scholar,* September 1974, 8.
65. Bettye I. Latimer, "Children's Books and Racism," *Black Scholar,* May–June 1973, 21.
66. Robert Macbeth, interview with author, Miami, Florida, 26 March 1989.
67. Macbeth and Bullins put out the story that Kingsley B. Bass, Jr., was a young man killed in the Detroit uprising. When the word got out that Bullins was the play's author, he and Macbeth "revised" the story to say that the viewpoint of the play was "through the eyes of one who could have been killed in the Detroit uprising." Macbeth said in an interview with the author (26 march 1989) that Bullins did not want his name on the play because he knew that it was going to be controversial.
68. The first New Lafayette Theatre at 132nd Street and 7th Avenue (site of the "Old Lafayette Theatre" of the thirties) was set on fire, allegedly by Donald Washington, on 31 January 1968. Washington allegedly was seeking revenge for Macbeth's having thrown him out of the theatre during a book party for Harold Cruse's *The Crisis of the Negro Intellectual.* Washington had been involved in a factional dispute between the Revolutionary Nationalists and the Cultural Nationalists.
69. Robert Macbeth, telephone conversation with author, 22 October 1992.
70. Unless otherwise stated, all quotations from the symposium are from "Lafayette Theatre: Reaction to *Bombers,*" *Black Theatre #4,* 1969, 16–25.
71. Larry Neal, "Toward a Relevant Black Theatre," *Black Theatre #4,* 1969, 14.
72. Ibid.
73. "LeRoi Jones Talks with Marvin X and Faruk," *Black Theatre #2,* 1969, 14.
74. Ben Caldwell, *Mission Accomplished,* in *The Drama Review,* Summer 1968, 51.

75. Hayward Henry, Jr., "Toward a Religion of Revolution," *Black Scholar*, December 1970, 27.
76. Ibid.
77. Calvin Bromlee Marshall III, "The Black Church: Its Mission is Liberation," *Black Scholar*, December 1970, 13.
78. Henry, "Toward a Religion of Revolution," 30.
79. Imamu Amiri Baraka, *A Black Value System* (Newark, N.J.: Jihad Productions, 1969), 13–14.
80. Andrew Billingsley, "Edward Blyden: Apostle of Blackness," *Black Scholar*, December 1970, 8.
81. Baraka describes "Insurrection and Misplaced Love" as an early version of *A Black Mass:*

> [The pantomime] begins with [the brother] actually creating himself, creating himself in the sense that when it comes on, he's making salat, in the sense that he is a creature of his own conception when he is asking for help from his Creator, in the larger sense of being, like talking about the Lord of the Worlds. Then it introduces how the beast comes on through the brother's weakness, and the brother finally abusing his power and going to sleep and the devil crawling out of the cave and taking over, taking all the things from him. Then he wakes the brother up and has all his skills and his powers, because he doesn't know he has the powers – he's been asleep – and the eventual reclaiming, after generations, successive generations. Finally the generation comes to reclaim the powers and then takes his rightful place in the world again (Marvin X, "An Interview with LeRoi Jones," *Black Theatre #1*, 1968, 21–2).

82. Ibid.
83. Robert Macbeth, *A Black Ritual, Black Theatre #2*, 1969, 8–9.
84. Hoyt W. Fuller, "General Black Theater Round-Up," *Black World*, April 1971, 26.
85. Ed Bullins, *The Theme Is Blackness* (New York: Morrow, 1972), 3–4.
86. Martha M. Jones, review of *Black Terror, Black Creation*, Spring 1972, 13.
87. "Honky-baiting" material required the presence of white people for its impact. "Black theatre," explained critic Kushauri Kupa, eventually became:

> primarily concerned about Black people and their problems, not utilizing the stage to hurl insults at whites sitting in seats in Black theatres that Black community people should be occupying. This preoccupation with attacking white people from the stages of Black

community theatres went out with the sixties. Our job now is to move ahead with the job of building *Black* minds, not doing what amounts to little more than 'revolutionary' protest plays (Kushauri Kupa, "Closeup: The New York Scene," *Black Theatre #6,* 1972, 39–40).

88. Peter A. Bailey, "Spotlight on the Black Theater Alliance," *First World,* January/February 1977, 52.

89. Baraka said that he abandoned *Kawaida* because it was feudalistic, one-man domination; male chauvinism given legitimacy as 'revolutionary'; and metaphysics. The feudalism charge stemmed from the ideology's

reactionary adherence to various forms of African dress and [to] learning a few Swahili words, [which could not have effected] black liberation. There is – right now even this very moment – a need for a cultural revolution, but the culture must be that of the black masses, given revolutionary focus and, as a whole, part of the actual political thrust itself. . . . [T]he reactionary nature of much of the *Kawaida* doctrine could not help but affect us negatively. For one thing, it encouraged a feudalistic, even dictatorial style of leadership. It was never my nature to be as absolute in my pronouncement as was called for by Maulanaism. . . . *Kawaida* was and is, if it still exists, a *religion.* On one level this had its tactical uses – e.g., it enabled us to go into many of the prisons as *priests* and teach black nationalism. . . . These three deeply rooted error led to many others, for which these were the base" (*Autobiograhy,* 298–9).

90. Neal, "Toward a Relevant Theatre," 14.

91. The Wheatley Players of Cleveland, directed by Henry Marone, performed *The Gospel Glory* in 1974, billing it as the world premiere of a lost Hughes play. The play had been performed in 1962, however, at the Temple of the Church of God in Christ in the Bedford-Stuyvesant district of Brooklyn.

92. Tom Dent, "New Theatres in the South Join Hands," *Black World,* April 1973, 93.

93. Unless otherwise stated, all quotations from *Song* are from Amiri Baraka, *Song,* in *New Plays for the Black Theatre,* ed. Woodie King, Jr. (Chicago: Third World Press, 1989), 1–15.

94. LeRoi Jones, *Madheart,* in *Black Fire,* ed. LeRoi Jones and Larry Neal (New York: Morrow, 1968), 588.

95. Amiri Baraka, *Selected Plays and Prose* (New York: Morrow, 1979), 144.

96. Marvin X, "Interview with LeRoi Jones," 20.

97. Ibid.
98. All quotations are from P. J. Gibson, *Konvergence*, in *New Plays for the Black Theatre*, 1–15.
99. All quotations are from Ben Caldwell, *Birth of a Blues*, in *New Plays for the Black Theatre*, 37–44.
100. Whitney Smith, review of *Down on Beale Street*, *Commercial Appeal*, 2 August 1985.
101. Ron Wynn, review of *Down on Beale Street*, *Commercial Appeal*, 21 May 1988.
102. Daniel W. Owens, *The Box*, in *New Plays for the Black Theatre*, 18.
103. Baraka, *A Black Value System*, 1.
104. Porter Anderson, review of *Praise House*, *American Theatre*, September 1990, 8.
105. Ibid.
106. Ibid.
107. Suzi-Lori Parks, *The Death of the Last Black Man in the Whole Entire World*, *Theater*, Spring 1990, 82.
108. Ibid., 89.
109. Ibid., 85.
110. Ibid., 84.

3. THEATRE PEOPLE: SOME SPLENDID EXAMPLES

1. Dr. Thurman W. Stanback, telephone conversation with author, 10 November 1992.
2. Ruby Dee, "The Tattered Queens," in *Anthology of the American Negro in the Theatre*, ed. Lindsay Patterson (Washington, D.C.: Publishers Company, 1968), 131.
3. Ibid.
4. Ibid., 134.
5. Manuel Noah, review of *Richard III*, *National Advocate*, 21 September 1821, 1.
6. Although not given the credit, Charles Mathews and Manuel Noah really originated the Negro minstrelsy. Mathews dramatized Noah's article describing Hewlett's *Richard III* performance. Mathews said that he had seen Hewlett perform Hamlet at the African Grove Theatre in 1822, and he claimed to be interpreting that performance in his "A Trip to America" (1824), a one-man show composed of anecdotes, monologues, songs, and impersonations. A comparison of Mathews's text with Noah's *Richard III* review shows,

however, that Mathews plagiarized Noah's article. Noah, then, wrote the very first Negro minstrel material for the stage in 1821.

7. *National Advocate*, 8 May 1824, 1.

8. Frances Cress Welsing, "The Cress Theory of Color-Confrontation," *Black Scholar*, May 1974, 32–40.

9. Herbert Marshall and Mildred Stock, *Ira Aldridge: The Negro Tragedian* (Carbondale: Southern Illinois University Press, 1968), 118–28.

10. Errol Hill, *Shakespeare in Sable: A History of Black Shakespearean Actors* (Amherst: University of Massachusetts Press, 1984), 24.

11. Marshall and Stock, *Ira Aldridge*, 117.

12. Ibid.

13. William Wells Brown saw Aldridge perform several roles in England in 1849. Brown first saw him play Othello at the Royal Haymarket. He thought Aldridge was "the best Othello that has ever been seen": "[T]he audience, with one impulse . . . [rose] to their feet amid the wildest enthusiasm." Brown was equally enthusiastic about Aldridge's Hamlet, which Brown said "charmed ears" and "arrested tongues": "The voice was so low and sad, the grace so consummate, that all yielded themselves silently to the delicious enchantment" (William Wells Brown, *The Black Man's Genius and Achievements* [New York, 1865], 118). Although Brown saw Aldridge in several other roles, he thought that Aldridge's Hamlet was the best – better even than Charles Kean's Hamlet. Brown reported that Aldridge's audiences at *Othello* and *Hamlet* gave him "wild and enthusiastic" standing ovations. (William Edward Farrison, *William Wells Brown: Author and Reformer* [Chicago: University of Chicago Press, 1969]), 118–19).

14. Farrison, *William Wells Brown*, 118–9.

15. William Wells Brown, *Narrative of William Wells Brown, an American Slave, Written by Himself* (London, 1848), 17.

16. Robert C. Toll, *Blacking Up: The Minstrel Show in Nineteenth-Century America* (New York: Oxford University Press, 1974), 212.

17. Ibid., 212–13.

18. Ibid., 213.

19. Alice Childress, "A Candle in a Gale Wind," in *Black Woman Writers*, ed. Mari Evans (Garden City, N.Y.: Anchor Press/Doubleday, 1984), 112–3.

20. John O. Killens, "The Literary Genius of Alice Childress," in *Black Woman Writers*, 132.

21. Henry T. Sampson, *Blacks in Blackface: A Source Book on Early Black Musical Shows* (Metuchen, N.J.: Scarecrow Press, 1980), 70.

22. Ibid., 82.

23. Ibid.
24. Ibid.
25. Toll, *Blacking Up*, 214.
26. Sampson, *Blacks in Blackface*, 82.
27. Beth Turner, "Charles Fuller: Black Pride, Integrity, Success," *Black Masks*, September/October 1987, 5.
28. For many insights concerning psychology, I am indebted to Dr. Charlotte Kennedy, Department of Psychiatry, University of Tennessee Medical School, Memphis.
29. According to Wesley,

    Working under Ed Bullins was better than anything I could have hoped for. He was in the middle of the entire Black Arts Movement. In 1969, Ed offered me the job of Managing Editor of *Black Theatre Magazine*, which was being published by the New Lafayette Theatre. Consequently, I was able to quit my airline job and run the magazine. Through Ed I met Quincy Troupe, Baraka, Sonia Sanchez, Jane Cortez, Etheridge Knight, and Larry Neal (Charles Turner, "Howard U., Broadway and Hollywood, Too: Richard Wesley," *Black Masks*, March 1985, 8).

30. Alvin Poussaint and Carolyn Atkinson, "Black Youth and Motivation," *Black Scholar*, March 1970, 44.
31. Sampson, *Blacks in Blackface*, 381.
32. Tony Preston, "A Different Yardstick: Progress in Black Theatre as Measured by the Lives of Two Illustrious Actors, Rosalind Cash and David Downing," *Black Masks*, January/February 1989, 4–7.
33. Caroline Jackson, "L. Scott Caldwell: Laughter in One Hand (The Tony in the Other)," *Black Masks*, Summer 1988, 5.
34. Charles H. Nichols, ed., *Arna Bontemps–Langston Hughes Letters: 1925–1967* (New York: Dodd, Mead & Co., 1980), 197.
35. Donald Bogle, *Brown Sugar: Eighty Years of America's Black Female Superstars* (New York: Harmony Books, 1980), 44.
36. Ibid., 43.
37. Paul Robeson, *Here I Stand* (Boston: Beacon Press, 1958), 31.
38. Ibid.
39. Ibid.
40. Ibid.
41. Eartha Kitt believed she was boycotted because at a luncheon with Lady Bird Johnson she had denounced the Johnson administration's involvement in Vietnam. Kitt said that an "angered President

Johnson did all he could to wreck her career, instructing the FBI to gather a dossier on her. Club and cafe owners were pressured into canceling engagements" (Bogle, *Brown Sugar,* 128).

42. Lena Horne, "Forty-five Years in Movies and Entertainment," *Ebony,* November 1990, 98.

43. Victor Daly, "Green Pastures and Black Washington," *Crisis,* May 1933, 106.

44. Ed Bullins, *The Theme Is Blackness* (New York: Morrow, 1973), 10.

45. Amiri Baraka, *The Autobiography of LeRoi Jones/Amiri Baraka,* (New York: Freundlich Books, 1984), 298.

46. Amiri Baraka, "The Congress of Afrikan People: A Position Paper," *Black Scholar,* January–February 1975, 2–15.

47. Haki R. Madhubuti, "The Latest Purge: The Attack on Black Nationalism and Pan-Afrikanism by the New Left, the Sons and Daughters of the Old Left," *Black Scholar,* September 1974, 46.

48. Sampson, *Blacks in Blackface,* 363–4.

49. Beth Turner, "For Sustained Excellence: Frances Foster," *Black Masks,* Summer 1985, 10.

50. Caroline Jackson, "South African Zakes Mokae: An Actor Against All Odds," *Black Masks,* October 1985, 3.

51. Sampson, *Blacks in Blackface,* 94–6.

52. Ibid., 417.

53. Marshall and Stock, *Ira Aldridge,* 197.

54. Hill, *Shakespeare in Sable,* 17.

55. Sampson, *Blacks in Blackface,* 335.

56. Cited in Mervyn Rothstein, "Star of 'The Piano Lesson' Who Found a New Life Onstage," *New York Times,* 19 April 1990, C-23.

57. Stephen McKinley Henderson, telephone conversation with author, 1 January 1991.

58. Maurice Henderson, "Margaret Avery: A Place among the Stars," *Black Masks,* Summer 1987, 4.

59. Ron Dortch, telephone conversation with author, 14 February 1991.

60. Judith Green, review of *Othello, San Diego Union-Ledger,* 31 August 1990, D-1.

61. Robert L. Benedetti, *The Actor at Work* (Englewood Cliffs, N.J.: Prentice-Hall, 1981), 226.

62. Ibid., 168.

63. Ernest R. Hilgard, Richard C. Atkinson, and Rita L. Atkinson, *Introduction to Psychology* (New York: Harcourt Brace Jovanovich, 1971), 416.

64. Unless otherwise noted, all citations about defense and coping mechanisms are from Hilgard et al., *Introduction to Psychology*, 442–63.
65. It is alleged that both Hewlett and Cole committed suicide, probably because of their thwarted ambitions. Hewlett supposedly inhaled gas in 1831. Cole suffered a nervous breakdown in 1910, and, although an excellent swimmer, he drowned in 1911. Marshall and Stock, *Ira Aldridge*, 38; and Sampson, *Blacks in Blackface*, 73.
66. Sampson, *Blacks in Blackface*, 93.
67. Ibid., 91.
68. Malik, "From Harlem's Teer, An Old Story Made New," *American Theatre*, September 1990, 64–5.
69. Douglas Turner Ward, telephone conversation with author, 5 December 1990.
70. Beth Turner, "Cyril Nir: Black, British, and Shakespearean," *Black Masks*, April/May 1989, 8.
71. "*A Different World* Star Glad Cosby Is Hiring Darker-Skinned Blacks," *Jet*, 10 December 1990, 35.
72. Mabel Rowland, ed., *Bert Williams, Son of Laughter: A Symposium of Tribute to the Man and to His Work by His Friends and Associates* (New York: Negro Universities Press, 1969), 129.
73. Ibid., 191.
74. "Charles Dutton Lauds Grads Who Got Degrees in Prison," *Jet* 1 July 1991, 36.
75. Rowland, *Bert Williams*, 192.

4. THE GOVERNANCE OF THEATRE ORGANIZATIONS

1. Ossie Davis, "The Flight from Broadway Back to the 'Harlems,' " *Negro Digest*, April 1966, 15.
2. Ibid.
3. Ethel Pitts Walker, "The American Negro Theatre," in *The Theatre of Black Americans*, ed. Errol Hill (New York: Applause Theatre Books Publications, 1987), 252.
4. Francesca Thompson, "The Lafayette Players" (Paper delivered at the Fourth Annual Conference on African American Theatre, Baltimore, Md., 9 April 1987), 10.
5. The Skyloft Theatre was later revived.
6. Constantia W. Jackson, "Between the Pages," *Krigwa Group Theatre Bulletin*, February 1948, 3.

7. The Negro Little Theatre became considerably less active in 1942. Many of its male actors served in World War II. According to the historian Guilbert A. Daley, 1942 was also the year that the then-director Sheldon B. Hoskins left to become ballet master for Billy Rose's Broadway production of *Carmen Jones*. Hoskins, a graduate of Columbia University, had developed the youth theatre of the Negro Little Theatre. His specialty was using the popular clown images of the African American musicals comedies to present the African American struggles for equality. For one much-celebrated dance recital on June 2, 1939 – attended by Maryland's governor Herbert R. O'Conor – Hoskins choreographed a dance that told the story of lynching with such force that, according to critic Ida Peters, "the audience literally sat on the edge of their seats" (Ida Peters, "Remembering Sheldon B. Hoskins," *Baltimore Afro-American*, 24 June 1978, 17). The lighting designer Samuel N. Phillips revived the Negro Little Theatre in 1946 to produce its final play, *Blind Alley*. Phillips, who had joined the theatre in 1937, photographed most of its productions. (The author is indebted to Mrs. Gloria Phillips, his widow, for sharing hundreds of his photographs.)

8. DuBois to the director of the New York Public Library, in DuBois Collection, Library of Congress, Washington, D.C.

9. The OET budget deficit in 1991 was reduced from $66,000 to "less than $20,000." The company presented three plays during the 1990–1 season. See Sharon Walton's letter to the editor, *American Theatre*, February 1991, 55.

10. Samuel Wilson, Jr., interview with the author, Baltimore, Md., 12 September 1987. The author is greatly indebted to Mr. Wilson for permission to study the books and archives of the Arena Players.

11. Camilla Sherrard, interview with author, Baltimore, Md., 22 September 1987.

12. The Arena Players subscribed to the Southern Arts Federation notion that fifteen to twenty-five members were adequate for the board of a developing organization. See *Southern Arts Federation: Tap III Consultancies* (Atlanta, 1990), 5.

13. Peggy Dye, "Peace and the Sword: Inside the Abyssinian Baptist Church with Reverend Calvin O. Butts, III," *Village Voice*, 12 June 1990, 15.

14. Phillip A. Bell published in New York City in 1837 the *Weekly Advocate* (later the *Colored American*), edited by the Reverend Samuel A. Cornish. Bell founded in 1865 the *Elevator* in San Francisco. According to one tribute, Bell was "a fine dramatic critic. He wrote several

articles for the California daily papers, criticizing Kean, Macready, Forrest, and others" (I. Garland Penn, *The Afro-American Press and Its Editors* [Springfield, Mass.: Willey & Co., 1891]), 98.

15. Dierdra Dyson, "Black Theatre Roundup: Chicago," *Black World*, April 1975, 28.

16. OyamO [Charles F. Gordon], "Black Theatre: Another Perspective," *Black Masks*, April/May 1990, 6.

17. The Song of Solomon 1:13.

18. The Arena Players followed Southern Arts Federation recommendations concerning scheduling meetings, preparing agendas, and holding annual meetings. The Players established dates for its regular meetings at the annual meeting. Regular meetings were scheduled only for the period of the time that would be needed to accomplish the limited purpose of a particular meeting. Because meetings started and ended on time, members arrived punctually and remained throughout the meeting. At least seven working days in advance of the meeting date, the Players prepared and sent on to board members an agenda, along with any material that was pertinent to the agenda. Members received a telephone reminder of the meeting at least twenty-four hours in advance of the meeting. Annual meetings, where votes on important or complex issues were avoided, were held just prior to the meeting that approved the budget for the fiscal year.

A board member's term of service, according to the Southern Arts Federation, should be limited to six years (two consecutive three-year terms, or three consecutive two-year terms). There might be two "classes" of memberships, including one-year, two-year, and three-year terms.

The Players, just as the Southern Arts Federation recommended, expected its boards members to believe in and to be an active advocate for the organization; to subscribe to and to attend all performances; to attend all board meetings; to serve actively on at least one standing committee; and to be *both* a dollar *giver* and a dollar *getter.*

19. Amiri Baraka, *The Autobiography of LeRoi Jones/Amiri Baraka* (New York: Freundlich Books, 1984), 202–29.

20. Camilla Sherrard and Clifton Sherrard, interview with author, Baltimore, Md., 22 September 1987.

21. Clifton Sherrard, interview with author, Baltimore, Md., 22 September 1987.

22. *McCree Theatre: Planning Process Project Summary*, 8 May 1990, 4–5.

23. John Nash, telephone conversation with author, 31 May 1992.

5. DEVELOPMENT

1. Peter Bailey, "Spotlight on the Black Theater Alliance," *First World*, January/February 1977, 50–2.
2. Beth Turner, "North Carolina Black Repertory Company: Look Out N.Y.," *Black Masks*, March/April 1987, 2.
3. Bailey, "Spotlight on the Black Theater Alliance," 51–2.
4. Turner, "North Carolina Black Repertory," 2.
5. Larry Neal, "Toward a Relevant Black Theatre," *Black Theatre*, 1969, 14–15.
6. "Star of Ethiopia," DuBois Collection, Library of Congress, Washington, D.C. (hereafter DuBois Collection).
7. Some actors like Charles Burroughs and Richard B. Harrison enjoyed giving readings so much that they spent considerable time during the twenties and thirties reading to students in secondary schools and colleges. Burroughs, in fact, made a living by reading Shakespeare. After appearing in *The Green Pastures* (1930) at Tuskegee, Harrison said that he was "more proud that the students liked his performance and the play than of any applause he had received at Times Square" (Walter C. Daniel, *"De Lawd": Richard B. Harrison and The Green Pastures* [New York: Greenwood Press, 1986], 144).
8. Several colleges invited guests artists to appear with their students. During 1921, the Howard Players, for example, invited the actor Charles Gilpin and the director Jasper Deeter (artistic director of the Hedgerow Theatre outside of Philadelphia) to work with its students in the Washington, D.C., premiere of Eugene O'Neill's *Emperor Jones* (1920). The production was so successful that O'Neill invited two of the students (Bernard Pryor and Matthew Shield) to take prominent parts in the national touring company of the play.
9. Because most African American theatres are nonprofit organizations, they might seek marketing assistance from those media outlets willing to donate their services. Besides the radio and television stations, newspapers, and magazines that offer *pro bono* assistance, public relations, advertising, and marking firms; printers; and production companies do so as well. Because these firms must spread their support throughout the community, however, theatres should limit their requests.
10. Gary Anderson, "Black Theatre: The Next Generation," *BTNews*, Summer 1991, 4.
11. Citing a U.S. information survey, Anderson reported that African Americans used radio for 49.70 percent of their information. Other

distribution means were word-of-mouth (24.30 percent), television (10.65 percent), print (9 percent), and other (6.35 percent).

12. DuBois promoted *The Star of Ethiopia* in Philadelphia in 1916 by giving prizes to people selling the largest number of tickets above one thousand. One hundred dollars was the first prize. Other prizes included a fifty-dollar second prize for the highest number of tickets sold between 500 and 1,000 tickets; a twenty-five-dollar third prize for the highest between 200 and 250; a ten-dollar fourth prize for the highest between 100 and 250; and five-dollar fifth, sixth, and seventh prizes for the highest between 50 and 100. To ensure accountability, DuBois asked for references from pastors and respected citizens. DuBois Collection.

13. The New Lafayette Theater's workshop consisted of writers and actors recruited from the surrounding Harlem neighborhood. The performers were called the Black Troop. Among their earliest plays were *The Portrait* by Neil Harris, *Sometimes the Switchblade Helps* by Milburn Davis, and *Black Cycle* by Martie Charles.

14. Among the one-acts performed by Black Arts/West of Seattle in 1971 were *Da Minstrel Show, Days of Thunder, Nights of Violence,* and *Guerilla Warfare* by Curtis Lyle; *Poor Willie* by Aaron Dumas; and of *Black Power Every Hour* by Ana V. Thorne.

15. The Arena Players co-sponsored the contest with the local CBS affiliate, WMAR-TV. The contest limited the plays to one setting and a maximum of four characters. More than one hundred entries were received in 1988.

16. Although the Eugene O'Neill Center in Connecticut offers a criticism program each summer, the program is neither Afrocentric nor beginner oriented. Because most African American newspapers hire beginning African American reporters, who take on theatre reviewing because of interest – not preparation, specially designed criticism programs are needed.

17. The Watts Writers Workshop pioneered the audience-as-critic technique. During some readings in 1969, sponsors asked people to vote their preferences for the most enjoyable poet. Richard Wesley, "An Interview with Playwright Ed Bullins," *Black Creation,* Winter 1973, 8–10.

18. Clayton Riley, "The Role of the Critic of the Sixties" (Paper delivered at the First National Conference on African American Theatre, Baltimore, Md., 20 April 1983), 4.

19. Budgetary restraints forced Howard University to close the Children's Theatre in 1992.

20. Hazel Bryant, "Improving Black Technical Theatre through Technical Training Programs" (Paper delivered at the First National Conference on African American Theatre, Baltimore, Md., 20 April 1983), 14.

21. The major coalitions of theatre companies – listed in order of founding dates – were the Organization of Black American Culture in Chicago (1967), the Black Theatre Alliance of New York (1971), the Coalition of Black Revolutionary Artists of Chicago (1972), the Southern Black Cultural Alliance (1972), the Black Theatre Alliance of Chicago (1974), the Audience Development Committee of New York (1973), the Midwest Afrikan-American Theatre Alliance (1976), the Black Arts Council of Dallas (1984), the Black Theatre Collective of New York (1986), the San Francisco Area Multi-Cultural Production Fund (1988), and the African Continuum Theatre Coalition (ACT Co) in Washington, D.C. (1989).

22. Eugene Perkins, "Chicago: Crisis in Black Theater," *Black World,* April 1973, 31.

23. Ibid.

24. Delano H. Stewart, artistic director of the Bed-Stuy Theater, spearheaded the drive to form the Black Theatre Alliance of New York (BTA), which consisted of Ernie McClintock's the Afro American Studio Theater, Hazel J. Bryant's the Afro-American Total Theater, Roger Furman's the New Heritage Repertory Theater, Lubaba Lateef's Brownsville Laboratory Theater, and Buddy Butler's Theater Black. With funding from the New York State Council of the Arts and the National Endowment for the Arts, BTA secured offices and personnel (Joan Sandler was founding executive director, Duane Jones the succeeding director, Peter A. Bailey later associate director, and Kathleen Rose administrative assistant). Within six years, the BTA grew to forty-eight members, including nineteen dance companies.

25. Useni Eugene Perkins founded both the Black Theater Alliance (BTA) of Chicago and the Midwest Afrikan American Theatre Alliance (MAATA). BTA consisted of the Black Heritage Theatrical Players, directed by Reverend Spencer Jackson; the Ebony Talent School of Total Theater, directed by Walter Bradford (writing), Tony Llorens (music), Julian Swain (dance), and Harold Johnson and Virgie Blakely (drama); Kusema, directed by Van Jackson; Kuumba Workshop, directed by Val and Francis Ward; La Mont Zeno Community Theater, directed by Pemon Rami, who agitated for the founding of BTA (Chicago); the Experimental Black Actors Guild,

directed by Clarence Taylor; the New Concept Theatre, directed by Lawrence Kabaka; and Theater in Prison, directed by Abena Seiwaa (Joan P. Brown).

The Midwest Afrikan American Theatre Alliance included theatres in Illinois, Ohio, Wisconsin, and Indiana. Among its founding members were Lois P. McGuire, Cynthia Pitts, and Vivian Womble. Members in 1992 included the Afrikan American Theatre Alliance, Chicago, Larry Franklin Crowe, president; African American Studio Theatre, Detroit, James Reed Faulkner, director; Saginaw Black Cultural Alliance, Saginaw, Michigan, Nellie Jo Brooks, director; Hansberry-Sands Theatre, Milwaukee, Willie Abney, director; Alaringo Theatre Company, Maywood, Illinois, Adekola Adedapo, director; ETA Creative Arts Foundation, Chicago, Abena Joan Brown, director; Milwaukee Inner City Arts Council, Milwaukee, Denise Crumble, director; St. Louis Black Repertory Company, St. Louis, Ron Himes, director; Kalamazoo Civic Black Theatre, Kalamazoo, Michigan, John McCants, director; Association for the Positive Development of Afrikan-American Youth, Chicago, Useni Eugene Perkins, director; Milwaukee Inner City Arts Council, Milwaukee, Cynthia Bryant Pitts, director; Madame C. J. Walker Urban Life Center, Indianapolis, Josephine Weathers, director; and Vivian Womble Players, St. Louis, Vivian Womble, director.

26. Vivian Robinson, Renee Chenowith, Doris Smith, Winifred Richardson, Jeanne Weeks, and Carlos Freeman founded the Audience Development Committee (AUDELCO), a voluntary organization that served all community and professional theatres in New York City.

27. The Southern Black Cultural Alliance (SBCA) was founded in 1972 at Mary Holmes College in West Point, Mississippi. SBCA consisted of the Theater of Afro-Art and the "M" Theater in Miami, the Black Arts Workshop of the Arkansas Arts Center in Little Rock, the Urban Theatre in Houston, the Last Messengers in Greenville, Mississippi, and *NKOMBO* magazine in New Orleans.

28. The Black Arts Council of Dallas was founded by the Afro-American Alliance (1977) and the Afro-American Players. GloDean Baker founded the Afro-American Players.

The Black Theatre Collective of New York was founded by the Alonzo Players, AUDELCO, the Billie Holiday Theatre, *Black Masks* Publication, Black Spectrum Theatre, Frank Silvera Writers' Workshop, H.A.D.L.E.Y. Players, National Black Theatre, New Federal Theatre, Negro Ensemble Company, O'Lac, Richard Allen Center for Culture and Art, New Heritage Repertory Theatre, and the

Theodore Ward Theatre Collection. "New Black Theatre Collective," *Black Masks,* Summer 1986, 11.

29. John L. Moore III founded the African Continuum Theatre Coalition in 1989 in Washington, D.C. Among its members were the American Theatre Project, Ed Bishop, founder; the Encore Theatre Company; Everyday Theatre Youth Ensemble, Susie Solf, founder; the Creative Ascent, Amelia Cobb Gray, founder; PM/2 Productions, Michael Howell, Theophilus Lee, and Elliott Hill, founders; HOME: Theatre New Columbia, Reginald Metcalf and Joni Lee Jones, founders; the Serenity Players, Doris Thomas, founder; and the Enough Said Children's Theatre, Esther Anglade, founder.

30. Samuel A. Hay founded the National Conference of African American Theatre, Inc. (NCAAT) in 1983. Themes of the annual conferences have included "Black Theatre of the Sixties" (1983), keynoted by the playwright Amiri Baraka; "Black American Protest Drama and Theatre" (1985), Errol Hill (John D. Willard Professor of Drama and Oratory at Dartmouth College), keynote; "The Afro-American Folk and Cultural Tradition in Theatre" (1986), The Honorable John Horne, minister of culture, St. Vincent's, keynote; "African American Theatre Companies" (1987), Woodie King, Jr., director of the New Federal Theatre of New York, keynote; "Theatre in Black Higher Education" (1988), Margaret J. Seagears, executive director of the White House Initiative on Historically Black Colleges and Universities, keynote; "Theatre Criticism by and about African Americans" (1989), Darwin T. Turner, Distinguished Professor of English and chair of Afro-American Studies at the University of Iowa, keynote; "The African American Actor" (1990), Douglas Turner Ward, artistic director of the Negro Ensemble Company in New York, keynote; "African American Musical Theatre" (1991), Clay Chavers, Esq., keynote; and "African Americans Backstage," (1992), Kathy A. Perkins, professor of theatre at the University of Illinois at Urbana-Champaign, keynote. The papers can be found in the organization's archives in Riviera Beach, Florida.

31. Founded by Barbara Montgomery and Mary Alice in 1983, Black Women in Theatre had chapters in New York and Los Angeles. The group sponsored seminars and conferences aimed at improving the image and the lot of African American women in the arts. It also held events to help the underprivileged.

32. Directed by Anna Kay France, the International Women's Playwrights Conference was held at the State University of New York at Buffalo in 1988. Women playwrights from countries including Nige-

ria, the United States, Brazil, Australia, Sri Lanka, Norway, Japan, and South Africa came together to compare experiences and present plays.

33. Ethel Pitts Walker founded the Black Theatre Network in 1986. Its early meetings were held as part of the National Black Arts Festival in Atlanta and the National Black Theatre Festival in Winston-Salem, North Carolina. The first independent meeting was held in 1992 in Detroit.

34. Directed by A. Michelle Smith, the ten-day National Black Arts Festival in Atlanta exhibited at its second annual meeting in 1988 such visual artists as James Lesesner Wells, Bill W. Walker, Roland Freeman, John Moore, Faith Ringgold, Beverly Buchanan, Marion Hassinger, Romare Bearden, Jacob Lawrence, Charles White, and Hale Woodruff. Among the dance companies were Bill T. Jones/Arnie Zane & Co., Capoeira Roda de Angola, Dance! Atlanta! Dance, Dance Expressions of the Diaspora, and Marie Brook's Children's Dance Research Theatre. The poets included Amiri Baraka, Pearl Cleage, Wanda Coleman, Mari Evans, Haki Hadhubuti, Kalamu ya Salaam, Sonia Sanchez, and Askia Muhammad Toure. The musical groups were the African Percussion Ensemble, Atlanta Jazz Series with Bureau of Cultural Affairs, Atlanta Symphony Orchestra, Gospel Concerts, Olatunji and HIs Drums of Passion, and Salsa Meets Jazz. Among the theatre organizations and artists were the Manhattan Theatre Club, Jomandi Productions, Philadelphia's Freedom Theatre, Knoxville's Carpetbag Theatre, and Avery Brooks in *Robeson*.

35. Such personalities as Oprah Winfrey, Lou Gossett, Jr., Ruby Dee, Ossie Davis, Cicely Tyson, and Roscoe Lee Browne joined with approximately fourteen thousand theatre people to entertain and conduct business with each other. "The 1989 National Black Theatre Festival," *Black Masks*, Summer 1989, 8.

36. Growth in the number of categories of the AUDELCO Awards signaled their popularity and importance. AUDELCO presented its first awards in 1973 in only six categories: lighting, set design, male/female acting, directing, and pioneers. Five other areas were added in 1974: stage managing, producing, choreography, playwright, and musical directing. Best supporting actor and actress in 1975 increased the total categories to thirteen. Since 1987, additional categories include sound design, outstanding performance in a musical/female and male, and outstanding musical creator (original music and/or lyrics). Seventeen people currently look forward to the benefits to their professional careers occasioned by this award.

37. The National Conference on African American Theatre has given Mr. Brown Awards to individuals who have made notable contributions to the development of African-American theatre. A student, friend, or colleague reads a paper on the recipient's accomplishments. The winners have been A. Clifton Lamb and S. Randolph Edmonds (1985); Thomas D. Pawley III and May Miller Sullivan (1986); Anne Cooke Reid and Winona Lee Fletcher (1987); James W. Butcher (1988); Frederick O'Neal (1989); Dick Campbell (1990); Abram Hill (1991); and Ralph T. Dines (1992).

38. New Orleans hosted the 1976 Festival of the Southern Black Cultural Alliance. Performances were given by the Urban Theater of Houston, directed by Barbara Marshall; the Theater of Afro-Arts and the "M" Theatre, directed respectively by Wendell Narcisse and Sam Williams; the Orlando School of Performing Arts, directed by Pat Moore; the Congo Square Writers Union in New Orleans, directed by Chakula Ja Juan and Adella Gautier; Ahidiana; Ethiopian Theater of New Orleans, directed by Monroe Bean; Badia Dance Company of Firmingham, directed by Donna Edwards; Beale Street Theatre in Memphis, directed by Levi Frazier; and Carpetbag Theater of Knoxville, directed by Wilmer Lucas.

39. Duane L. Jones, who died July 22, 1988, made an immense contribution to the development of African American theatre. He was the director of the Macguire Theatre at the State University of New York at Old Westbury on Long Island. He was also the artistic director of Hazel Bryant's Richard Allen Center for Culture and Art, and the editor of *Caribe* magazine. He acted in films (*The Night of the Living Dead, Ganja and Hess*, and *Beat Street*) and on television ("Good Luck, Mr. Robinson"). His directing credits extended from the classics (*Antigone*) to jazz opera (*Sojourner*). During his tenure as president of the New York Black Theatre Alliance, membership grew to seventy-five dance and theatre companies. Niamani Mutima, "Duane Jones: A True Believer," *Black Masks*, October/November 1988, 4–5.

40. Dr. Helen Armstead-Johnson, director of the Armstead-Johnson Foundation for Theater Research, supplied stage ephemera and artifacts to exhibitors throughout New York state. A sample of the photographs from her collection, among the largest of its kind, is in her monograph *Black America on Stage* (New York: City University of New York, 1978).

41. *The BTN Black Theatre Directory* was available for ten dollars in 1992 from Addell Austin Anderson, president; Black Theatre Network; P.O. Box 11502; Fisher Building Station; Detroit MI 48211.

42. *The BTN Black Theatre Directory* broke down the listings into forty geographical areas. It provided not only the usual name, address, and telephone available but also each individual's organizational and union affiliations, as well as his or her specialties – from Arts Administrator (AA) to Vocalist (VO). The listing of theatre companies included contact person, year founded, kinds of tours (city, state, or U.S.), and company types (amateur, semiprofessional, or professional). A description of the purposes and objectives of black theatre organizations accompanied that listing. The only feature not included was a list of recent plays by African Americans, a quite useful section in the 1968 New York *Black Theatre Alliance Directory.*
43. Bailey, "Spotlight on the Black Theater Alliance," 50.
44. "The Funding Crunch: Black Theaters in Crisis," *Black Masks,* Summer 1985, 1.
45. Alisa Solomon, "BACA Folds: Another Theater Forced to Close," *Village Voice,* 25 June 1991, 96.
46. Don Shewey, "The Buck Starts Here: Six Interviews with Corporate and Foundation Funders," *American Theatre,* March 1991, 30.
47. Ibid., 31.
48. Frank Rich, review of *Black Eagles, New York Times,* 22 April 1991, B-5.
49. Ibid.

CONCLUSION

1. Beth Turner, "Beyond Entertainment," *Black Masks,* June/July 1991, 4.
2. Jonathan D. Sarna, *Jacksonian Jew: The Two Worlds of Mordecai Noah* (New York: Holmes & Meier Publishers, 1981), 50.

Select Bibliography

Except for relevant books and articles by and about W. E. B. DuBois and Alain Locke, the bibliography is restricted to books on the history and criticism of African American theatre.

Abramson, Doris E. *Negro Playwrights in the American Theatre, 1925–59*. New York: Columbia University Press, 1969.

Aptheker, Herbert, ed. *The Correspondence of W. E. B. DuBois. 3* vols. Amherst: University of Massachusetts Press, *1973*.

Archer, Leonard C. *Black Images in American Theatre*. Nashville: Pageant Press, 1973.

Baraka, Amiri. *The New Nationalism: Kawaida Studies*. Chicago: Third World Press, 1972.

   The Autobiography of LeRoi Jones/Amiri Baraka. New York: Freundlich Books, 1984.

Belcher, Fannin S., Jr. "The Place of the Negro in the Evolution of the American Theatre, 1767–1940." Ph.D. diss., Yale University, 1945.

Benston, Kimberly W. *Baraka: The Renegade and the Mask*. New Haven: Yale University Press, 1976.

Bigsby, C. W. E. *Confrontation and Commitment: A Study of Contemporary American Drama, 1959–1966*. Columbia: University of Missouri Press, 1968.

Bogle, Donald. *Brown Sugar: Eighty Years of America's Black Female Superstars*. New York: Harmony Books, 1980.

Bond, Frederick. *The Negro and the Drama*. Washington, D.C: Associated Publishers, 1940.

Broderick, Francis L. *W. E. B. DuBois: Negro Leader in a Time of Crisis*. Stanford, Calif.: Stanford University Press, 1959.

Brown, Sterling. *Negro Poetry and Drama*. Washington, D.C.: Associates in Negro Folk Education, 1937. Reprint. New York: Atheneum, 1969.

Brown-Guillory, Elizabeth. *Their Places on the Stage: Black Woman Playwrights in America*. New York: Praeger, 1988.

Butcher, Margaret Just. *The Negro in American Culture*. New York: Knopf, 1956.

Christian, Barbara. *Black Feminist Criticism: Perspectives on Black Women Writers*. New York: Pergamon, 1985.

Clarke, John Henrik, Esther Jackson, Ernest Kaiser, and J. H. O'Dell, eds. *Black Titan: W. E. B. DuBois: An Anthology by the Editors of Freedomways*. Boston: Beacon, 1970.

Cruse, Harold. *The Crisis of the Negro Intellectual*. New York: Morrow, 1967.

Dent, Thomas C., Richard Schechner, and Gilbert Moses. *The Free Southern Theater by the Free Southern Theater*. Indianapolis: Bobbs-Merrill, 1969.

DuBois, Shirley Graham. *His Day Is Marching On: A Memoir of W. E. B. DuBois*. New York: Lippincott, 1971.

DuBois, W. E. B. "The Renaissance of Ethics: A Critical Comparison of Scholastic and Modern Ethics." MS, 1889. James Weldon Johnson Collection. Yale University Library, New Haven, Connecticut.

"The Drama among Black Folk," *The Crisis*. August 1916, 11–14.

"Can the Negro Serve the Drama?" *Theatre Magazine*, July 1923, 12.

"The Krigwa Little Theatre." *The Crisis*, July 1926, 134.

The Autobiography of W. E. B. DuBois, Edited by Herbert Aptheker. New York: International, 1968.

A Pageant in Seven Decades. Pamphlet, n.d. Reprint. In *Speeches and Addresses, 1890–1919,* edited by Philip S. Foner, 21–72. New York: Pathfinder Press, 1970.

"How to Celebrate the Semicentennial of the Emancipation Proclamation." U.S. Congress. Senate. *Senate Report No. 31.* 62d Cong., 2d sess. Reprint. In *Speeches and Addresses, 1890–1919,* edited by Philip S. Foner, 226–9. New York: Pathfinder Press, 1970.

"On Being Black." *The New Republic,* 18 February 1920, 338–41. Reprint. In *Speeches and Addresses, 1920–1963,* edited by Philip S. Foner, 3–9. New York: Pathfinder Press, 1970.

"Shall the Negro Be Encouraged to Seek Cultural Equality?" In *Report of Debate Conducted by the Chicago Forum, March 17, 1929.* Pamphlet, n.p, n.d., 3–9. Reprint. In *Speeches and Addresses, 1920–1963,* edited by Philip S. Foner, 47–54. New York: Pathfinder Press, 1970.

"The Colored Audience." *The Crisis,* September 1916, 217. Reprint. In *The Seventh Son: The Thought and Writings of W. E. B. DuBois,* edited by Julius Lester. Vol. 2, 52. New York: Vintage Books, 1971.

"Criteria of Negro Art." *The Crisis,* October 1926, 290–7. Reprint. In *The Seventh Son: The Thought and Writings of W. E. B. DuBois,* edited by Julius Lester. Vol. 2, 312–21. New York: Vintage Books, 1971.

Dusk of Dawn: An Essay Toward an Autobiography of a Race Concept. New York: Harcourt, Brace & World, 1940. Reprint, New York: Schocken Books, 1971.

"The Negro and the American Stage." *The Crisis,* June 1924, 56–7. Reprint. In *The Seventh Son: The Thought and Writings of W. E. B. DuBois,* edited by Julius Lester. Vol. 2, 310–12. New York: Vintage Books, 1971.

"The Negro in Literature and Art." *Annals of the American Academy of Political and Social Science* (September 1913): 233–7. Reprint. In *The Seventh Son: The Thought and Writings of W. E. B. DuBois,* edited by Julius Lester. Vol. 1, 452–63. Vintage Books, 1971.

"A Philosophy for 1913," *The Crisis,* January 1913, 127. Reprint. In *The Seventh Son: The Thought and Writings of W. E. B. DuBois,* edited by Julius Lester. Vol. 2, 379–80. New York: Vintage Books, 1971.

"Protest." *The Crisis,* October 1928. Reprint. In *The Seventh Son: The Thought and Writings of W. E. B. DuBois,* edited by Julius Lester. Vol. 2, 58. New York: Vintage Books, 1971.

"The Art and Art Galleries of Modern Europe." MS., c. 1894–6. F. L. Broderick transcripts, Schomburg Collection. New York Public Library, New York. Reprint. In *Against Racism: Unpublished Essays, Papers, Addresses, 1887–1961 by W. E. B. DuBois,* edited by

Herbert Aptheker, 33–43. Amherst: University of Massachusetts Press, 1985.

DuBois, W. E. B., and Alain Locke. "The Younger Literary Movement." *The Crisis,* February 1924, 161–2.

Evans, Mari, ed. *Black Women Writers (1950–1980): A Critical Evaluation.* New York: Anchor Press/Doubleday, 1984.

Fabre, Genevieve. *Drumbeats, Masks, and Metaphor: Contemporary Afro-American Theatre.* Translated by Melvin Dixon. Cambridge, Mass.: Harvard University Press, 1983.

Farrison, William Edward. *William Wells Brown: Author and Reformer.* Chicago: University of Chicago Press, 1969.

Fletcher, Tom. *The Tom Fletcher Story: One Hundred Years of the Negro in Show Business.* New York: Burdge & Company, 1954.

Gayle, Addison, Jr. *The Black Aesthetic.* New York: Doubleday/Anchor Books, 1971.

Harris, Leonard, ed. *The Philosophy of Alain Locke: Harlem Renaissance and Beyond.* Philadelphia: Temple University Press, 1991.

Harrison, Paul Carter. *The Drama of Nommo.* New York: Grove, 1972.

Hay, Saumel A. "Alain Locke and Black Drama." *Black World,* April 1972, 8–14.

Hill, Errol. *Shakespeare in Sable: A History of Black Shakespearean Actors.* Amherst: University of Massachusetts Press, 1984.

,ed. *The Theater of Black Americans.* 2 vols. Englewood Cliffs, N.J.: Prentice-Hall, 1980. Reprint. New York: Applause Theatre Book Publishers, 1987.

Holmes, Eugene C. "Alain Locke – Philosopher, Critic, Spokesman." *Journal of Philosophy* (28 February 1957): 113–18.

"Alain Locke: A Sketch." *Phylon,* Spring 1959, 82–9.

"The Legacy of Alain Locke." *Freedomways,* Summer 1963, 293–306.

Johnson, James Weldon. *Black Manhattan.* New York: Knopf, 1930. Reprint. New York: Atheneum, 1969.

Jones, LeRoi, and Larry Neal, eds. *Black Fire.* New York: Morrow, 1968.

Locke, Alain. "Steps toward the Negro Theatre." *The Crisis,* December 1922, 66–8.

"The Ethics of Culture." *Howard University Record,* January 1923, 178–85.

"Review of *Goat Alley.*" *Opportunity,* February 1923, 30.

"Negro Speaks for Himself." *The Survey,* 15 April 1924, 71–2.

"Max Reinhardt Reads the Negro's Dramatic Horoscope." *Opportunity,* May 1924, 145–6.

"The Concept of Race as Applied to Social Culture." *Howard Review,* June 1924, 290–9.

"Enter the New Negro." *The Survey,* 1 March 1925, 631–4.

"Youth Speaks." *The Survey,* March 1925, 659–60.

"The Drama of Negro Life." *Theatre Arts Monthly,* October 1926, 701–6.

"The Drama of Negro Life." In *Plays of Negro Life,* edited by Alain Locke and Montgomery Gregory. New York: Harper & Bros., 1927.

"The Gift of the Jungle." *The Survey,* 1 January 1927, 463.

"The Negro in the American Theater." In *Theatre: Essays in the Arts of the Theatre,* edited by Edith J. Isaac, 290–303. Boston: Little, Brown, 1927.

"Art or Propaganda?" *Harlem,* November 1928, 12–13.

"The Negro's Contribution to American Art and Literature." *Annals of the American Academy of Political and Social Science* 140 (1928): 234–47.

"The Negro in American Culture." In *Anthology of American Negro Literature,* edited by V. F. Calverton, 248–66. New York: Modern Library Series, 1929.

"Black Truth and Black Beauty: A Retrospective Review of the Literature of the Negro for 1932." *Opportunity,* January 1933, 14–18.

"On Being Ashamed of Oneself: An Essay on Race Pride." *The Crisis,* September 1933, 199–200.

"Jingo, Counter-Jingo, and Us." *Opportunity,* January and February 1938, 7–11.

"The Negro's Contribution to American Culture." *Journal of Negro Education* 8 (July 1939): 521–9.

"Broadway and the Negro Drama." *Theatre Arts,* October 1941, 745–52.

"Autobiographical Sketch." In *Twentieth-Century Authors,* edited by Stanley Kunitz and Howard Haycroft. New York: Wilson Company, 1942.

"Understanding through Art and Culture." *Africa Today and Tomorrow,* April 1945, 23.

"Self-Criticism: The Third Dimension in Culture." *Phylon,* 1950, 391–4.

"The Negro and the American Stage." *Theatre Arts,* February 1926, 112–20. Reprint. In *Theatre Arts Anthology,* edited by Rosamond Gilder. New York: Theatre Arts Books, 1950. Reprint. In *Anthology of the American Negro in the Theatre: A Critical Approach,* edited by Lindsay Patterson, 21–4. New York: Publishers Company, 1968.

"Negro Youth Speaks." In *The New Negro,* edited by Alain Locke. New York: Albert & Charles Boni, 1925. Reprint. New York: Atheneum, 1969.

The Negro and His Music and Negro Art: Past and Present. Washington, D.C.: Associates in Negro Folk Education, 1936. Reprint. New York: Arno Press and *The New York Times*, 1969.

ed. *The New Negro.* New York: Albert & Charles Boni, 1925. Reprint. New York: Atheneum, 1969.

Long, Richard. "Alain Locke: Cultural and Social Mentor." *Black World*, November 1970, 87–90.

Marshall, Herbert, and Mildred Stock. *Ira Aldridge: The Negro Tragedian.* Carbondale: Southern Illinois University Press, 1968.

Mitchell, Loften. *Black Drama: The Story of the American Negro in the Theatre.* New York: Hawthorn Books, 1967.

Moon, Henry Lee. *The Emerging Thought of W. E. B. DuBois.* New York: Simon & Schuster, 1972.

Patterson, Lindsay, ed. *Anthology of the American Negro in the Theatre.* New York: Publishers Company, 1968.

Rampersad, Arnold. *The Art and Imagination of W. E. B. DuBois.* Cambridge, Mass.: Harvard University Press, 1976.

Reardon, William R., and Thomas D. Pawley, eds. *The Black Teacher and the Dramatic Arts.* Westport, Conn.: Negro Universities Press, 1970.

Sampson, Henry T. *Blacks in Blackface: A Source Book on Early Black Musical Shows.* Metuchen, N.J.: Scarecrow Press, 1980.

Southern, Eileen. *The Music of Black Americans: A History.* 2d ed. New York: Norton, 1983.

Toll, Robert C. *Blacking Up: The Minstrel Show in Nineteenth-Century America.* New York: Oxford University Press, 1974.

Turner, Darwin T. "W. E. B. DuBois and the Theory of a Black Aesthetic." *Studies in Literary Imagination* 7 (Fall 1974): 1–21.

Washington, Johnny. *Alain Locke and Philosophy: A Quest for Cultural Pluralism.* New York: Greenwood Press, 1986.

Williams, Mance. *Black Theatre in the 1960s and 1970s: A Historical-Critical Analysis of the Movement.* Westport, Conn.: Greenwood Press, 1985.

Woll, Allen. *Black Musical Theatre: From "Coontown" to "Dreamgirls."* Baton Rouge: Louisiana State University Press, 1989.

Index

Printed in the United States
42934LVS00005B/49